Creating Constitutionalism?

Creating Constitutionalism?

The Politics of Legal Expertise and Administrative Law in England and Wales

Susan Sterett

Ann Arbor
The University of Michigan Press

Published in the United States of America by
The University of Michigan Press
Manufactured in the United States of America
♾ Printed on acid-free paper

2000 1999 1998 1997 4 3 2 1

A CIP catalog record for this book is available from the British Library.

Library of Congress Cataloging-in-Publication Data

Sterett, Susan Marie.
Creating constitutionalism? : the politics of legal expertise and administrative law in England and Wales / Susan Sterett.
p. cm.
Includes bibliographical references and index.
ISBN 0-472-10630-9
1. Great Britain—Constitutional law. 2. Rule of law—Great Britain. 3. Judicial review of administrative acts—Great Britain. 4. Political questions and judicial power—Great Britain. 5. Emigration and immigration law—Great Britain. I. Title.
KD3989.S74 1996
342.41—dc21 96-40116
CIP

For Jack
with thanks

Acknowledgments

I am grateful to many people for assistance with this project in its various stages. The University of California at Berkeley provided financial support and an excellent library. The University of Edinburgh provided support and a congenial atmosphere in which to consider administrative accountability, the rule of law, British politics, and legal reasoning. Michael Adler, Ruth Adler, Zen Bankowski, Anthony Bradley, David Garland, Christopher Himsworth, Neil MacCormick, David Nelken, and Jeremy Waldron at Edinburgh contributed valuable discussion and opportunity for reflection. Lawyers practicing in the field of administrative law generously spoke with me about their work. Bruce Feldthusen, Bob Kagan, and Harry Scheiber provided useful comments on different drafts of this project. The State University of New York at Binghamton provided some research funds and support. Jason Sullivan provided helpful research assistance. Malcolm Litchfield, Chuck Myers, and Kevin Rennells at the University of Michigan Press all provided helpful editorial assistance. My family will be pleased that this book is done, which I appreciate. Marianne Constable, Lucy Salyer, and I have discussed concerns regarding history, due process, and accountability for years, discussions that shaped this project. Martin Shapiro taught me to take for granted that administrative accountability is part of politics. Jack Tweedie has read more drafts of more material than either he or I could count. With Jack I learned the significance of one more rep and for that I dedicate this book to him.

Contents

Introduction

In December of 1981 I was a tourist in London. Just after arriving I went to listen to Parliament debate. The House of Commons was arguing about a recent court decision. The Law Lords, constituting the highest appeals court in England, had struck down as illegal a London local government policy subsidizing transport fares. Local officials had run for election on the basis of the policy, giving it the catchy name Fare's Fair. Members of the Conservative party repeatedly asked if the Labour party would tell the London metropolitan government to obey the law.

From an American perspective, much is odd about that experience, though I realized very little of that in 1981. The national legislature was debating a court decision concerning a policy that a city had enacted. The dispute was between the London metropolitan government and a subgovernment. The lack of federalism could hardly be more evident; Congress seldom debates disputes between New York City and Staten Island. Yet part of what colored the debate was an argument in favor of local autonomy. Also, a decision from the highest court was unusual enough to be debated by the whole House of Commons. The U.S. Congress is not primarily a debating body, and Congress as a whole would not often spend much time debating a particular court decision, certainly not one regarding public transportation outside the context of segregation. Furthermore, Britain is not supposed to have anything like American judicial review, through which courts can overturn government policies. What had the courts done? One part of the debate centered on the obligation of the London government to obey the law, meaning the decision by the Law Lords. Why were complex policy disputes between levels of government framed as obligations to obey the law? The level at which governments should subsidize transport was not the primary topic for debate.[1] Instead, the debate emphasized the authoritative face of law: courts made decisions that all had an obligation to obey, not question.

The debate in Parliament that day would exemplify many of the policy disputes that occurred throughout the 1980s and into the 1990s in Britain; the expectation that the courts matter has colored political discussion. The courts were particularly significant in public debate regarding local government finance. In other areas their decisions were part of an effort to shape how resources were distributed at the case level, primarily in homelessness, immigration, and schooling. Legal rights embodied in part in court decisions have been understood to be an increasingly important part of British governance (Loveland 1991; Tweedie 1989; Paterson 1982). Some of what matters about the role of court decisions in governing administrative state policies in Britain is just what I saw: Parliament debates issues the courts decide in part simply because the courts decided them. While this became very visible in the 1980s, courts and law as part of the administrative state, imposing standards on the administrative state, have been part of political debate in Britain throughout the twentieth century. Sometimes it has broken into public debate; at other times the questions have been maintained only in more dry discussions in the legal literature. In a time of increased attention to constitutionalist accountability in western postindustrial states it is worth understanding the meanings of law as imposing accountability. That debate in Parliament over Fare's Fair and the obligation to obey the law was not new.

Other national states in Europe established constitutional courts after World War II, leading to a politics of constitutionalization throughout Europe (Stone 1992). The European Court of Justice and the European Court of Human Rights have also led to the increased presence of courts as part of national policymaking in Europe. While Britain has reluctantly acceded to judgments from the two European Courts, it has been the state most resistant to enacting explicitly a constitutionalist politics and a special court that would judge politics according to some fundamental principles. That resistance could lead to a conclusion that having courts judge state policies has simply not been of interest to the British and therefore is not worth discussing when discussing the constitutionalist politics of Europe. However, a consistent postwar thread of concern among legal academics, sometimes emerging into wider public debate, has been that Britain needed a different kind of political institution to impose accountability on an administrative state. Because Parliament has seen no reason to enact any basic statutes giving courts that power, the interest in and advocacy of court-based politics has come out in more subtle ways. Those include writing textbooks so to advocate the resources available in the common law, amplifying judgments the courts make that concern basic principles of administrative state power, and turning a technical revision of remedies into a seeming-power to challenge Parliament.

By 1995 the British overwhelmingly favored some form of bill of rights and some form of entrenchment of such rights (Worcester 1995). The Labour party has committed to incorporating the European Convention on Human Rights if it forms a government. As a result of earlier years of more subtle advocacy, the legal profession addresses those questions by claiming expertise and citing judicial decisions critical of administration as examples of what judges could do with a bill of rights.

Legality in an Administrative State

Legal elites in Britain have criticized executive branch officials when officials have not wanted to expand legal control of state power for behaving contrary to British legal and even constitutional tradition. Legal elites have done so without benefit of a written constitution to which they can appeal in Britain. The resistance the central state has displayed to expanding legal accountability has required resisting pressure from legal elites and sometimes a wider public. That and the disgruntled debate over the place of courts exhibited in the Fare's Fair debate raise the question of why statutes have not seemed to invite judicial review of administration as they sometimes have in the United States. To ask that question immediately requires reaching beyond court decisions in explaining the rule of law in an administrative state. Instead, explaining the legal strategies of governance, a more wide ranging problem, is important.

Explaining choices about the place of legal strategies in governing is to explain constitutionalist choice. That is true in the straightforward sense that legal elites in debate have seen problems like Fare's Fair as raising constitutional problems. It is also true analytically. Constitutionalism as an analytic concept refers to a reliance on words as a touchstone for shaping governing practices (Harris 1982; Hartog 1987). That framework invites investigation of political debate reaching well beyond individual court decisions. It invites investigation of a legal field, in this case administrative accountability through law. A legal field incorporates all the actors who refer to each other and take each other into account with regard to decisions. The legal field of law in administration, then, refers to administrators, the legal elites who have argued about accountability, and Parliament when it has considered accountability. Explaining constitutionalist choice is more amorphous than explaining how courts have applied a particular constitutional provision. But doing so is necessary. Choices made regarding the role of legal accountability in the administrative state shape the problems the courts find before them. Therefore, understanding how law has mattered requires understanding the choices made well before the courts hear cases.

Choices about legal accountability became part of the political contest in the early twentieth century in Britain as local governments gained authority in slum clearance and the central government took on responsibility for social welfare programs. With the emergence of early social welfare programs, British legal elites worried about the rule of law and what it meant in an administrative state. They tried to raise their concerns in a way that stripped them from their dense political context: legal elites tried to elevate legality, or reliance on law and courts, as the right way to govern, one that the new programs were undermining. Relying on law and the courts was to be above the substance of the political fray over social welfare programs. Periodically since the early twentieth century legal elites have been able to play on more widespread cultural concerns about state power. In the 1930s and 1950s the state provided major inquiries into state power and what forms of legal accountability should apply.

From an American perspective, the concern with the place of law in an administrative state as a constitutional problem could be surprising. Americans are accustomed to thinking of the U.S. Constitution as explaining the significance of law in governing in the United States. The Constitution sometimes seems so important that it becomes the source of explanation for why other countries do not do things as the United States does. Indeed, the U.S. Constitution as well as the European Convention on Human Rights have played that role in British debate over the place of rights in governance. However, this approach misunderstands the American case. Administrative practices are governed more by statutes and political disputes over their meaning than by the Constitution.[2] In the United States the Fifth and Fourteenth Amendments provided the first grounds for building procedural requirements into administrative agency action, but they are not the primary reference point now. If even in the United States appeals to the right way of governing appear in arguments about statutes rather than only the Constitution, it would seem that a state does not need to have a written constitution for constitutionalist arguments to appear. A written constitution is not the only possible reference point for governing administration, even in the United States. Perhaps some explanation of the concerns of legal elites and the way those concerns have or have not been enacted is necessary other than the lack of a written constitution. The task for this study is to discover how administration is configured through constitutional discourse without written limits to which to appeal. That requires explaining and understanding disputes over statutes, not just judicial decisions. I will analyze how ideals of legality are made and maintained in an administrative state.

Legality as Institutional Choice

This study therefore requires some understanding of what *legality* might mean. Philip Selznick, an early leading scholar of legality in organizations, has defined *legality* as "the gradual reduction of arbitrariness" (1969). This definition is very open ended. That has substantial advantages for my study. It allows me to investigate the disputes over what constituted the best way to enact legality within state organizations rather than taking the issue as settled. Lon Fuller in his 1969 book *The Morality of Law* laid out criteria for what he considered a fully achieved legal system. These criteria are useful as elaborations of what it means within legal ideology to reduce arbitrariness through law. These criteria stipulate that laws must be (1) announced; (2) before they are applied; (3) understandable; (4) noncontradictory; (5) possible to meet; (6) not too frequently changed; and (7) administered as they are stated. Leaving aside whether Fuller's criteria are either necessary or sufficient for whether something counts as law, Fuller states aspirations that are common in the governing rhetoric of Western states.[3] As we will see in this study, that a government is not abiding by these precepts has sometimes provided a framework for critique in political debate in Britain.

Legal strategies of governing administration provide an excellent site for analysis of constitutionalist discourse (Shapiro 1988). First, administrative practices govern much of our lives today. They govern who may immigrate and settle, who gets what kind of public housing, and what counts as pollution under environmental law. Second, analyzing the legal control of administration immediately turns one away from looking to provisions of a written constitution as the most important elements shaping choices, even in the United States. Therefore, it is implausible to attribute the limited emphasis on legal accountability in Britain primarily to the lack of a written constitution.

To explain constitutionalist choice requires two parts. First, we need to understand the cultural framing of the problem. Second, we have to explain why, within the cultural framework, some options have become part of political settlement and others have not.

Individuals and State Organization

Cultural concerns about the rule of law in Britain have been framed as questions of the individual against the state throughout most of the twentieth century. This approach takes as a model the individual property holder whose holding precedes the state rather than being constituted by it. Even Fare's Fair was understood in law to be about the fiduciary responsibility of the Greater London Council to spend its taxpayers' money wisely. A dispute between levels of government regarding transportation subsidies became a dispute about the individual property holder against the state.

In accepting the importance of the individual property holder commentators took for granted that the citizens who might not be treated fairly were male. Examples that conservatives used to illustrate bureaucratic unfairness from 1929 onward drew upon professions dominated by men, such as medicine. Social insurance programs were generally not at first believed to require any particular legality-based form of fairness for their clients. Even so, social insurance programs were based on a gendered division of labor; they had been designed based on a household consisting of a male breadwinner and a woman who did not work for pay (Pederson 1994). So, even when consideration of procedures that would make distribution of national insurance benefits fair came up explicitly in the 1950s, they then primarily concerned fairness for a male working class. Even the 1950s dispute that triggered discussion of bureaucratic unfairness centered on a man asserting property rights; the property was land he had gained through marriage to a woman who would have inherited the land had the government not bought it. Programs affecting women more directly were largely outside the realm of judicial evaluation. Gender and race only became more visible with the emergence of claims of race and sex discrimination in the 1970s and the commitment of some scholars and lawyers to concerns about what legality might mean in those areas (Kenney 1992). Even with that reluctance statutes have provided some grounds for review. Furthermore, the traditional common law remedies were consolidated into a remedy called judicial review in 1978. That remedy, more than ordinary appeals under statutes, has raised in Britain the question of the potential to apply legal principles of fundamental fairness to the government through the courts.

Even in the early twentieth century, before new statutes constituted claims concerning antidiscrimination and most immigration issues, the framing of the individual against the state excluded substantial issues. It excluded local government efforts to distribute milk to children, a need-based social welfare concern of the women in local government who seldom had reason to talk abstractly of state power. In 1909 in Britain local governments gained the authority to condemn buildings for purposes of town planning. While the individual against the state might capture the perspective of a building owner, it did not necessarily capture the different perspectives possible among those for whom the state would build or regulate housing. The central government would by 1911 have programs creating unemployment insurance, health insurance, and old age pensions (Orloff and Skocpol 1984; Hollis 1987). Some of these programs would also lead to disputes in the courts. Political struggles of the time provided a rich context for these programs. Unions uneasily made peace with social welfare programs, though such programs threatened to displace union-provided benefits (Orloff and Skocpol 1984). Local governments in taking responsibility for the quality of housing for the poor and the purity of milk engaged activists in volunteer sectors as well as their own socialist officials. To frame the rule of law as a way of protecting individuals against the state makes for a tremendous ideological narrowing of the grounds of discussion about constituting state power.

Even so, leftist lawyers and conservatives alike accepted this property-based framework from the 1930s through the 1950s, when the role of law in the administrative state was the subject of extensive debate. Both agreed that individuals had interests opposed to that of the state. For socialist-leaning lawyers, the interests of the state had to take precedence. Because unions have been so thoroughly integrated into the Labour party, the interests of the state could mean, socialist lawyers hoped, the interests of working people making social welfare claims when the Labour Party was in power. For conservatives, the interests of the individual had to take precedence. They had to receive properly cautious procedural protection before the state could do such things as regulating that property or condemning it for public housing. In accepting the framework the socialist lawyers conceded a great deal. They also could be relentlessly consistent. While what they often meant by a socialist legality was that they hoped administrators would give benefits readily, they also could believe that the interests of the state were opposed to the interests of any one benefits claimant as well. Administrators had to take into account all claimants, which could mean that individual benefits claimants still had no particular rights (see, e.g., Titmuss 1971).

The attention to the individual against the state took as fundamental class-based cleavages in society. It does little to appreciate issues that come out of what are often called "the new social movements"—for example, claims for antidiscrimination on the basis of sex or race. In those cases the concerns of the claimant about discrimination can be against a public entity such as local government. However, the claims can also be against private parties such as employers or landlords, looking to the state for redress rather than having interests fundamentally opposed to the state. State agencies can (and do) handle discrimination claims, or any other claims, badly, but the interests are not necessarily fundamentally opposed. Nor does this address the interests of immigrants; sometimes states want to draw immigrants in and sometimes they do not, making the interests of immigrants partly constituted by state policies of inclusion and exclusion.

Finally, the framework does not take organizational issues between levels of government or different agencies seriously. Yet interorganizational issues are the ones that have emerged in the 1980s and 1990s as crucial in administrative governance in Britain. Fare's Fair after all could be productively understood as a question of the relationship between central, metropolitan, and local governments. The individual against the state hardly captures the complexity of the issue; "the state" was hardly something unified. The frameworks have changed somewhat to account for the emergence of new issues but only implicitly. And immigration in particular seldom appears in "general" discussions of administrative law and political accountability. While it addresses state power in what is perhaps one of the most biting international political issues today, it does so for low status groups and it does so outside the often taken for granted private property framework.

In the midst of social policy change raising rule-of-law questions, lawyers struggled to justify their version of correct governance by finding continuity with the past. A legal argument generally considered to be persuasive even within western legal systems is an appeal to traditional governance, claiming that one has the true interpretation of the law as embodying political tradition. In doing so legal elites deployed the meaning of the past ideologically; appeal to tradition was persuasive.[4] As we will see, legal elites relied on law quite selectively. Because the early-twentieth-century debate has proven of ongoing significance, both in terms of what it excluded and in the appeal to an ambiguous history, the first chapter of this study addresses the debate over administrative power and how legal scholars appealed to history to justify their understanding of the role of parties in an administrative state. Chapters 3 and 4 address reform efforts in the 1950s and from the 1960s onward.

The legacy of the narrowing of debate is evident in Britain today. The late 1980s saw an expansion of interest in a new and written constitution for Britain. Part of that was a discussion of administrative power. Constitutionalism has been perceived as a question of imposing limits on what state institutions can do to people. The courts then are discussed as though they are not part of the state, and whether they can hold the rest of the state to prohibitions becomes the central question. The discussion has attended in part to protection of individuals, but the individuals most likely to rely on judicial review in Britain, immigrants, have not often been addressed as part of constitutionalist accountability. Discussion has instead addressed the core political issue in Britain, the control of central government. It has not been conceived as a question of reorganization of the state but instead of how to place legal limits on the central state.

As I have briefly outlined, the question of how to treat individuals in an administrative state has been an important one in British legal debate throughout the twentieth century. Not surprisingly, those who have been concerned have tried to make their beliefs part of legal governance in Britain. Efforts to get statutes enacted through Parliament as well as struggles over the meaning of British legal-political tradition have provided important contests. What remains is to explain why and how perspectives on legality have or have not been incorporated into governance.

Explanatory Choices: Culture, Attitudes, and Structures

While this is a study of Britain, I want to address why different political systems choose differently about legality in administration. Three levels of explanation are relevant: the significance of cultural values, the importance of judicial attitudes, and the importance of institutional organization and opportunities. To the extent that the imposition of legality has been studied, the primary explanation has rested in cultural differences. Americans are understood to have a culture that believes in legal rules and rights. Conversely, the British are understood to have a culture that is deferential and governs in a much more conciliatory way than through law (Vogel 1986). However, that explanation rests very much on what the comparison country is. Mary Ruggie has explained British policies with regard to working women as resulting in part from a culture that is individualist, relying on rights drawn from a common law tradition (1983). The shiftiness of exactly how "individualist" and confrontational Britain is should draw the explanation into question. Furthermore, the British have not routinely deferred to state power. Far from being distinctive to the United States, anxiety about state power is a widespread western phenomenon (March and Olsen 1989). Indeed, its very pervasiveness provides multiple opportunities for assessing exactly how the British have addressed these anxieties, for the concerns recur.

The cultural values explanation too readily takes values as uniform and static. An explanation derived from cultural values makes it difficult to explain change. Culture is a helpful framework for understanding the questions that have been asked more than the answers that have been offered (Laitin 1986). The debate over the meaning of Fare's Fair is a cultural debate. Within it some might think the problem is anti-Labour judges; others might think the problem is a local government that does not obey the law. People operating from these perspectives would reach different conclusions about what the problem is and what should be done about it. Explaining the institutionalization of legality, then, requires turning to the ways choices are made within that cultural framework (Taylor 1989).

If the cultural explanation is valuable but limited, perhaps it is important to turn to the gatekeeping institutions, the institutions that shape forms of legal accountability. In addressing legality it would first seem most obvious to turn to the courts. Choosing what one wants to explain often shapes what type of explanation seems most relevant. When court decisions are seen as the crucial thing to explain rather than as one element in a legal field, the attitude of the judges on the bench often seems to be key to understanding the place of law in governance (Paterson 1982). Indeed, most twentieth-century critiques of the role of courts in governance in Britain have focused on the admittedly extremely narrow class background and training of judges (Hutchinson 1985; McAuslan 1983; Griffith 1991; Robson and Watchman 1981). Everyone acknowledges that judges have room to make choices. In law and administration, they can make choices in favor of claimants, in favor of central state organizations, or in favor of local governments. They can make choices to distribute benefits generously or not. Studies have pointed out repeatedly that the courts in Britain preferred through the mid-1960s to defer to state officials unless the person facing them actually was a private property holder rather than a benefits claimant (Hutchinson 1985; McAuslan 1980). After the 1960s, the consensus seems to be that the judges have been eager to impose greater restrictions on government officials, largely in reaction to emerging critiques of British government as ineffective and unaccountable.

However, focusing on judicial attitudes ignores all the limits on what gets to court. Statutes can make it easy or difficult to complain; they can state standards that seem to invite judges to read legal duties into the statutes or they can emphasize discretion. While judges have choices to make, they only have a limited range of choices, and they can only choose in the context of the cases that come before them. Focusing on variations in judicial attitudes takes for granted the rules defining the standards the courts can use in reviewing administrative action.

Neither the explanation from cultural values nor one from judicial attitudes attends to the political institutions available for reconstructing political authority through legality. That leads to an alternative explanation of political discontent, one that explains choices in terms of how existing political institutions provide opportunities, diagnoses of problems, and possible solutions to those problems. An explanation focusing on political opportunity structure is as applicable to state choices about legality as it is to anything else. In the British political system the state has had substantial ability to select who will participate in policy negotiations and on what terms, outside of producer groups. Challenge to state policy via litigation is only one of the many opportunities that historically largely have not been available in Britain; it is worth explaining why. The option of objecting to politics through legal challenge has largely been closed off in Britain and not solely because Britain has no written constitution. Nor is it because no one has raised the possibility of legal challenge. To the extent it has not been closed off it has been used. The courts have suggested since the 1960s that they might be amenable to hearing challenges, and legal commentators have amplified those signals. People have relied on the courts to challenge central state policies. This use of legal challenge also draws explanations resting on widespread cultural preferences into question. The British refusal to use legal forms to hold administrators accountable has quite proximate causes in twentieth-century party and state institutions. While there are common cultural strategies for addressing problems, their availability as a matter of common sense has explanations that rest in part on available institutional opportunities.

Legal elites have pressed for greater imposition of legality. They have been cautious in what they have asked from Parliament and the executive. They have had good reason to be; few in politics ask for much more than is even remotely possible to achieve. In Britain central government ministers also sit in Parliament, and Parliament has little ability to enact anything the central ministries would reject. The ministries in turn have little reason to impose limits on themselves. Strategies in addition to requesting statutory changes, then, are also necessary for enacting legality. The profession can advocate more subtle changes through readings of the law.

Lawyers and judges interpret and reinterpret legal decisions and traditions. These practices have substantially shaped choices about legality. *Fare's Fair* represented a choice to read past decisions as though they imposed statutory duties on local governments. *Fare's Fair* in turn has been reinterpreted in the legal community to be not just about transport but about the duty of a local government to take everyone's interests into account. Even in Britain, where law is more narrow and technical than it is in the United States, litigation contests interpretations of the law. That happens not just through direct challenges but also through reinterpretation in courts and legal scholarship. The context of the European Court of Human Rights has in particular meant that in arguments before the court even the British government has had substantial reason to argue that domestic law is actually very rights-based, offering extensive legal remedies for wrongs. Attending to the struggles over interpretation embedded in the profession illuminates the possibilities as well as the constraints in law. Lawyers, including legal commentators, are therefore significant in understanding what is made of the law (Gordon 1984). Both struggles to get statutes enacted and struggles over interpretation are important to understanding the imposition of legality.

Limits to Creating Constitutionalism and Challenging Those Limits

In exploring disputes about legality as constitutionalist questions, an important question is how one gets constitutionalism embodied in new contexts. That project is now receiving global attention with what seems to be in Europe the growing significance of the European Court of Justice and the European Court of Human Rights as well as the collapse of the Eastern bloc after 1989, where constitutions have become widely discussed (Elster 1991). It is both more difficult and easier than one would think at first to embody a state that relies on words, particularly words representing legality, as touchstones for governing. It is more difficult because simply writing down prohibitions of government action cannot accomplish the whole task, though it is often taken to be the heart of constitutionalism. Without institutional support for them, prohibitions on government action mean little. Examples abound in American history: even the prohibition on restricting the freedom of speech in the First Amendment to the U.S. Constitution leaves open what that freedom is. That means, for example, that when red scares limiting freedom of speech have been popular in the United States and have had elite political support they have often met with little resistance from the courts (Murphy 1979; Navasky 1980).

Recent constitutionalist debates have focused on prohibitions and how they would be enforced, particularly in Britain. Yet much of what is important in governance is how action is made possible: the forms it will take and how power is shared (Nonet 1969). Therefore, treating constitutionalism as a simple matter of writing down some prohibitions, even if a court can enforce those prohibitions, misses much of constitutionalism.

While a focus on prohibitions misses some of the difficulties of instituting constitutionalist practices, a focus on the hostility of the state to changing anything misses some of the openness in legal systems. It is somewhat easier to make aspects of a constitutionalist government than the written constitutional prohibitions model supposes. It is difficult to create a legal system that is wholly closed to challenge. At minimum one can ask that the government live up to its own principles. Implicitly most legal professionals believe in some of the basic precepts of legality. In Britain the vagueness of principles of legality—that laws not be retrospective, that people be treated equally—actually means that the government can be criticized for not adhering to legality.[5] Without any specific provisions to appeal to, constitutionalism can, paradoxically, become quite wide. In Britain, for example, the abolition of local governments in the 1980s was called a constitutional problem by critics, though local governments have no clear constitutional status and throughout the twentieth century central government has imposed limits on them (Ashford 1983; Graham and Prosser 1990; Barron and Scott 1992).

Legal forms sometimes help to construct critiques of governing practices; rule-of-law ideals provide some resistance to state authority. *Fare's Fair* exemplifies the government's emphasis on the obligation to obey the law and the legal-political authority of governing officials. But sometimes the central government loses. The possibility of using the language of the authority of law to criticize what the government does as illegal makes it possible to resist the central executive through its own law. Even more than that, the belief that law should embody some amorphous principles of right governing makes it possible to critique the state as fundamentally unfair in conflicts even when the central executive does not lose. E. P. Thompson noted that long ago the claim to common law rights in England provided resistance to central state policies (1991); now a more general sense of what governing principles should be proves appealing. The possibility of using law as a challenge to dominant practices sometimes depends in part on its meaning as authoritative and clear.[6] Without some expectations that law has those characteristics, it would not be possible to criticize the government for not adhering to the law. Such criticism is useful in Britain for embarrassing the government. Of course, governments are not always easily embarrassed, and embarrassment does not always affect political choices.

In Britain the lack of explicitly stated constitutional principles means that if judges rule against government policy in a particular case the government can be criticized for its inability to follow its own laws. It has little grounds for criticizing the judges when the government itself has insisted that judges are completely independent. Nor can it say that the judges misapplied some fundamental principle, for the polity has none written. When the government wins, critics can claim that the victory was nothing more than a further demonstration of the problem of having narrowly professional judges in a system without fundamental rights. Paradoxically, the very professional narrowness and deference to the government that makes the courts seem so politically unengaged in Britain means that a victory in court against government officials is often newsworthy.

I particularly focus on this aspect of law in immigration in chapters 5 and 6. In immigration lawyers have joined with other activists to work to gain favorable interpretations from the courts. In examining this I examine the meanings of law as available for resistant political activity.

The emergence of the rule of law as the basis of a critique of governing practices has been a theme throughout the twentieth century in Britain. Early in the century it was important to those criticizing the political effort to create a social welfare state. In the latter part of the century this critique has been important to those critical of the Conservative government in power since 1979. It has been particularly important to those who have challenged the immigration practices of the government. With the elevation internationally of human rights discourse, most relevantly in Britain through its participation in the European Convention on Human Rights, British legal elites have drawn on an ambiguous and non–rights based political-legal history to find a homegrown basis for human rights. Much of the basis for these claims has developed through the law made to hold administrators legally accountable for their actions.

Victories in court in immigration provide a framework for thinking about the usefulness of litigation in resisting state authority. Victories are small. They do not overturn all the immigration rules but allow one client to stay in the country, sometimes only for a limited time. In thinking about this type of resistance some scholars have raised the concern that it loses sight of the overall problem. In immigration, whether individual claimants in Britain can stay is only one part of the desperate conditions of conflict in the world creating the large number of refugees.[7] To focus on small losses and victories is a refusal to recognize systematic forms of domination (Hartsock 1990). Indeed, it is individuating and profoundly apolitical.

Immigration lawyering is a good site to examine this claim. British immigration law is explicitly restrictive and racist; the justification for limits are that assimilation is necessary to good race relations and assimilation can only occur when there are a limited number of immigrants. British law is the most restrictive in Europe with regard to refugees (Zolberg, Suhrke, and Aguayo 1989). That restrictiveness is unlikely to dramatically change. However, immigration lawyering directly and sometimes collectively engages state power. The usefulness of the connection between the work for clients and the broader issues is for the reader to assess; I would argue that, like much of the lawyering for social change in the United States, the connection is profound and important.

On Not Being British

In explaining the limits to instituting legal accountability as well as the possibility of challenge to those limits I am not addressing a primarily British concern. Rather, the questions come from an American interest in why legality is instituted and an interest in explanation that is not identical with the advocacy of change one might do in one's own culture. I do not mean to address directly the very urgent questions before Britain now, for example, whether market and management forms of accountability are better than constitutional-ist ones (Barron and Scott 1992). I do not mean to analyze whether the judges are "really" fair nor whether the British system of complaint processing is adequate to satisfy people nor, finally, whether Britain should have a written constitution and what should be in it. Rather, I mean to ask and explain how a polity makes a rule of law and then what gets made of it. I want to attend to the complex meanings of law possible even in a unitary Western industrialized state that emphasizes law as obedience to state power. In this effort I want this study to contribute to debates about the role of culture and institutions in making legal systems. I also mean to contribute to the opening of the study of public law in political science to question how the rules of the game are made.

By analyzing the politics of legality we can learn how different justifications for rule can become embedded into institutions. We can also learn how centralized democratic institutions do or do not organize to accommodate liberal rights. As countries throughout Europe consider rights-oriented regimes, it is worth understanding how their creation depends on the institutions from which they emerge.

Where We Go from Here

Because it is important to understand how legal scholars have understood the twentieth-century debate, chapter 1 outlines the early-twentieth-century discussion of accountability in the administrative state. This discussion includes the role the courts were taking and what forms of administration were excluded from consideration. Chapter 2 provides an overview of the law that framed the debate concerning the role of courts and legality for the 1950s' consideration of legal accountability. Chapters 3 and 4 discuss efforts to impose structures of legality on administration and why they failed. Throughout I attend to how those participating in debates understood the nature of the British state. In chapter 5 I discuss how discontent with the British state has been translated from the 1980s through the 1990s both into law and into interpretive understandings of what constitutionalism means in Britain. Chapter 6 addresses immigration, which has provided the biggest part of the case load for the courts in administrative law but has been excluded from the discussions in chapter 5 of "general" accountability issues. Chapter 7 concludes with analysis of the limited constitutionalism in Britain and of the usefulness of law as a rethinking of state power.

CHAPTER 1

Party Politics and Courts: Using History

Introduction

Throughout much of the twentieth century, parties in Britain were united on the importance of state spending programs, though they have done their best to disagree with each other. In the early twentieth century, these new spending policies required new forms of governance to implement and legitimate them. In making new policies the parties drew on familiar traditions to make a new governance, one based on what has been called collectivism. The story of the emerging elite partisan consensus in Britain around collectivism both as a way of making policy and as the ideal for the substance of policy is a familiar one in European comparative politics. But what to do with courts and their presumed focus on the individual posed a problem in governance for the parties, and collectivism posed a problem for the lawyers. That story is not familiar. This chapter explores the use of history by lawyers to justify understandings of what made governance legitimate with the emergence of an administrative state in the first half of the twentieth century.

Legal texts and interpretations of history are cultural documents, to be interpreted for an understanding of how the legal elites writing them explain and justify the state in their society.[1] Historical and legal normative argument were ideologically charged, unavoidably so. Elizabeth Mertz has argued for a similar approach to studying the ideological interpretation of cultural history: "[L]anguage is socially grounded, structuring and being structured by social context. In studying legal texts, we see the dynamic translation and creation of social relations as they are explained—an explanation that speaks of history, and justifies social change."[2] English legal history was rich enough to support appeals to British practice, tradition, or legitimating principles when advocates were trying to justify quite divergent approaches to administrative law and courts. Two important aspects of British legality—the independence of the judiciary from the executive and the courts' reliance on precedent—had ambiguous histories upon which critics of the courts or executive could draw.

Lawyers' interpretations of the place of courts and law in the administrative state had what might be roughly considered Conservative and Labour variants, though not all lawyers who spoke on the issues actively identified with one party. Both sides believed in the importance of legality as adding legitimacy to governing. Class implications of different interpretations of legality were evident to participants, though lawyers more identified with the Labour party raised that point. Gender, however, was largely invisible to those who argued about the meaning of legality. The early-twentieth-century administrative state in Britain had different implications for men and women; gender was not an irrelevant category (Pederson 1994). Both sides arguing about legality were exclusively male; women were not allowed into the legal profession until 1919. Even after that women did not have a base in university work, so they had no place from which to articulate abstract concerns about state power. Women were involved in the welfare state and governance in Britain in the early twentieth century. But, rather than concerning themselves with abstract questions of state power, women worked in local government administering new programs of slum clearance and food purity (Hollis 1987). Therefore, most of this chapter concerns the construction of legal accountability and state power through elite men's understandings. Those understandings often took to be irrelevant to questions of state power social welfare work at the local level, in which women did engage and of which women were clients.

Both sides in the lawyers' debate concerning state power deployed British history and their understanding of legal professionals' norms for governance to interpret changes and justify their positions with regard to administrative power. Partisan commitments intertwined with interpretations of legal history to explain what was necessary to achieve legality in an administrative state. The effort to interpret how the administrative state should work continued the consolidation of legal scholarship as a field independent of practice, a process that had begun in the late nineteenth century (Sugarman 1986).

Without an understanding of the policy context and the organization of politics emerging in the first part of the century it is not possible to understand the debates concerning legality. After outlining the policy context I will turn to an outline of the court system and to how lawyers criticized the courts and government.

Policies and Governance

To legal elites watching politics in the early twentieth century, party affiliation did not seem to determine whether Britain would have state-sponsored social welfare programs. Both the Conservative and the Liberal parties had been important in establishing some of Britain's social spending programs. Programs such as family benefit, unemployment insurance, and sickness insurance operated before World War I; Britain's first Labour government only came to power in 1929 (Beer 1969, 302–13; Heclo 1974, 105–26). That early part of the twentieth century saw wide-ranging changes in the organization of politics; social welfare programs came about as the result of a broad conjunction of forces. They included the growth of trade unions and the expansion of suffrage to include working men, the advocacy by elites of social welfare programs, and the availability of a civil service that could work to deliver promises the parties made (Heclo 1974; Orloff and Skocpol 1984; Pederson 1994). Socialist elites formed the Fabian Society, committed to a planning-based amelioration of the economic dislocations of capitalism. The significance of the growing importance of economic sectors in governing, especially the trade unions, was highlighted by the extension of suffrage in 1928. In addition to social spending programs such as pensions, unemployment insurance, health insurance, and disability insurance, governments in the first part of the twentieth century enacted housing programs that allowed local governments to condemn unfit housing. Furthermore, the coalition governments during the 1930s and early 1940s, led by the Conservatives, ran many of the major industries such as coal (Morgan 1985). The industries were not nationalized, but they were subject to considerable direction from the central government. Conservative ministers were important in the decision to manage the economy and direct major industries during the Depression and the war (Beer 1969, 278–98). The Conservative party did not make a full commitment to the welfare state until after the 1945 election in which Labour swept into power; that election seemed to make welfare policies an irrevocable part of British politics. But it was under a Conservative government that Beveridge issued his 1942 report that came to be considered a founding document of the welfare state in Britain. The ferment that was part of the creation of social welfare programs seemed to involve new forms for the organization and articulation of interests.

In creating new policies, British parties found they required different politics: they needed justifications for new modes of governance. In justifying policies that took collectivist approaches to addressing social problems, Labour and Conservative conceptions of state power converged. Both parties drew on traditions and arguments familiar in British politics, but they ignored or played down aspects of British politics that did not contribute to their interpretation of state power.

By the twentieth century, both parties had come to believe that democracy through general elections was the legitimate mechanism for choosing a government. Once this choice was made, the ministries were responsible for choosing policies, and they could only be called to account through questions and votes in Parliament. All of the government's ministers, or heads of the executive departments, were members of Parliament, so their control over policy was not undemocratic. Instead, tightly uniting the executive and Parliament seemed to be required to ensure that electoral demands became policy.

The parties had different understandings of relations between elections and governing: Conservatives believed the electorate was to ratify or reject a government's past policies, determining whether or not it should entrust the leaders with office again, while Labour and Liberals believed the electorate was to select a future line of policy by choosing between the parties. Party discipline was essential to both conceptions of democracy; members of Parliament were to ratify their party leaders' policies. Parliament ought to ratify leaders' choices rather than criticize them, according to the Labour party, because it was the only way to remain true to the electorate's choice and, according to the Conservative party, because the ministers were the leaders. But in neither conception of democracy would the general citizenry or the backbenchers (the Members of Parliament who were not ministers) play an active role in formulating policy throughout a government's tenure. It was essential to both conceptions that the government—the ministers—retain the power to make and change policy with little hindrance from any other institution (Beer 1969, 69–104). Good governance required centralization of control for both parties, though their justifications differed.

Justifications for both parties' understandings of the role of Parliament and elections in governance drew on traditions and the remaking of traditions from at least the eighteenth century. However, they drew selectively on tradition to justify their practices. Tories ignored Radical understandings of British politics from the nineteenth century that emphasized the importance of the electorate in choosing policy; Socialist democracy rejected Tory support for order and hierarchy maintained properly through a governing class. Whether relying on Tory or Radical justifications for parties, law administered by courts raised problems for the control of politics by parties in Parliament. The longstanding doctrine of Parliamentary sovereignty provided a historical grounding for an interpretation of state power that allowed the creation of executive programs and control.

However, parliamentary sovereignty had an ideological tradition too. Traced back to Hooker and Hobbes in the sixteenth and seventeenth centuries, it had once been a religious doctrine. Unified sovereignty would make impossible principled claims of resistance to the state by equating the duty of the polity with humanity's duty to God (Carty 1991, 186–87). That grounding would erode in the late nineteenth century, leaving a rationalist effort to reconstruct the importance of parliamentary sovereignty without legal limits.

Difficulties in calling such a system democratically accountable also were not commonly noted, though selecting a party with its whole package of policies every several years hardly makes for a clear statement of preferences on any individual policy. Instead, the intellectual-political problem was to make such a system legally accountable without disrupting democratic accountability. The two seemed to be at least potentially compatible rather than in conflict. Other existing state institutions posed some challenge to democratic accountability, but they too could be incorporated within party purpose.

The Civil Service

The organization of the civil service seemed to facilitate political accountability rather than pose a problem. After 1855, Britain had a civil service organized at least nominally under rational bureaucratic principles. Entry and promotion worked according to merit as evaluated by educational credentials rather than party politics, and the civil service did not change personnel with every election. Rather than moderating partisan politics through expertise, as the American civil service was supposed to do after late-nineteenth-century reforms, the British civil service's political neutrality was to serve party purpose. A neutral body could implement Labour or Conservative policy (not just a technically correct policy), ensuring that party purpose was not sidetracked by civil servants' preferences or priorities.[3] The early organization of the civil service did indeed make it easier for governments to make promises based in programmatic commitments rather than particularistic patronage (Skocpol and Weir 1985). While the civil service has been criticized as too committed to establishment values, it has enabled parties to enact their policies.

The House of Lords

However, the unelected House of Lords occupied a difficult position by the early twentieth century: in the Conservative conception of the state, it could judge and argue about policy because it was a group of natural leaders. As the Conservatives became more committed to election as a basis for choice of government, the Lords became less justifiable. They certainly did not fit Labour conceptions of governance based on electoral control. After a statute changing the power of the Lords was enacted in 1911, the Lords agreed not to hinder the enactment of government policy (Ashford 1981, 263–64).

Local Governments

Control of local governments raised particular problems with parliamentary sovereignty, party control, and national mandates. Local governments had had substantial autonomy in choosing and administering policy through the early nineteenth century (Eastwood 1994). Indeed, local notables governing through assizes and quarter sessions were responsible for what we would now consider judicial, legislative, and administrative tasks (Baker 1979, 21–27; Eastwood

1994). A series of social crises concerning poverty and crime as well as ideological shifts led to increasing control and later reorganization of local governments by parliamentary policy initiatives from the mid–nineteenth century onward (Eastwood 1994).

To the extent twentieth-century democracy required centralized control and planning, local governments could no longer appeal to local democracy as a justification for their rule. In an extreme version of the new collectivism, all problems ought to be resolved by reference to national purpose, and local governments ought to be considered as administrators for central policy. The tension between the legitimacy of local autonomy and parliamentary sovereignty was not resolved, as abstract issues seldom are in practice. Local governments in the early twentieth century were vibrant sources of policy initiatives within parliamentary frameworks (Hollis 1987). Drawing on traditional practices and existing administrative channels, the parties used local governments to administer new state programs in the beginning of the century (Ashford 1980, 167–68, 273–74, 287). Statutes enacted by Parliament either created new local boards out of existing authorities or relied wholly on existing local government for administration. For example, the Housing Act of 1909 allowed local authorities to condemn buildings if they were not inhabitable. It provided for an appeal by the building owner to a centrally created Local Government Board (Ashford 1983).

Tribunals

New programs in the early twentieth century created appellate boards like the Local Government Board as well as myriad tribunals to hear appeals against case-level administrative decisions. Unemployment insurance, medical insurance, regulation of rents, and compulsory purchase of property were all created, expanded, or modified in the early twentieth century, and all had local tribunals to which people could complain if they did not like a decision (Farmer 1974). Tribunals have had specific subject matter jurisdiction. Housing appeals tribunals have heard appeals regarding public housing claims. National insurance tribunals, developed alongside the national insurance program from 1911 onward, decided claims regarding national insurance only, such as old age insurance, unemployment benefits, and medical insurance. Tribunals partook of a longstanding tradition within the trades in Britain of settling disputes according to internal standards "without the law" (Arthurs 1985). Governments have justified these boards and tribunals by arguing that they can make appeals more widely available than do the general jurisdiction courts; appeals to tribunals can also be cheaper to administer and cheaper for claimants. Officials have also understood tribunals to subsume administrative decision making to public purpose; what that means has been contested over time. Tribunals have been faster, less expensive, and more informal than courts have been. That can mean they provide speedy and accessible justice or that they ignore any legal rights of claimants and legitimate departments' decisions without really reconsidering them (Genn and Genn 1989).

Because tribunals decided individual cases, they could directly raise questions about the role of courts in governing new administrative programs. Many tribunals did not require legal representation. They were designed to be more informal than were the general jurisdiction courts. They generally have had two members and a chair. By design they were also to have some range of interest representation: departments would appoint the members, but, for example, trade unions could nominate a member to social security tribunals. In keeping with the aim of representation and informality, tribunals did not have to be staffed by lawyers. However, by the mid-1950s lawyers chaired some tribunals as a matter of departmental practice (Baldwin, Wikeley, and Young 1992, 19, 127). Departments were more committed to appointing lawyers in the tribunals that administered universal benefits such as national insurance than in programs that were means tested. National insurance programs were based on a family model that required a male breadwinner and a "dependent" spouse (Pederson 1994); therefore, these tribunals were marginally more committed to legality in decision making through their staffing and were more likely to be deciding men's claims. In means tested programs, need more than legal right provided the justification for the program and therefore permitted lay decisions (Baldwin, Wikeley, and Young 1992, 127). Lay people decided cases but only after training from the relevant government department.

The importance of national elections and national purpose highlights tensions between party ideologies and major institutions, including the House of Lords and local governments. It does not address what problems legal accountability has raised for party government, nor does it address how legal scholars told counter or complementary stories to put the courts and legality together with party government. Parliamentary sovereignty could run headlong into other practices in British governing. Outlining the organization of the higher court system is the task of the next section; a discussion of how the lawyers read the history of that system in the context of party government will follow.

Courts and Collectivism

Judges and lawyers had partisan commitments, but in conjunction they developed understandings of and loyalty to the legal system and their versions of legal fairness. That loyalty provided counterweight to the appeal by both parties to British practice as a justification for centralization in the ministries. Judges and legal scholars drew on their own versions of British political tradition to argue against the expansion of executive and parliamentary power.

Conservative lawyers appealed to a tradition of neutral, nonpartisan judgment by the common law courts, independent from the executive, rather than to a tradition that emphasized leadership and central control, as the parties were emphasizing. Lawyers explicitly identified with the Labour party or more informally committed to socialism appealed to legal neutrality as an aspiration. That aspiration, the same ideal that more conservative lawyers took as a reality, provided a critique of judgments of the courts that were against trade unions or against collectivist programs for public housing (Jennings 1936). Discussions of how to incorporate legality in the administrative state began in earnest in the late 1920s. It ran through the mid-1930s and came up again after World War II.[4] But to understand that discussion, it is necessary to outline the legal history lawyers interpreted. The commitment of the legal profession to precedent and continuity made it important to lawyers to interpret the past in a way consistent with their vision of the future. While socialist lawyers were sometimes more eager to find new forms of legality for an administrative state, they too used the past to criticize more recent judgments of the courts. Conservative lawyers in particular concerned themselves with finding a historically justified position against party governance. The elements of judicial nonpartisanship that were key to those discussing the administrative state were judicial independence and the reliance on precedent.

The discussion of the place of courts in administration has drawn on the legal system of England and Wales. Scotland differs in the place accorded to courts in governing administration in some respects. Those differences have become politically more important with the ebb and flow of political concern about independence for Scotland from England and Wales. The differences have seldom provided a significant framework for discussion of British constitutionalism, which has been a source of some understandable complaint from the Scots. Indeed, Professor J. D. B. Mitchell, an important participant in the discussion of administrative state legality in the 1950s and 1960s, wrote from Scotland but did not make it a focus of his discussion (see, e.g., Mitchell 1967). Because this study focuses on a map of the intellectual terrain, I will not closely address the muddied and complex relationships between the centralization of the British state and the status of Scotland. I will largely focus on developments as understood for England and Wales.

A. V. Dicey launched the debate in 1885 with his rendering of the British political system. He published his *Introduction to the Study of the Law of the Constitution* (1920), a description of the British political system that emphasized British courts' complete and eternal separation from political judgment. He wrote that Britain, unlike France, had no administrative law, nor should it. Administrative law was, to Dicey, a way of subjecting officials to special rules, exempting them from ordinary citizens' liability for wrongs they committed. The only protection for individuals in an administrative state was to forbid recourse to special courts and special rules. The ordinary courts relying on ordinary common law rights would protect people from the administration. Administrative law would not. With this book he would become a continuing ground for British constitutional discussion in the twentieth century.[5] Dicey's perspective immediately raised problems with party governance. For, if the rule of law meant the courts could evaluate executive action, ministers or even local governments as administrators for ministers might not always win.

Anthony Carty has illuminated Dicey's work by arguing that Dicey cut parliamentary sovereignty away from its seventeenth-century basis in theology. Dicey instead found an arbitrary point of creation for the doctrine of parliamentary sovereignty (Carty 1991). He made acceptance by the people only a contingent fact of parliamentary sovereignty, contingent on the emergence of representative democracy (201–3). But Dicey's insistence on the fundamental and incontrovertible status of parliamentary sovereignty has, according to Carty, made for the legal-political tradition in Britain that provides no principled consent or rights-based grounds for criticizing law (1991). Tracing the ambiguities that Dicey erased is an important task in understanding the authoritarian face of law in Britain. But, as subsequent chapters will show, the law itself provides principled grounds for critique, making the task less hopeless even from within British cultures than Carty would suggest.

The judicial independence that A. V. Dicey and other lawyers celebrated was, as far as it existed, a rather recent achievement.[6] It is difficult to determine what it means, for judges are appointed by the executive, they chair commissions investigating major public policy issues, and members of the Law Lords comment on legislation. Robert Stevens recently has stated most aptly the difficulty of assessing what independence means, concluding that "while the independence of the judiciary is casual at best, the English have a strong commitment to the independence of individual judges," meaning that it is inappropriate to try to influence judges in cases on which they are sitting (1993, 5).

For much of British history judges had advised members of Parliament on legislation. Judges in Britain have historically not had recourse to parliamentary materials to interpret the intent or purpose of a statute before them. That way, so the justification has gone, they decide the law, not what someone meant the law to be. However, the judges were once presumed not to need to look at parliamentary materials to discover the purpose of the law because they knew the legislation well from preparing it (Baker 1979, 181–82). It was not initially a practice that allowed the courts to simply adhere to some uncommitted plain meaning of the words of law, as it later has been treated (Cross 1977). Judges in the House of Lords continue to comment on legislation under consideration (Stevens 1993, prologue, chap. 1).

The High Court

The courts in one form or another had long been part of British governance. The High Court, the central trial-level court of the common law, had existed since the twelfth century. It had been created to administer the king's justice over local and lesser courts (Baker 1979, 15–18; Shapiro 1981). It consisted of divisions, and by historical accident the King's or Queen's Bench Division heard most of the common law claims. This control over the law did not go uncontested; those who were discontent with the *Bleak House* aspects of English law made way in the nineteenth century for internally and locally developed judgment by institutional rules—by Poor Law boards and merchant boards (Arthurs 1985). Since 1875 the court has had an official president, the Lord Chief Justice, who has been in charge of administering the courts and has chosen panels to sit on cases. Before 1875 the lord chief justice had only informally been used as the title for the chief justice of the King's Bench (Baker 1979, 46–48). The King's Bench Division was responsible for reviewing cases that courts of lesser jurisdiction and local courts had decided. At its discretion arising from the monarch's prerogative, it could review via the prerogative writs decisions of any lower tribunal for error. By the turn of the twentieth century, several writs were available to supervise lower courts and administrators—prohibition, certiorari, and mandamus were those most often used for reviewing administrative decisions. Though they had arisen for different purposes and had different rules governing their applicability, their reason for existence as a group was to impose the common law on lower courts, including administrative boards, and to ensure that the courts stayed within the law. As new administrative programs were created, statutes gave the King's Bench jurisdiction to supervise them (Baker 1979, 123–24). Lower courts have over time been reorganized; the primary general civil jurisdiction lower courts now are the county courts.

English law has long made a distinction between appeal and review: under a statutory appeal a court would check to see if a decision maker had made an error of law. Under review, it could only check to see if the lower court or administration had decided outside its jurisdiction. The courts could review for decisions that were ultra vires, or outside the power of the decision maker. They could also review for violations of natural justice, or a duty to decide fairly. The latter is largely a grounds for review of procedure, addressing for example whether a decision maker had heard the case before deciding. The writs provided only for review. The distinction may be difficult to maintain, but it is often used by the courts in explaining the standard of review they use. Traditionally, the court could only review for error on the face of the record of the lower trial court; it could not reconsider all the evidence. If the lower court had not explained its decisions, there was nothing for the Queen's Bench to review (Baker

1979, 123–24; Wade 1994, 35–38). The High Court can review the decisions of county courts and administrators; appeal from county courts and some tribunals such as the Lands Tribunal goes to the Court of Appeal.

The Court of Appeal

Since 1873 when the Court of Appeal was created, appeal lay from the Queen's Bench to the Court of Appeal. It heard appeals, rather than simply a request for review, from a lower court. The judges who staffed it were the lords of appeal (Baker 1979, 122–23). In the twentieth century some administrative tribunals were created with a right of appeal directly to the Court of Appeal. These special tribunals eventually have included the Lands Tribunal (1949), hearing complaints regarding administrative handling of property issues; the Employment Appeals Tribunal (1965), which has heard disputes regarding labor law; and, since 1993, the Immigration Appeals Tribunal.

The House of Lords

The House of Lords has long heard appeals from lower courts in some form; it has also formally been a legislative body. The House of Lords participated in both legislation and judgment through much of the nineteenth century, but the distinctions that might now make it seem odd to unify the two had either not been made or had been considered difficult to make even as late as the seventeenth century (Baker 1979, 180–81). Indeed, the common law embodied the right principles of governing; legislation was to follow it (Baker 1979, 169–70). Under such a conception of governing, there was nothing wrong with allowing the Lords to both legislate and judge cases. Though this theory of law declaration had virtually died out by the nineteenth century, uniting judgment and legislation in the House of Lords had not.

Not until 1876 did the government create by statute a separately staffed court within the House of Lords. Members were to be chosen for their legal qualifications. Called Lords of Appeal in Ordinary, they were responsible for deciding appeals from the Court of Appeal. They could also participate in some legislative debates in the House of Lords, so they were not solely judges barred from other aspects of political life (Stevens 1980, 1993).

Also through longstanding practice, the head of the judiciary—the Lord Chancellor—was a minister and a member of the House of Lords. The Lord Chancellor had always judged cases as well as sitting as a member of the House of Lords and working as a minister within the government. Like any other minister, by the twentieth century the government in power chose him. The government would choose a Lord Chancellor who was a member of the governing party, just as it would choose other ministers. Most Lord Chancellors have been

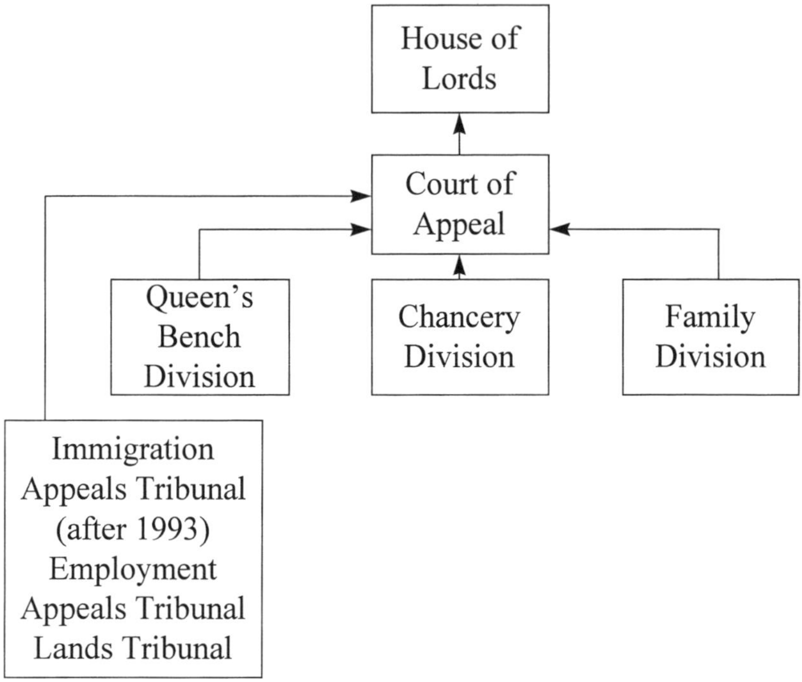

Fig. 1.1. Court structure

eminent lawyers, but they have also been chosen for political loyalty, and that trend continued with the entrenchment of party government in the early twentieth century (Baker 1979, 85–86). The complete independence of the judiciary so important to Dicey was not a simple description of the place of the courts in British governance.

Professional and Political Judgment

A late example came in what proved to be a particularly controversial case decided in 1915, *Local Government Board v. Arlidge* ([1915] A.C. 120). The Housing and Town Planning Act of 1909 required the board to hold an inquiry before it dismissed an appeal against a slum clearance order. The Local Government Board had decided to affirm a local authority's issuance of a clearance order against a building for being uninhabitable. The building owner challenged the decision on the basis that the board had not listened to him. The Law Lords on the panel deciding the case had all been active in the governing Liberal party

(Stevens 1980, 198). The Law Lords held that they could not require the local authority to disclose its report, nor could they require the board to hear the building owner in person, all on the grounds that the department was responsible only to Parliament. Those active in local government saw slum clearance orders as necessary for improving the health of the urban poor (Hollis 1987, 445–55). Conservative lawyers believed this kind of case gave them cause to worry about British governance: proper methods of governance through law were being subordinated to party purpose.

Arlidge would not just create concern among lawyers about what the governing parties were doing. It would invite concern among Conservative lawyers about what the courts were doing within party governance. Were they abandoning what lawyers portrayed as their traditional practice of judging and instead turning everything over to the parties? If they had not ruled in that way, would they be illegitimately working against the purpose of the legislation, usurping the role of government?

Professional criteria currently dominate the selection of judges for the High Court, Court of Appeal, and Law Lords. That is, judges are chosen from among experienced practicing barristers (Atiyah and Summers 1987, 339–53). That was codified in 1981 but had been a part of practice from about World War II. The emphasis on professional criteria is one part of the complex settlement that limits how much judges in Britain explicitly evaluate government choices on substantive grounds. The narrow professionalism is part of what legal scholars were willing to insist on as part of the independence of the judiciary. That professionalism is, of course, a political choice about the place of courts in governance. It also invites a kind of "debunking" approach to the law, holding that, despite much-vaunted neutrality, judges make politically relevant choices.

Choosing judges for their partisan political loyalties became less dominant in the twentieth century, but integrating judgment and legislation was not foreign to the English system. Professionalization through appointment of lawyers, development of a separate Court of Appeal, and creation of a separate staff within the House of Lords were important changes of the late nineteenth century in separating legal from partisan judgment. Parties could claim that the courts were one more institution that ought to subordinate itself to national purpose while still drawing on traditions in British governance to justify that argument. Legal scholars could point to a tradition within which courts could judge according to the common law separate from what the parties might want; indeed, doing so was crucial to rights protection in Britain (Craig 1990a). The ambiguous position of these institutions provided resources for the politicians to call on in their efforts to vest all authority in the ministries.

The point of this brief outline of the deployment of British courts, then, is to point out how partial any analysis would have been that held courts to somehow be the longstanding home of judgments that were more fair than those of the executive because they were independent of it. While that interpretation had some material to draw on, primarily the ideology of the common law, it flattened the ways that "independence" in part simply meant a different governing system. *Bleak House* warns of the problems of relying on the courts for fair judgment; the confusion resulting from technicalities and the length of time to judgment were very real. Accounts of judicial independence also misstate the ways executive and legislative politics had been tied to that of the judiciary. On the other hand, socialist-leaning lawyers who would emphasize the overruling importance of party and party purpose in legitimating governing were also flattening institutional tensions and the settlement that allowed judges some separate room to govern.

Adhering to common law precedent provided another linchpin of political neutrality in legal ideology. While linked to independence because it was a way of preserving the separation of the legal world from the political, it is worth discussing on its own. The use of precedent was also both a British tradition and a recent creation in the early twentieth century. And to the extent it had been a British tradition it had been confused and variously flexible. How to use precedent properly has been widely debated; that it was used has not. Though precedent as a source of law had long been an important English practice, accepted wisdom before the mid–nineteenth century had always been that if a previous decision was bad the court ought not to adhere to it. Precedent was also used differently according to the field of law: by the seventeenth century judges believed that property law required certainty, therefore reliance on precedent, more than contracts or tort did (Baker 1979, 172). So determining how cases ought to be used was far from simple; the historian J. H. Baker has described the judges' approach over the centuries as "a vicious circle" (1979, 174). Reliance on precedent expanded after the mid–nineteenth century, and the appellate courts declared themselves bound by their own decisions as well as by those of superior courts. The House of Lords settled on this theory in 1898; the Court of Appeal has only bound itself since 1944 (Baker 1979, 174–75). From the early twentieth century through midcentury, the use of precedent was understood to be essential and almost determining in legal judgment. Due to extensive criticism, the House of Lords changed its practice in 1966. The Law Lords issued a practice statement, stating that if justice required them to change an earlier decision they would ([1966] 3 All E.R. 77). The Law Lords have not explicitly used this power frequently, but it is available (Paterson 1983). Reliance on precedent no more has an ideologically clear history in Britain than judges' separation from Parliament, and therefore the executive, does. This ambiguous history provided resources for lawyers who wanted to criticize or support expansion of the administrative state.

Lawyers and Collectivism

Shortly after the turn of the century, Dicey acknowledged with regret that Britain had administrative law in the sense that administrators made decisions affecting individuals, often without recourse to the ordinary courts (1926). Administrative social spending and regulatory programs created Britain's regrettable move toward administrative law, according to Dicey.

Lawyers' concern with the growth of the administrative state was manifest throughout the late 1920s and 1930s. Just as politicians were looking for modes of governance that would fit with new policies, conservative lawyers were explaining that the new policies embodied wrongheaded modes of governance. Lord Hewart, the Lord Chief Justice, wrote a book in 1929 entitled *The New Despotism*, which sounded an alarm against the expanding powers of the executive branch of the state, including of course the ministries. Carleton Kemp Allen, a professor of law at Oxford, had similar concerns. He published a collection of articles he had written throughout the 1920s as a book in 1931, called *Bureaucracy Triumphant*.

Courts formed only one topic for these books: it is entirely possible to criticize administrative discretion without celebrating courts. But what courts were *for* and what Britain had lost by no longer relying on them to judge administration formed the background for much of the discussion regarding administration. Courts would not only hold bureaucracies to rules, according to Hewart and Allen, but in the process would create greater justice and distributive fairness. Hewart and Allen implicitly believed courts should never enforce the substance of rules made by Parliament and administrators that foolishly and arbitrarily governed people's business. To do so would contravene common law tradition. Yet to interfere would, in new interpretations, contravene parliamentary sovereignty. To maintain both the common law and parliamentary sovereignty required seeing common law rules as simply apart from political choice. Hewart and Allen pointed to court decisions of the late nineteenth century that had required administrators to provide hearings and justify policies, decisions they sorrowfully noted the courts by the 1930s seemed to ignore. Those earlier decisions, to Allen and Hewart, epitomized what the courts could offer within an administrative state. They could stop injustice, a term so taken for granted that it went undiscussed.

Hewart and Allen wrote of Britain's fall from grace. They believed the British had been well served and well protected by the courts, which exercised no power but protected people from party and administrative government, which did hold power. But Britain had fallen from its great tradition of allowing individuals free rein through the common law by expanding administration, and the courts had acquiesced. A prime example in such a discussion was *Local*

Government Board v. Arlidge, the housing condemnation case in which the court held it could not overturn the Local Government Board's decision.

Not surprisingly, the historical context in which Hewart and Allen were working made "protecting individuals" from the arbitrariness of government not as politically neutral as they would have had it. During the period they refer to vaguely as the high-water mark of judicial review, the late nineteenth century, the courts were imposing civil liability for trade union activity, including picketing. The courts were protecting businesses from trade union organizing. In 1901 the House of Lords issued the *Taff Vale* decision, which made picketing impossible by imposing a very heavy fine. The decision was notorious and it was an issue in the 1906 election. After the election Parliament gave a very clear signal to the courts that these judgments were profoundly political and unacceptable. Despite the courts' certainty, the antiunion decisions were not separate from political disputes and simply legally right. Parliament enacted the Trade Disputes Act, which explicitly made picketing legal and not subject to civil penalties.[7] While neither Hewart nor Allen focused on labor law, those disputes from earlier in the century clearly provided a background for their discussion.

Allen and Hewart both had many stories to tell. The stories were often examples of what they saw as unfair bureaucratic rules. Hewart wrote that

> the treatment of the panel doctors under the Health Insurance Acts is pure despotism. The doctors are liable at the mere discretion of the official who acts for the Minister of Health, to be ruined professionally by being struck off the panel, or, as a lesser punishment, to be fined to an arbitrary extent. In one instance a fine of £1000 was imposed on two doctors who carried on business in partnership. "Excessive prescribing," an offence wholly unknown to the law, which consists in prescribing for the patient medicines that are either too expensive in quality or too liberal in quantity, is one of the things for which a doctor may be penalised. (1929, 30)

Hewart also cited statutes that allowed ministers to change a statute if it turned out to be inconvenient; any orders from the department under these statutes would be treated "as if enacted in this Act." Examples included the Patents, Designs and Trade Marks Act of 1883, the Housing Act of 1925 (allowing demolition of buildings and reconstruction), and the Unemployment Insurance Act of 1920 (allowing the minister the power to do anything "necessary or expedient" to bring the act into effect). In saying that these statutes and practices were unknown to the law, Hewart was taking as part of the natural order the common law, as though it had no political implications whatsoever. It was simply the law.[8]

In response to the argument that such discretion was necessary for new government programs, Lord Hewart wrote:

> The complaint is not that rules and regulations are made, though they are made, to be sure, in the most embarrassing multiplicity. The complaint is that they are made at such a stage, in such a form, and in such circumstances as to deprive, at one and the same time, both Parliament and the Law Courts of any real authority in relation to them. . . . The conclusion is irresistible that it is manifestly the off spring of a well-thought-out plan, the object and the effect of which are to clothe the Department with despotic power. (1929, 159)

Lord Hewart was not part of any elite cross-party collectivist consensus.[9]

Hewart wanted to find a solution that would accommodate the growth of administrative programs, but he found it difficult. He certainly did not advocate an administrative court, an institution Dicey had feared, because it would further reject individual rights and favor administrative purposes. Hewart argued that it was vital to the protection of the citizens that the ordinary courts remain available to hear complaints against administration. He also did not want any changes made in the judiciary. An independent judiciary, which he believed Britain had, was entirely different from a political one, and maintaining the distinction was also crucial to saving the citizens from administration. In arguing against a Ministry of Justice, he wrote:

> Sooner or later, and rather sooner than later, it is to be expected that the office of Minister of Justice would be held by somebody who, without the smallest disrespect, might be described as a mere politician. His interest in law, and in the traditions of the law, would be neither more nor less than that of any other member of the Cabinet. Instead of being at one and the same time a member of the Judiciary, profoundly conscious of his duties to the Judiciary, and a member of the Executive, profoundly conscious of his duties to the Executive, he would be a member of the Executive alone. . . . Does anybody fail to perceive what, in the long run, would be likely to happen? (1929, 110–11)

Lord Hewart found the answer obvious: more despotism, subsuming rights to administrative convenience. The only solution he could find that would keep the courts out of party politics as his constitutional principles required was a supervisory committee in Parliament. It would inspect all bills to make sure they were not giving even more power to the ministries. Lord Hewart, like many other lawyers, believed in the correctness as a matter of governance, or politics, of allocating judgships according to lawyers' criteria. But his argument made it no less a political choice; like other lawyers, he was arguing for a mode of governance that he believed to be disappearing quickly. Yet his implicit model of governing in Britain, with independent courts holding the executive to the law, was a highly selective political story.

Lord Hewart continued to raise his concerns about a ministry of justice. In a debate in 1934 over a minor bill expanding the number of judges, he fulminated against political appointments to the judiciary. He argued that the importance of the civil service raised the specter of a ministry of justice, in which a lawyer would not head the judiciary (Stevens 1993, 37).

Lord Hewart tilted his description of the judicial tradition in Britain in accord with his belief that governing through the common law courts was the right way to govern. He was not falsifying British tradition any more than those who emphasized electoral accountability were; he simply emphasized a different tradition. But the Lord Chancellorship had always been a "political" appointment, in the sense Lord Hewart feared in a ministry of justice, chosen by each new government. It was only recently that the Law Lords and the Court of Appeal had been taken out of what he called politics, the debate over policy, and had been staffed according to professional criteria. The Law Lords still argued for amendments to bills in accordance with what they saw as sensible legal requirements in their capacity as members of the House of Lords. Though the vision that Hewart held was not an entirely accurate version of British politics, it seemed to present an important and often valid criticism of British politics to politicians, as we shall see.

While Hewart might have had the spotlight, Conservative discourse did not monopolize the concern with legality. Socialist-leaning lawyers were also concerned with legality, but the element of the British political system they emphasized was parliamentary sovereignty—that Parliament could do anything but the physically impossible. The executive was accountable to Parliament; at some uncertain point perhaps the ministries or their officials might violate Parliament's law, and the courts could judge. While conservative lawyers also acceded to parliamentary sovereignty, their emphasis was different. The socialist-leaning lawyers' emphasis on Parliament fit with the rise of party doctrine better than did the approach of the conservative lawyers. Socialist lawyers emphasized legality within the administration—avoiding *Bleak House* by allowing for internal appeals, tribunals, and review. They did not abandon a lawyers' concern for legal accountability. W. A. Robson of the London School of Economics (LSE) was concerned with attending to legality within administration (Robson 1928 [reissued 1970], 1975). He began to teach a course on administrative law in 1929 at the LSE. In 1933 he moved the course from the Politics Department to the Law Faculty. It was an important topic, he believed, to incorporate into the education of state managers and lawyers. But legality could be brought to bear on administration from inside—not through courts that, in the guise of being nonpartisan, refused to allow Labour governments to change the rules governing property rights. From Robson's early efforts to rethink and teach administrative law the LSE became associated with internal concerns in administrative law while Oxford became associated with approaches emphasizing courts.

But the debate about legality did not stay in the common rooms of Oxford Colleges and the LSE. It certainly engaged at least elite attention. It was possible to mobilize concern by talking about bureaucratic unfairness, even when the programs seemed to be part of generally supported policy shifts. Largely as a response to Lord Hewart's book, the Lord Chancellor of the Labour government established an ad hoc Committee on Ministers' Powers in 1929. It included eight lawyers, three former ministers, three Labour Members of Parliament, and two law teachers, including Harold Laski, a prominent socialist teacher of law and politics at the LSE. The terms of reference from the Lord Chancellor directed the committee to consider ministers' powers under delegated legislation and in making judicial or quasi-judicial decisions. It was "to report what safeguards are desirable or necessary to secure the constitutional principles of the sovereignty of Parliament and the supremacy of the Law."

The Committee reported in 1932, after the Labour government had fallen and a coalition government had come into power (Cmd. 4060, 1936). It did not recommend any fundamental changes in the administrative legal structure. Drawing from Lord Hewart's *New Despotism* (1929), the Committee recommended that there be a standing committee in Parliament to supervise all delegated legislation and all bills that gave ministers lawmaking authority. Legal form was the concern; the committee did not need to specialize in any particular substantive area. The reason administrators had so much power, according to the Committee, was that Parliament just did not pay attention. The idea that ministers and upper-level civil servants chose to write statutes with extensive discretion received little credit. A new committee in Parliament would be able to attend to the details of the proper form of rule. Hewart had been concerned about formalities, but implicitly the substance of rules had concerned him most. That is, whether or not Parliament had enacted it, he did not think "excessive prescribing" of medicine should have a penalty attached precisely because it had not been a common law offense.

The expansion of discretionary power was consistent with both Labour and Conservative party conceptions of the British constitution, and ministries relied on it. The ministers publicly deplored excessive bureaucratic power, and simply by appointing the Committee they showed some support for limiting bureaucracy. Yet neither statutes nor practice that relied on extensive discretion arose mysteriously from nowhere: at least some ministers had to believe that granting such authority was necessary and right. If legitimate rule hinged on centralization of control among the ministers, who were accountable to Parliament and the electorate, statutes could and ought to grant extensive power to them. It certainly would pose less of a problem to democracy than allowing the judges to supervise programs, which was one of the socialists' points. But it was easy to mobilize elite opinion, Labour and Conservative, against authority granted to departments, as the response to Hewart's book had shown.

Though the Committee on Ministers' Powers received considerable attention, its proposals did not go far. The committee in Parliament was not established, and the Committee had not wanted to recommend very much else for fear of encroaching either on the "rule of law" (which meant that no new courts ought to be created) or on legitimate ministerial privilege.

In an article published after the Committee reported, W. A. Robson wrote: "The Committee started life with the dead hand of Dicey lying frozen on its neck" (1932, 351). The supremacy of law meant, in British terms, the power of the common law courts to supervise administrative action. The socialist lawyers were certain that the independence of the common law courts worked against social programs (which in turn had been endorsed by Parliament) and that the terms of reference of the Committee worked against institutional innovation. Despite being commissioned by a Labour government, the Committee did not represent Labour lawyers' views about legality—which would have looked to the expansion of legality from within. The closest it came was in the attempt to reconcile rule-of-law concerns with parliamentary sovereignty by recommending a supervisory committee in Parliament.

Curiously, for all their vehemence the socialist-leaning and conservative lawyers were united on the subject of problems with administrative government. Socialist lawyers were also worried about the rise of administrative government and how individuals were to be protected. A Labour government had established the Committee on Ministers' Powers, prompted by Lord Hewart's book. The lawyers simply disagreed on the instruments to achieve protection for individuals and which individuals needed protecting. Each saw a threat to legitimate governance in the others' proposals. To the socialists, Dicey's argument that there was not and ought not to be an administrative law in Great Britain not only put the common law courts in the way of implementing socialist programs but it maintained vast areas of Crown privilege, leaving individuals without remedy against wrongs the government committed. For example, Robson, a prominent socialist lawyer, argued in response to the Committee's report that in addition to the Crown's immunity from tort liability there were

> a whole series of other privileges given to the executive in the courts of law: by statutory measures such as the Public Authorities Protection Act; by common law doctrines founded on ancient prejudices, such as nonfeasance, whereby a public authority cannot be made liable for damages for

> the nonfulfilment [*sic*] of a public duty, even though injury results to one or more citizens; by the self-limitation of the courts of law, which impels them to refuse to investigate entire fields of executive action; by the archaic forms of procedure which have usually to be adopted whenever the activity of the Government is questioned in the courts of law. (1932, 356)

The only possible remedy for the problem was to create a new system of courts. To conservatives, a system of courts explicitly within the executive would only leave individuals more at the mercy of administrators' concern to get things done quickly and cheaply; it would directly violate Dicey's prescription for fairness.

The same arguments, problems, and perceptions arose once again to the level of public debate in a public investigation in 1957, which I will discuss in chapter 3. Britain has undergone consideration of administrative government and administrative reform periodically, as the United States has. As March and Olsen have usefully argued in the case of the United States, these episodes are symbolically important, though it is predictable that they would not accomplish very much. They enact cultural anxiety about powerlessness within a faceless state and end with a reassurance that something has been done. Because the problems are often intractable, because those involved often do not want to change practices, and because in Britain the government controls reforms, these periodic considerations seldom change very much (March and Olsen 1989).

The socialist-oriented critique of the courts and the common law emerged more strongly during the 1930s. W. I. Jennings of the London School of Economics saw nothing neutral or fair about the courts' emphasis on private rights. He emphasized the importance of courts not imposing independent judgment on administrators (1933, 219–34). He argued that the redistributive policies of a welfare state were intended to change the property rights people had, so that courts' claim to be protecting individuals in a politically neutral way was actually hostile to administrative programs. Traditional legal judgment, with its emphasis on precedent, therefore abrogated parliamentary sovereignty. If the courts refused to allow change, they were illegitimately usurping democratic choice. Jennings tackled head on the substantive implications of Hewart's formal critique of the executive's power to make law.

In a 1936 article in the *Harvard Law Review,* Jennings argued that recent decisions by the courts regarding housing legislation were charged with the political preferences of the courts. In one case, a local authority had ordered the demolition of two houses that it had declared were unfit for human use. After demolishing the buildings, the local authority would be required to build new housing. The owner of the houses sued, arguing that he ought to be allowed to turn the two unfit houses into one usable house. The Court of Appeal held that the authority had to allow the owner to do so. Regarding the housing decisions, Jennings commented:

> It must be remarked, in parentheses, that with a few exceptions that have now been removed by the Housing Act, 1935, no property owner suffers loss under the Housing Acts unless he has been making a profit from insanitary property which Parliament has, since 1890, consistently held to be antisocial. The late Minister of Health, now Lord Kennet, has said that a person is no more entitled to compensation for bad houses than he is entitled to compensation for bad meat. (1936, 437)

The courts, according to Jennings, simply disagreed with Parliament and the minister of health about the importance of abolishing unfit housing. Under parliamentary sovereignty they had no business making their preferences law. That approach to the problem with the courts fit with the partisan approach to governing.

Similarly, Harold Laski argued (1938) that what passed for commitment to lawyerly values, which were supposed to be neutral between competing political programs, covered judges' hostility to the substance of social welfare programs. Judges were remote from the way ordinary people lived their lives, with commitments fundamentally at odds with a politically legitimate and chosen welfare state. What Allen and Hewart saw as a commitment to the right way of ruling, separable from the content of policies, Laski and other socialists saw as disguised and illegitimate opposition to government policies.

The lack of a realist movement among legal scholars in Great Britain has long been noted and deplored.[10] But Jennings and Laski borrowed explicitly from the American realist or sociological jurisprudence movement in arguing that what the judges were doing was nothing less than elevating personal political beliefs into law, beliefs that were out of touch with modern social needs.[11] Harold Laski saw in the British courts a duplicate of the American Supreme Court, which until 1937 usually struck down state and federal legislation regulating working conditions.[12] He argued that the British courts had erected something akin to a Fourteenth Amendment against welfare legislation in Great Britain. The British courts refused to accede to the spirit of their times just as American courts had:

> Exactly as the Supreme Court of the United States made itself, above all in its hostility to the New Deal of President Roosevelt, a kind of super-legislature engaged in the enunciation of political doctrine under guise of legal procedure, so the High Court in England is engaged in a similar task. Its opportunities, of course, are smaller here; it cannot forthrightly annul an Act of Parliament. But it is at least willing to build up a kind of four-

> teenth amendment in this country, and to use it as fully as it can to set a barrier across the road of any social change of which it happens to disapprove. (Laski 1938, 313)

Similarly, Jennings concluded his study of housing decisions by writing:

> It has been said that the task of the judge is to interpret the law in accordance with the recognized technique, and not to concern himself with matters outside the law. This is, of course, the old fallacy that there is a correct interpretation of every rule, and that the task of the judge is to give that interpretation. It is, in other words, the "slot machine" theory in a new context. It is hardly necessary to reply that all interpretation on "doubtful" points is in fact legislation. If this is admitted the question to be answered is whether the legislation of the judge is to run with the stream that flows from the legislature or against it—whether, in other words, he is to seek to forward the policy of Parliament or to thwart it. It is clear that the present rules of interpretation permit, and the peculiar ideas of lawyers sometimes lead, the judges to decide counter to the ideas which lie behind social reforms. (1936, 454)

Though Jennings ascribed the problem to lawyerly values, he meant the judges in power. They were the ones he indicted. He, as well as other socialists, was a member of the bar and believed in bringing to bear legal forms in ways that were sympathetic to the clients of social programs.

Jennings and Laski could cite cases to support their positions just as Allen and Hewart could. Laski pointed to *Roberts v. Hopwood* ([1925] A.C. 578), in which the House of Lords had struck down a local authority's decision to set its employees' minimum wage equal for men and women at £4 per week. That set wages above market rates and in equalizing pay for men and women violated standard practice. The statute allowed the local authority to set wages as they "think fit," but the Law Lords said local authorities were not to use it to advance "socialist and feminist principles."

To head off critiques that people such as Jennings and Laski posed, more traditional legal scholars worked very hard to establish a rational legal order. Scholars continued to insist ever more loudly that law was separate from politics. Textbook writing provided one important way of trying to strip the law of its political implications (Sugarman 1991).

That rationalizing effort was especially important because the judges were engaging issues that were not simply internal to the profession. The Law Lords in *Roberts v. Hopwood* had a very real reason for concern about both feminism and socialism. Numbers of women were elected to and active in local government in the early part of the twentieth century. Women worked on local government social welfare committees, inspecting milk and working on housing for the poor (Hollis 1987). Women had been active even before they got the parliamentary franchise, which women over thirty won in 1918 and the rest of adult women won only in 1928 (Thane 1993, 343, 350). In the first two decades women and some socialist men had laid the groundwork for issues like the minimum wage by working in local government and conducting studies of poverty, expressing concern for a minimum family wage that might allow children to drink good milk and women to stop working when they bore children. Indeed, feminists were divided on the issue of a family wage; Eleanor Rathbone, a social worker, supported equal pay for men and women. To make up to those who had to support families, from 1917 on she worked on a campaign for a family allowance, which would be granted for children (Wilson 1977; Lewis 1983a; Pederson 1994). Sylvia Pankhurst, a feminist activist, established a nursery in the East End of London in 1914 (Rowbotham 1973, 114–17). Women were very involved in settlement houses in the poor sections of London, though their participation did not lead to political or civil service office, as it did for men (Skocpol and Ritter 1991). Women in the voluntary sector did much of what we might now consider welfare work (Koven 1993, 94). Equal pay and welfare were clearly feminist and socialist issues.[13] The association between socialism and feminism in turn intersected with concern about the importance of traditional gender roles. Between World War I and World War II British social elites expressed great concern about resurrecting and reinforcing gender roles, within which women were not involved in public life (Kent 1993). To the extent the concern about legal accountability was about central state control of local governments and committees, which it was in part, the issue concerned how the part of the state most involving men, the central state, would control the part of the state more associated with women and women's concerns, the local state.

However, the integration of labor unions into the party structure was strong enough that as social welfare programs were enacted they upheld the model of a family wage-earning man rather than providing explicit support for motherhood (Pederson 1994; Skocpol and Ritter 1991, 89–92). But that result did not mean that feminism did not appear to be a real concern to judges at the time. There was simply no political institutional route for women to take wherein they might have been asked to confront questions of state administration and legal rights.

These political disputes had also been part of the groundwork for *Arlidge,* the 1915 housing case in which the courts had held the Local Government Board to be only responsible to Parliament. *Roberts,* in 1925, received considerable press as one episode in an ongoing dispute regarding Poplarism, or local autonomy for the purposes of pursuing socialist policies. Poplar was the name of the local council from which *Roberts* emerged.[14] *Roberts* animated debates concerning the role of the courts as well as that of central and local democracy. The control of local governments provided one of the themes of the creation of British party purpose as the reference point for governing; hostility to local government would reemerge in the 1980s as some were again both financially constrained and resistant to central government (Weir 1992; Harvey 1989). Struggles between local and central governments have had a continuing thread in law upon which to draw (Sugarman 1983).

Feminist activists were involved in political disputes regarding new social welfare schemes that sometimes relied upon state bureaucratic creation and often involved women's volunteer work (Hollis 1987; Kean 1990). These were just the issues that evoked the concern among male academic lawyers about the form of government. Feminist emphases on informalism and assistance, perspectives developed very much within social-work studies rather than law, lent support to the socialist approach to legal fairncss—one that was concerned with courts striking down welfare legislation by limiting the powers of the myriad boards being created. However, emerging social-work perspectives did not lend themselves to as much concern with legal form as some of the Oxford and LSE men expressed. This division between social-work perspectives and legal perspectives occurred in part because women were not admitted into the legal profession until 1919. Feminist lawyers were not developing the experience to pronounce on legal form that some few, such as Josephine Goldmark and Florence Kelley, had developed in the United States.[15] Women were also much more excluded from higher education generally in Britain than they were in the United States in the early twentieth century (Skocpol and Ritter 1991, 81). While feminist activity fit into the early-twentieth-century debate on social welfare and bureaucracy, implicitly drawing on justifications for state power and deference that the new policies required, the formal debate was not as much of a concern. However, another aspect of the interest in informalism was a mistrust of state power that would not have neatly supported the powers of the tribunals that socialist men often favored.

Laski concluded his analysis of the courts by writing: "Every period of rapid social change confronts the danger that its legal habits may not keep pace with the political decisions it has to interpret" (1938, 323). And he interpreted these bitter and deep political divisions in just this apolitical light: courts were standing in the way of the march of progress.

Jennings and Laski justified their critiques of the courts with the parties' understanding of the British constitution: every decision was to be integrated into a party program legitimated through Parliament and the ministries. But just as Hewart and Allen distorted British political history to emphasize the importance and political neutrality of the courts, Laski and Jennings were focusing on the recent ascendancy of parties in their appeal for legitimacy. Although by the 1930s a strict doctrine of precedent prevailed in the courts, legal theory had previously allowed courts to reverse decisions because they were wrong and judge legislation according to a common law sense of right and wrong. And, as Jennings noted, that common law sense protected property rights the governments had been in the process of changing.

Lawyers claim expertise in an area in part by using and claiming legal language of their own (Halliday 1987, 261–67); that was largely the strategy of the conservative lawyers. However, another strategy is to make that wavering distinction between law and politics in one's own favor; certainly that was the practice on all sides in this debate. Jennings could argue that the courts, in the guise of being legal and using legal language, were just enacting conservative politics. This political conflict conducted in inextricably mixed partisan and legal terms only became more intense after the 1945 election.

The 1945 Labour Government

Administrative programs and the problem of administration for individuals were well established by 1945. The election in that year, the first general election since 1935, startled those who followed the political weather; Samuel Beer has called it a "crushing and unexpected" defeat for the Conservatives (1969, 302). The Labour party came into power. Socialism, a radical new form of government that seemed alien to some of the British elite, had come to Britain. It promised a set of programs that seemed much more far-reaching than anything the earlier Labour government had attempted. As discussed previously, this did not represent a radical shift from earlier governments in terms of welfare state programs. Conservative and Liberal governments had offered welfare programs in the past (Heclo 1974,105–26). But in the elite perception it was a startling break with the past. The election encouraged the Conservatives to accept fully and expand the welfare state once they regained power in 1951 (Beer 1969, 302–3, 353–54).

The new government intended to offer welfare programs moving away from needs-based criteria and toward universal application, but even that effort was based on a report commissioned by the previous Conservative government. The Beveridge Report, as it was called, has been considered the founding document of the welfare state in Britain. The Conservative ministers had endorsed it when it came out in 1942, though it was something of an embarrassment to them because it moved far beyond their intended social policies (Beer 1969, 306; Morgan 1985, 20).

What did seem completely new, so different that it heralded a new form of governance in Britain, was nationalization. Nationalization had been in the Labour party's constitution since 1919, but the party had not had a specific plan to nationalize industries until 1937 (Morgan 1985, 94–95). The new government intended to nationalize coal, iron and steel, gas, railways, the Bank of England, and medicine, to name most of the industries. These programs were not even strongly opposed by those most immediately affected, though the unions were not particularly enthusiastic. Only the leadership of the British Medical Association strongly opposed nationalization of health care; rank and file doctors supported it (Morgan 1985, 156–60).

The Labour government also intended to create an extensive program of urban renewal, land use planning, and public housing. The Town and Country Planning Act of 1947 gave it the authority to do so, but the program did not go as far as Labour wanted. It was left to the Conservatives from 1951 on to build much of the public housing, an achievement it was proud of. Land use planning programs and urban renewal touched on property law, an extremely well-developed area of law because it governed property relations and there were resources to support litigation in the area. Land use had been an important part of challenges to administrative programs in the courts in the 1920s and 1930s.

Lawyers continued to write on the problems of bureaucracy. Sir Carleton Kemp Allen published a book in 1945 entitled *Law and Orders.* It picked out examples of petty bureaucratic rules and jeered at them as unworthy of a government, using, of course, examples from before the Labour election. But the book was well timed. Judges and conservative lawyers thought their worst fears had come true, and socialist-leaning lawyers also began to argue more vigorously that Britain ought to seriously consider legal forms in the new governance.[16] The perception that British governance had changed dramatically influenced judges in their continuing evaluation of their place in the political system. The need to attend to individuals and legal forms in the pursuit of public purpose began to seem even more important than it had been in the 1930s.

That perception of change substantially influenced lawyers' evaluations of courts, legality, and judicial review in postwar Britain. It promoted the thought that courts were not doing anything to protect individuals in the new state, and it was the spur to a great amount of writing on how to reform administration and bring legality to it. Lawyers relied on a distinction between law and policy to find an area in which courts could legitimately judge without encroaching on political judgment. That distinction in itself was a recent one, though all lawyers agreed it was an important part of British governing. The judicial insistence on such a separation was only consolidated during the interwar period, in conjunction with the rise of collectivism as the format and justification for governing in Britain (Atiyah 1979, 660–66). Lawyers were working against a governing system that would allow little room for judicial decisions. A cathartic dispute over the relations between law and policy in the administrative state occurred in the 1950s and provides the topic for chapter 3. Once again, Britain, led by a legal elite largely excluded from state power, would consider control in an administrative state.

Parliamentary control and ministerial accountability to Parliament have continued to justify a highly centralized and discretion-holding administrative state. In all of what is considered in the United States to be the new social regulation, such as water and air pollution control and workers' safety, statutes have delegated to departments and officials the authority to make policy. Departments or boards seldom make publicly announced rules; instead they negotiate with individual businesses the standards to which they will adhere and renegotiate them when the time seems right (Grant 1985; Hawkins 1984). The Thatcher administration tried to change corporatist consultation, though the primary result might have turned out to be the exclusion of trade unions. Party democracy and ministerial responsibility to Parliament justify discretion.

The administrative tribunals that were a part of early British administration have also expanded. They hear appeals from case-level administration. There are dozens of different tribunals hearing thousands of cases annually. They range from the Milk Marketing Board tribunals, which hear appeals regarding milk prices, to the Supplementary Benefits Appeal Tribunals, which hear appeals regarding welfare benefits. In 1980, the latter heard more than forty-five thousand appeals (Baldwin, Wikeley, and Young 1992). While the debate about legality in the courts has rolled on, the tribunals have been created within the executive to decide inexpensively complaints regarding individual administrative decisions. If administrative law is the law administrators make, Britain has administrative law. If it is the law the courts make in judging what administrators do, Britain also has administrative law. Both have been the site of political contest and fractured protest against a centralized and controlling government. Administrative law in the courts both enacts and criticizes the practices of centralization of control in Parliament that were consolidated in the twentieth century.

We will see the strains in court doctrine in chapter 2, in an examination of postwar doctrine alongside the patterns of cases regarding administration. Chapter 3 will address how the concerns about legality in administration once again gained a governmental investigation, as they had in 1932.

CHAPTER 2

Postwar Judging of Administrators

Introduction

British legal history allowed interpretations that could address the different concerns legal elites raised from the 1930s onward about changing British governance. Courts made decisions that scholars could in turn fit into that context of concern. The courts are often called passive in the 1946–64 period and active after 1964 (e.g., Paterson 1982, Wade 1994, Craig 1994) in their review of administrative decisions. This chapter will discuss postwar legal decisions and doctrine, pointing out that there was considerable ambiguity in both the pattern of decisions and the language of the judges. Case law, however, was fit into a framework that also emphasized elite cultural anxiety. For postwar judicial review has been considered a set of decisions that only deferred to the elected government, using the justification of partisan democracy all the way down to the level of local administrative officials. The party version of governance, in which decisions by all institutions were to be subsumed to parliamentary sovereignty, seemed to have taken over the judges with a vengeance: there was no law to apply, not even in favor of claimants of state benefits. In off-the-bench comments judges sometimes argued that, much as they regretted it, Britain no longer relied on legality in governance.[1] The few cases in which the courts—primarily the Court of Appeal—explicitly held they could not judge seemed to represent the abdication of law. The judges, far from resurrecting a barrier to the administrative state based on their professional commitments, seemingly tried to ensure that they would not find any law anywhere. Elites raised the concern that Britain would have no rule of law in an administrative state. That issue could seem particularly stark in the postwar context because states in continental Europe, far from explicitly deciding that courts had no role in the modern state, were instituting new constitutional courts (Stone 1992).

Under the constitutional doctrine of parliamentary sovereignty, courts' role in reviewing administrative action was not clear. Courts could not hold statutes to be unconstitutional. However, acceptance of parliamentary sovereignty has subtle effects in the interpretation of statutes constituting administrative programs. To the extent that Britain was a parliamentary democracy only accountable through political judgment, courts perhaps ought to refuse to hold administrators to any guiding standards contained in statutes. Certainly statutes promoted that view. Lord Hewart was right when he said that statutes did not tell administrators what to do. Standards in statutes have conferred considerable discretion on ministers and local authorities. Under some, orders have been valid "if the minister so directs." Despite British assertions about reading statutes for their plain meaning, these words do not speak for themselves. Judges have to read them through presumptions or arguments about how the state works and what justifies governance. They could interpret such statutes as though they were completely in line with the centralization of control within the ministries, as party doctrine emphasized. Or they could interpret statutes in such a way that a minister could only direct something reasonable—reading the statute as though it created binding legal duties.

Indeed, there was some doctrinal basis for such a reading. British judicial review works with two basic doctrines—ultra vires and natural justice. Ultra vires means that courts can hold an administrative action to be outside of the bounds of the statute and therefore outside the administrator's powers. That is the most dramatic of court powers. Natural justice is akin to American due process. It requires, at minimum, that "the one who decides must hear" a case. It also requires impartial decision makers in disputes that look like individual cases (Wade 1994, chap. 15). These are common-law doctrines. Finally, judges need not draw explicitly on any common-law doctrine to interpret the meaning of a statute—for instance, what the rules governing conferral of a pension meant and whether the administrators had gotten it right.

The story of judicial abdication is partly alarmist. It derives from concerns that the new administrative state would mean there was no law to apply; people sometimes look for support for their greatest fears. At the same time scholars were deploring decisions, they were also arguing that common law provided resources for the courts to use in deciding so that judges could impose law on government without making new law. The story of abdication is important, not least because it so thoroughly shaped perceptions of what the problem of legal accountability is. But it does not attend to all that was happening; it virtually ignores the cases in which the courts simply applied their interpretation of the law without pronouncing on the nature of parliamentary governance. The standard story focuses on the judges as the source of legality, taking statutory discretion as given. This story about judges holds that after about 1964 the courts became willing to impose accountability on administrators once again. This second half of the story also relies on a few leading cases. However, it also ignores much of the courts' work in which they interpreted what they assumed to be ordinary legal rights. It also takes for granted the background of statutes that did or did not facilitate review.

There are two stories to tell. One story involves the cases academic lawyers highlighted as emblematic of the role of courts between 1946 and 1964.

The other story focuses on the patterns of cases that the courts decided. Both stories are important. Perceptions shaped reform proposals, proposals I will address in chapters 3 and 4. An analysis of patterns of cases points out what was ignored in perceptions of judicial review, leading to insight about why some cases might have been ignored.

The alternative possibilities in the law—between discretion and legal rights—built in an immediate tension. Would the courts simply be following the law when they interpreted a statute so as to require a hearing or a unanimous vote before denying a benefit? Or would they illegitimately be encroaching on centralized policy and political control? The terms of the debate among academic lawyers were not about whether these two terms—*law* and *policy*—existed and were separable. Everyone agreed they were. Indeed, the distinction had become more solid between the wars, in part in response to collectivism (Atiyah 1979). The controversy concerned how far each ran. It is easy to see how any one decision by a court could immediately feed into a debate about the proper role of courts.

Judges did review decisions in longstanding programs such as income tax and property tax. Courts had "always" made these decisions and continued to do so. These decisions involved the case-level application of rules. Courts believed they could discover rules in these areas. These ordinary cases were the "law" end of Britain's distinction between law and policy. "Policy," dangerous for the courts in the perception of judges and legal scholars, sometimes involved case-level decisions regarding benefit programs, and it was often at issue in cases regarding a minister's choice about a program—where to site a new town, for example.

To state basic legal doctrine is also to misstate it, treating as definitive rules what were instead indications in only a few cases. The statement of definite rules from ambiguous cases has been part of the ideological work that has gone into the making of thought about constitutionality and state power. To highlight the courts' ordinary decision making I will first turn to an assessment of the overall patterns of claims in the courts between 1946 and 1968, the period in which the courts are understood to have abdicated judgment.

Writs and Statutes: Appeals and Review in the Courts

Britain has long had established channels for taking complaints regarding governance to the courts, both through procedures in particular statutes and through the writs. These channels did not disappear with the growing strength of the parties, though some politicians and scholars wanted to eliminate them for some issues. The availability of formal complaint had some longstanding legitimacy about it, but democratic party politics and administration posed a problem for the courts. How these channels worked is the topic of this section.

Not only substantive standards—"if the minister so directs"—regulate the decisions courts reach; rules for getting into court limit or make available judicial review as well. British law relies on two forms for challenging administrative decisions. Although some statutes attempted to exclude judicial decision making before 1958, others provided for appeals to courts from decisions by administrators or tribunals, informal administrative courts that have been designed to address cases in particular policy areas.[2] In these statutory appeals, either the administration or the person subject to administrative action might sue. For instance, under the Lands Tribunal Act of 1949 people who had a local authority make a compulsory purchase order for their land could appeal the decision to the Lands Tribunal, an administrative court. Other decisions could be appealed to the minister or appeals boards within the administration. Appeals from some specialized administrative courts, including the Lands Tribunal, would go directly to the Court of Appeal. Officials could also sometimes appeal to the courts after an administrative appeal. For example, tax officials could appeal adverse decisions of the tax commissioners, the highest administrative authority. Cases between local and central government, or local authorities and administrative boards, would have a similar structure, with local authorities appealing under a statute against a decision by a central ministry. The deciding authority could also refuse to decide a case, sending it instead to the court for decision.

Alternatively, a complainant could sue under the prerogative writs. Those dissatisfied with a decision an administrative authority had made against them would apply to the Queen's Bench (the High Court) under a writ. The process had two steps, unlike appeals under statutes. The court had discretion to grant or deny the application; if it granted the application, it would hear and decide the case. Certiorari, which orders the administrative authority to correctly decide under law, was the primary writ used until 1978 to supervise administrative action. Under the writs, the Queen's Bench would declare the law and order the deciding body to make a correct decision or the court would quash the decision of the administrative body as unlawful. The complainant using the writs would apply to the court for review of an administrative decision, with the final administrative decision maker—the tax commissioners or a tribunal, for example—as the second party to the suit. Under statutory appeal to an appeal tribunal the tribunal itself might not be party to the suit, but under the prerogative writs it would be, as the authority that the complainant claimed had decided incorrectly. Until 1978, when it was reformed, the writ system seemed terribly complicated, even to lawyers. Certiorari was only available for judicial, not administrative, acts, and the case law did not make the distinction very clear. People could fall between the requirements for different writs and find themselves unable to find a writ under which to ask for review (Law Commission 1976). Looking at all these cases, from the complaints local administrators brought under statutes to complaints brought under the writs against a minister, yields information on the patterns of cases that are brought and the ordinary cases the courts see every day. It gives a better picture of the courts' business than analysis of a few outstanding cases does. The Lord Chancellor's Office collects and reports the number of cases brought every year into the Queen's Bench Division, both appeals under statutes and review under the prerogative writs. Those numbers provide information on how relatively important review under statutes and review under the prerogative writs have been as well as on whether courts have allowed appeals.

There are some problems with using these numbers. The prerogative writs overstate the review given administrative issues; they include, for example, some applications for review of criminal law decisions that simply cannot be separated out of the Lord Chancellor's aggregate statistics. Even so, the Lord Chancellor's statistics allow a rough look at how many cases the courts have heard, how that has changed, and how often the courts have allowed complaints against administrators.[3]

In surveying the caseload of the courts, I have employed a broad understanding of administrative law: any challenges to central government's programs. A narrower understanding of administrative law is more common, and it is usually implicit. Often only cases that explicitly raise questions of governance in Britain—does Parliamentary sovereignty win, must administrators decide according to rules or according to their sense of the right decision, must administrators provide hearings, to whom are administrators accountable—are included in general administrative law.[4] This strategy is useful for creating a system of critical administrative law through courts' decisions, which has usually been the purpose of people discussing decisions, as we will see in the next chapter. But it is not useful for determining how administration is governed by courts. Meanings *law* and *governance* have in British politics can be elucidated by looking at the ordinary decisions, not only the extraordinary ones. An overview of the courts' caseload from the Lord Chancellor's statistics shows that they did indeed assume authority over the years. They did not abandon judgment.

The prerogative writs more than appeals under statutes are often taken to constitute the real judicial review, because they evaluate statutes by common-law principles rather than just checking whether the administrator substantively abided by the statute in assessing taxes, for example. The prerogative writs were not, however, the primary form under which people sought judicial oversight of administrative action before 1970. By far the largest numbers of decisions by courts were under statutory provisions for appeal against decisions regarding taxes and compulsory purchase orders and made as appeals under statutes. (Compulsory purchase orders are roughly equivalent to the American eminent domain power; the government buys someone's land, usually to redevelop it.) Through 1968 the number of prerogative writs heard was less than one hundred

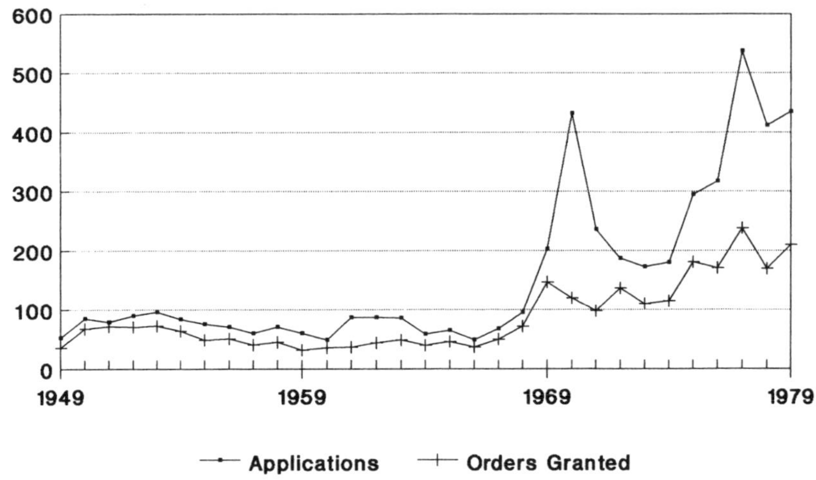

Fig. 2.1. Judicial review: applications and orders granted

per year. (See fig. 2.1.) Between 1950 and 1960 the number of statutory appeals each year varied between fifty and one hundred (fig. 2.2). For many years virtually all of these were reviews of compulsory purchase orders under the Town and Country Planning Act (first enacted in 1932, amended in 1944, 1947, and three times in the 1950s), the Housing Acts (enacted and amended five times between 1925 and 1957), or the Acquisition of Land (Authorisation Procedure) Act of 1946. In the years following 1966, the number of statutory appeals quickly increased due to the creation of industrial tribunals in 1964 by the Industrial Training Act. Tax cases, that is, appeals under tax statutes, comprised a dominant part of the administrative caseload of the courts; they added between forty and one hundred appeals per year through the mid-1960s to the numbers of appeals under statutes (fig. 2.2).

In other words, most appeals were property claims. Others have noted the significance of property to the courts (McAuslan 1980). However, that point is usually made to emphasize that the courts were sympathetic to property claims but not to others. That the courts would hear those claims presumably mattered in encouraging people to bring them to court. But it is worth noting that the cases did have to come to court and the judges themselves could not do that. Instead, the field of law was well developed; the legal profession's practice has historically rested in property (Abel 1988b). Claimants had the resources to bring cases, which in turn would encourage the courts to develop standards.

In addition to relying on the Lord Chancellor's statistics, I took a random sample of cases against administrative officials from the general law reports for

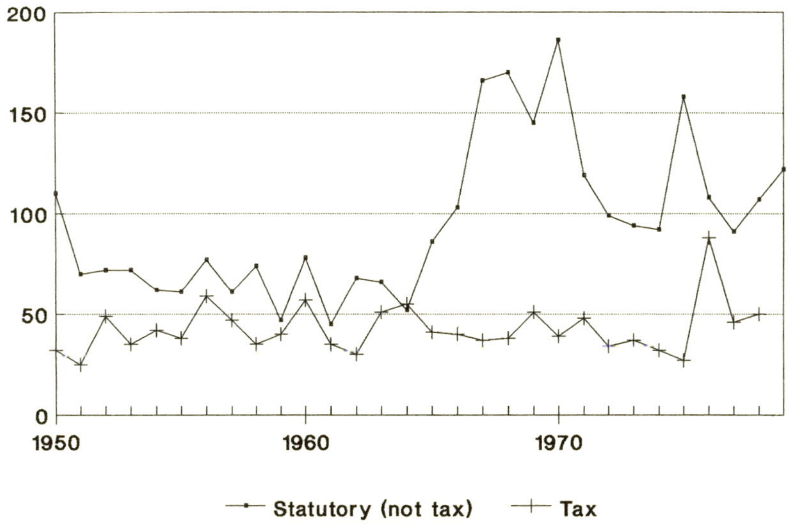

Fig. 2.2. Statutory appeals

every year from 1946 through 1970. I excluded cases regarding children in state care. While extremely important, the latter raise different issues than those addressed here. I sampled from the *Weekly Law Reports,* a general report that includes decisions from the Queen's Bench Division, the Court of Appeal, and the House of Lords. Lawyers choose the decisions to report, relying in part on a sense of what cases raise important principles of law. Many tax and land use cases are reported in specialized reports; my sample understates these cases as a percentage of the caseload of the courts. However, from the Lord Chancellor's statistics we have a sense of how predominant these cases have been. This sample, coded for subject and winners and losers, can give a sense of how often claimants won if interpreted cautiously and alongside doctrine. (To have enough cases to work with, I chose a sample level for each year that would yield at least twenty cases; for convenience in comparing numbers, I sampled either 100 percent or 50 percent of the cases.)

Appeals to courts in each year involved only a very small percentage of administrative decisions; no lack of decisions can explain the small number of cases in court. For example, in 1958 Supplementary Benefits (Social Security) Appeal Tribunals alone made twenty-eight thousand decisions. No cases from them appeared in the courts. In addition to tribunals' case-level decisions, ministers and administrators made policy making decisions: where new towns ought to be developed, what national health service priorities ought to be, and, later, how North Sea Oil ought to be developed.[5] Decisions setting regulatory policy are not discrete and cannot be counted. The rules themselves in part define decisions and state (or do not state) standards governing those decisions. The rules partly constitute the opportunity for taking a complaint to court. Therefore, a lack of complaints is neither evidence that there were no decisions nor evidence that people were happy or unhappy with decisions. Statutes set few guiding standards and seldom stated legal rights, the courts were unwilling to build independent standards, the prerogative writ system was a maze to negotiate, and many issues did not have groups or individuals organized to litigate them. The courts simply were not central to many administrative programs in the 1950s and 1960s. At the same time, they were closely involved in making decisions concerning property rights and taxation, with many appeals every year.

Perhaps more surprising, the courts also supervised wartime pensions and national insurance benefits, money that like private property could be seen as held through entitlement, therefore including legal standards for governing. For example, in *Minister of Pensions v. Horsey* ([1949] 2 K.B. 526), the court held that appeals regarding pensions for wartime injuries had to be decided by a unanimous tribunal; a majority vote would not suffice. The court explicitly drew an analogy with jury decision making, arguing that there was a serious risk of error in allocating pensions and that decisions must therefore be certain. The High Court similarly held in favor of a claimant for industrial injury benefits on legality grounds: the commissioner who heard the administrative appeal obtained evidence on his own initiative without telling the complainant. For that reason, the court held, the complainant had not received a fair hearing (*R. v. Deputy Industrial Injuries Commissioner ex p. Jones* [1962] 2 Q.B. 677).

In light of arguments about the "passivity" of the courts in the late 1940s and 1950s regarding administration, what is most striking about the aggregate statistics on the business of the courts at that time is how often complainants won against administration. Not only did the courts hear complaints. They overturned administrators. During the approximately twenty years that are supposed to mark judicial passivity in Britain after the war,[6] the administration lost a substantial percentage of the case-level complaints before the High Court. Courts allowed complaints under statutes between 15 and 44 percent of the time between 1946 and 1967, with no apparent pattern. The percentage of times the tax commissioners were overturned has varied over the years, and no strong pattern emerges. Appellate tax officials' decisions were overturned 34 percent of the time in 1950 and 46 percent of the time in 1967, varying between 17 and 55 percent in the middle years (see table 2.1.). These numbers do not directly translate into individual winners against the administration, the central concern in political argument. They cannot be read that way because either tax officials or taxpayers can appeal the tax commissioners' decisions. Tax commissioners hear appeals by taxpayers from tax officials' decisions. The loser—whether the tax official or taxpayer—can appeal the decision to the court. In either case the court

TABLE 2.1. Statutory Appeals

	Tax Appeals		Other Appeals[a]	
Year	Successes (%)	Total No. of Cases	Successes (%)	Total No. of Cases
1950	34	32	30	112
1951	36	25	28	71
1952	37	49	25	73
1953	49	35	21	72
1954	31	42	19	64
1955	29	38	31	61
1956	32	59	44	79
1957	38	47	33	61
1958	37	45	27	74
1959	45	40	40	47
1960	37	57	29	78
1961	17	35	29	45
1962	53	30	34	68
1963	43	51	26	66
1964	38	55	31	52
1965	41	41	34	86
1966	55	40	26	103
1967	46	37	15	166

[a] Excludes courts of summary jurisdiction.

was overturning an administrator, whether a case-level tax official or the tax commissioners. It is not surprising that courts would overturn government officials. People generally file cases only when there is some chance of winning. That is particularly true when there is a specialized and therefore knowledgeable bar, as there has been in tax law and land use, both of which have had enough business to have specialized case law reports and magazines reporting changes in law in part as implemented through the courts (see, e.g., Scrivens and Goodfellow 1955).

As table 2.2 shows, the majority of cases in the sample from the law reports involved taxes, land use, rates, and rent setting. In other words, cases in the postwar period overwhelmingly involved private property claims. It is not simply that courts were willing to protect private property, as the accusation that the courts are unremittingly conservative often claims. Rather, property claims constituted the primary caseload of the courts. If they were going to decide in favor of any individuals, they were going to decide in favor of property holders.

Review under the prerogative writs is easier to interpret in terms of a legal scholar's dichotomy, whether or not claimants won against the state. Virtually all claims are by an individual or business against an administrator, although some are between state agencies. In the 1950s, the Queen's Bench Division allowed between 47 and 73 percent of claims against administrative authori-

TABLE 2.2. Case Distribution by Subject (percent within periods)

Subject	1946–50	1951–55	1956–60	1961–65	1966–70
Tax	13	9	20	25	24
Land use	17	25	19	22	17
Rates	19	9	21	5	5
Rents	15	9	3	2	1
Public housing	4	2	3	4	4
Benefits	14	9	5	5	13
Employment	6	7	5	1	10
Licensing	3	5	4	9	4
Race	0	0	0	0	0
Prisoners	0	0	1	3	0
Immigration	0	0	0	6	5
Local government	1	2	2	3	1
Miscellaneous	6	20	16	14	14
N	92	88	89	86	101

ties in the prerogative proceedings. The Queen's Bench Division has steadily held in favor of claimants against the state (fig. 2.3). Such numbers indicate a willingness on the part of courts to evaluate administrative decisions rather than defer as a matter of principle.

Different understandings of the courts lead to different interpretations of these trends. Perceptions of what courts do matter: an increasing number of cases decided could contribute to a sense that they have become more active without legal reasoning or approaches changing dramatically. The change could be interpreted by those accustomed to looking solely to the courts as a shift in what judges do rather than in what people ask them to do.

The official story, focusing on the passivity of the courts in the 1950s and their choice to govern administration after 1964, misses general patterns of cases, ignoring the day-to-day business of the courts in land use and taxation appeals. Those cases represent the governance of private property, a key issue in Western industrialized states and one that is so accepted as at the heart of legal rights as to be readily ignored in assessments of how state power would change. That point invites a closer look at the choices courts have made in interpreting law as a matter of right as against a matter of complete government discretion.

Rights and Discretion in the Courts

While aggregate statistics can outline what the courts have been doing, they say little about how the courts justified what they did, which is always a task in

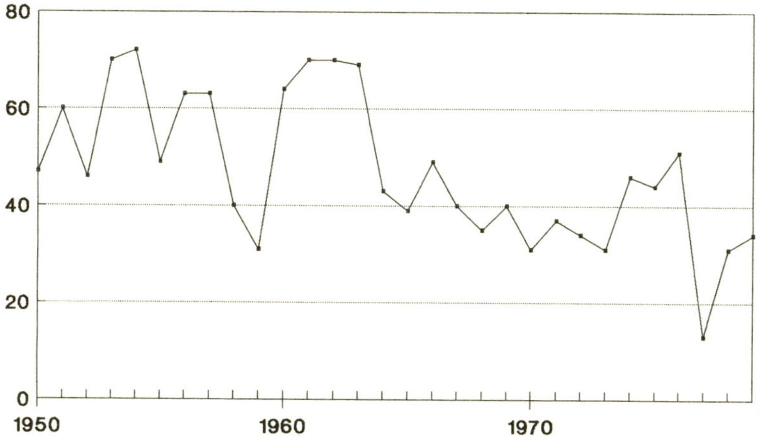

Fig. 2.3. Orders granted in prerogative proceedings (as a percent of the applications granted)

judicial review. What does it mean to say that the courts did not abandon judgment when commentators can point to cases in which they did? One possible response is that the courts just followed orders. They judged where statutes stated standards and did not where statutes did not. If the courts seldom ruled for claimants in public housing, and ruled more frequently for claimants in land use planning, then perhaps we should look to the statutes rather than the courts' reasoning. I want to illustrate how the courts reached the results they did rather than guess at what they did from win-loss rates. For, while statutes influenced judges' approaches to a case, they did not determine whether or not courts ought to read standards as legally binding. Courts had (and have) two types of arguments to draw upon in deciding administrative claims. One was explicit, the other often implicit, and they drew on the different arguments selectively. First, they could argue that Parliament had entrusted administrators and tribunals with discretion and the court ought to respect that.[7] That argument can appear most readily in cases against ministers' decisions, for ministers are most clearly subject only to the controls of political judgment. For example, in a case that the High Court decided immediately after the war, the complainant asked the Court not to allow the Minister of War Transport to decide that a highway, temporarily blocked by the minister under his emergency powers, could be permanently blocked. The statute did not say anything explicit about such an extension of powers; the statute allowed the minister to issue orders about highways "if he was satisfied" that it was necessary. The King's Bench held that it simply did not have the jurisdiction to consider whether the minister was satisfied (In re Beck and Pollitzer's Application [1948] 2 K.B. 339). That kind of reasoning could appear even in low-profile, case-level decisions, though because of the political justification of ministerial responsibility to Parliament it was most readily available in cases against ministers.

Alternatively, the courts could see problems of administration, whether compulsory purchase orders or benefits claims, as ones of getting the law right, something tribunals and administrators might not do and that courts needed to ensure. When courts took this approach, there was often very little argument about administrative authority or the need for discretion or the formal qualities of a rule, whether it was a statute or only delegated legislation. Instead, whatever the relevant provision was, the courts would interpret it as though it created enforceable legal rights against administrators.[8] The courts used legal analogies particularly in decisions regarding pensions that might be seen as earned; wartime pensions and national insurance tribunals provide important examples. As table 2.3 shows, while the numbers of benefits cases were often very small in the sample, individuals did win. In 1957, for example, the Court of Appeal reviewed a medical appeal tribunal's holding that a man was not entitled to full compensation for an injury to his eye (*R. v. Medical Appeal Tribunal ex p. Gilmore* [1957] 1 Q.B. 574). The court, based on the tribunal's record, held that the tribunal had misinterpreted its regulations; it had to assess how much he was entitled to for his total disability rather than only for the injury itself. This approach, one based on a sense of legal rights, by no means guaranteed that a complainant would win. It just meant that the court would do more than the judicial equivalent of shrugging its shoulders. It would apply administrative rules to see if decisions under them were justified.[9] Whether to read this type of case as part of administrative law or not is sometimes seen as difficult. For the case evaluates the application of a rule in a particular type of case, rather than evaluating the nature of British administrative authority. It creates no general principle except that administrators can err. But that is a key background presumption in reading statutes as though they create legal rights. Even in state benefits programs, courts were willing to hold for claimants against administrators.

TABLE 2.3. Cases Won by Individuals (by percent)

Subject	1946–50	1951–55	1956–60	1961–65	1966–70
Benefits	65 (13)	17 (8)	55 (4)	0 (4)	49 (14)
Land use	25 (16)	32 (23)	34 (17)	32 (19)	26 (17)

Note: Figures in parentheses are total number of cases.

With this approach to legal reasoning, the courts also sometimes read in requirements of evidence and procedure against administrators and ministers. They did this in case-level decisions, even in the period generally understood to be passive. After the Court of Appeal (overturning the King's Bench) held in 1947 that tribunals could make mistakes, and tribunals therefore could only decide to reject a claim for a pension unanimously, the King's Bench considered the converse case.[10] In 1949 the King's Bench held that tribunals could also only allow claims unanimously, not by majority.[11] Hardly spectacular, these decisions regarding blindness and voting in tribunals, and they do not explicitly appeal to the nature of British governance.[12] Instead, the courts presumed there were errors to be made, as there could not be in cases that only required political judgment. To assume there are errors to correct is an essential part of what it means to "apply the law." For if all accountability were subsumed under political judgment, there would be no law to apply and the tribunal would always win.

Cases in Political Argument

To know what the courts have been doing, an overview of their caseloads and the results they have reached is necessary. However, to understand how the courts have been perceived in politics, the few cases lawyers relied on to express their concern over the courts are more important. Some very few cases have formed the basis of arguments for reform. They have provided the threads commentators found they needed to weave an administrative law, and some have become the basis for judicial review in the fields that have emerged in recent years. To provide a solid understanding of the problems lawyers thought they faced in urging the courts to supervise administration during the 1950s and 1960s, as well as to outline the resources on which the courts have relied, this section will outline the decisions lawyers have believed to be important, ones that usually most explicitly considered problems of governance and elected officials' authority. This handful of cases I will describe does not comprise all of administrative law in the 1940s and 1950s, despite the way they have been treated. Not all the cases were initially greeted as essential to understanding administrative law, but as casebooks and articles multiplied they became the basis for scholars' construction of an administrative law. Even so, the courts, as the previous section showed, were critical of administrative decisions in many cases. Their work was just limited to particular fields, and there seemed to be little effort within the courts to build critical principles that applied across fields. However, claimants did win in particular disputes. I will contrast the reasons and particular decisions made with a brief description of the importance in the caseload of those types of decisions. In this section I will describe the patterns of cases not for their subject matter, as I did in the previous section, but for the issues the courts used them for: who was sued—central or local government, tribunals, or officers—and what justified holding for or against any of the types of officials.

Governance and Discretion

As I have argued, both parties considered discretion for elected officials to be essential to legitimate, democratic governance. Political officials had to be able always to make the best decision under the circumstances; the requirement that they justify their decisions to Parliament and eventually the electorate was a sufficient guide to choice. Many statutes relied on this view of governance. Local authorities were to distribute housing as they "saw fit"; ministers were to order the development of new towns if they were "satisfied" that they were needed. Under an interpretation of governance that adheres to partisanship and flexibility, such standards left no room for courts. On another interpretation they could: ministers might be required to have reasons to be satisfied.[13] Once again, we can see the traces of the debates regarding law and governance and the appeals to tradition made by both socialist-leaning and conservative lawyers. Either the law and courts were subject to parliamentary judgment, or the courts had a duty to find the law and decide according to it. Cases questioning whether "the minister is satisfied" in two land use planning cases illustrate perceptions of the deference given to administrative judgment in the 1940s and 1950s. They have been cited as typical of courts' approaches to administration in the 1940s and 1950s, despite all the compulsory purchase order and tax cases the courts decided.[14] Statutes gave the minister of town and country planning the power to make a compulsory purchase order if he was satisfied that the areas as a whole should be redeveloped. Two cases decided in the Court of Appeal in 1947, *Franklin v. Minister of Town and Country Planning* [1948] A.C. 87 and *Robinson v. Minister of Town and Country Planning* [1947] K.B. 702,[15] challenged ministers' decisions to buy land, claiming that the ministers could not show that the land was needed to fulfill the purposes of the statute. The ministers had not answered objections to the orders raised at local inquiries.[16] In both cases complainants lost in the Court of Appeal, though they had won in the High Court. The plaintiffs did not lose because the minister could justify the purchase. The court instead held that justification was entirely unnecessary. Lord Greene, now well known for his firm conviction that courts could not legitimately shape administrative decisions, wrote in *Robinson:*

> How can this minister, who is entrusted by Parliament with the power to make or not to make an executive order according to his judgment and acts bona fide (as he must be assumed to do in the absence of evidence of

> the contrary), be called upon to justify his decision by proving that he had before him materials sufficient to support it? (717)

With this question Greene summed up the explicit standard for judging central government's actions in the 1940s and 1950s. However, he did not represent in that statement how all cases were decided. As we saw in the previous section compulsory purchase order cases appeared before the courts and complainants won. While Lord Greene's reasoning fit with the alarm legal scholars had expressed concerning the party justifications of governance, it did not capture all of judging. For example, in a case just the previous year, the Divisional Court of the High Court held that a landowner in a compulsory purchase order case had not received an adequate hearing, and the decision had to be quashed for that reason (*Stafford v. Minister of Health* [1946] 1 K.B. 621). Cases such as *Stafford* contained no optimistic reasoning about the rule of law to counter Lord Greene's certainty that only ministers had any say in governing. Cases such as *Stafford* therefore did not so readily play into the lawyers' debate about the role of courts and legality in governing.

A 1948 case, *Associated Provincial Picture Houses Ltd. v. Wednesbury Corporation* ([1948], 1 K.B. 223), which reached the Court of Appeal, established what has since become the postwar standard for supervising administrative action across policy fields through the doctrine of unreasonableness.[17] Wednesbury, a local authority (local government),[18] licensed a movie theater to open on Sundays but said the theater could not admit children. Under the statute, the authority could license a theater to open on Sundays "subject to such conditions the authority think fit to impose." In other words, the statute did not clearly impose any conditions on the local authority at all. The theater challenged the authority's decision as unreasonable under the statute.

The Court of Appeal relied in part on justifications drawn from party governance to hold that the authority could refuse to allow children into the theater on Sundays. It held that the local authority could concern itself with the welfare of children (228). The other justifications reached beyond the particular issue. Lord Greene, who wrote the leading opinion in the case, argued that Parliament had delegated to the local authority the power to decide the case. The sovereignty of Parliament provided one strong justification for deferring to the local authority. Once the local authority's general action had been authorized by Parliament the court could not investigate the decision. He wrote:

> When an executive discretion is entrusted by Parliament in a body such as the local authority in this case, what appears to be an exercise of that discretion can only be challenged in a strictly limited class of case. As I have said, it must always be remembered that the court is not a court of appeal. When discretion of this kind is granted the law recognizes certain

> principles upon which that discretion must be exercised, but within the four corners of those principles, the discretion, in my opinion, is an absolute one and cannot be questioned in any court of law. . . . It is true to say that, if a decision on a competent matter is so unreasonable that no reasonable authority could ever have come to it, then the courts can interfere. That, I think, is quite right; but to prove a case of that kind would require something overwhelming. (230)

Lord Greene's reasoning did not appeal to the autonomy of local governments or the significance of local choice. Instead, local governments are nothing but an administrative arm to implement the will of Parliament. As noted in the previous chapter, there was a history of substantial local autonomy in Britain, but during the nineteenth century the reorganization of local governments meant that they did often administer central programs, though with substantial regional variation and initiative. These are the kinds of decisions that could concern legal commentators: the courts, the most conservative of institutions, when they got the chance, would completely capitulate to a centralized party version of governing.

The High Court did not believe there could be standards of administration not directly enacted by Parliament except that the authority could not act on a whim. The judge cited the example of firing a teacher because she had red hair (231) as an example of an illegitimate decision. So, while *Wednesbury* deferred to political choice in exactly the strong sense that concerned legal commentators, at the same time the opinion suggested that there were circumstances under which courts would hold that administrators had made the legally wrong decision.

Lawyers could emphasize different themes in the decision. While firing a teacher because she has red hair is neither a general policy-setting act nor a very telling example of what can go wrong in administration, the case contained other language for governing administrative action. Lord Greene wrote that, though this case did not pose the problem, in the future administrative action could be overturned if the decision maker acted "as no reasonable authority could act" or took "into account matters which it ought not to take into account." What the case meant clearly would depend on the way it was deployed in the future.

Wednesbury was not typical of cases against local governments. Most cases were appeals of compulsory purchase orders, rates decisions, or rent decisions, as we saw in the first section. A substantial portion of the cases have been against local authorities or their committees. As table 2.3 shows, individuals won in land use cases. Individuals also won against tribunals, which were often associated with local governments, as we will see in the next section.

As *Wednesbury* illustrates, at least the Court of Appeal in the 1940s and 1950s had a generous interpretation of what constituted a planning decision and how far democratic forms of accountability were presumed to extend. Those Court of Appeal judgments were taken to represent the law in that period. Lord Greene in *Wednesbury* had implied that an administrative decision made in bad faith would bring in the courts. But in a 1956 decision, *Smith v. East Elloe Rural District Council* ([1956] A.C. 736), a local government accused of acting in bad faith still won its case at all levels, from the Queen's Bench to the House of Lords, and not because the judges held that the accusation was unfounded. The statute allowed six weeks for a complainant to sue. The House of Lords, following the Court of Appeal in this compulsory purchase order case, deferred to the administration because the case had been brought after the expiration of the deadline, even though the complainant alleged that the authority had committed fraud. No court would construct an understanding of the statute that would allow it to evaluate the local government. Courts would follow clauses that limited judicial review, which two dissenting Law Lords found deplorable; they argued that actions in bad faith fell wholly outside statutory powers and therefore could not be governed by statutory time limits.[19] Interpretive principles used in common law could provide the arguments for governing in administration, they believed. That judges in some cases explicitly refused to use them was a terrible refusal to do the necessary job; some legal scholars agreed.[20]

Rules and Rights in Tribunals

Alongside its discretionary, closed, policy-making system Britain has established an enormous number of tribunals. The busiest ones have heard appeals from decisions of national health insurance officers or decided disputes between landlords and tenants, employers and employees, tax officers and business. An Immigration Appeals Tribunal has been part of the administration of immigration policy since 1971. Tribunals were designed to hear appeals from case-level decisions because they could decide quickly and they were much less formal than courts were, with less strict rules of evidence and no legal representation. They were often staffed by lay people and advised on departmental rules by a clerk from the department.

Some cases have involved challenges to the decisions that tribunals made. Tribunals have a peculiar legal position. They do a courtlike job of applying rules to particular cases when a client claims the administration has decided incorrectly. Yet they are creatures of the administration. Setting up tribunals was sometimes a clear political effort to reach faster, less expensive decisions than the courts could provide. But more than that, tribunals could provide a more "purposive" interpretation of statutes than courts would. What was meant by *purpose* was either that they would decide with administrators or that they would decide in favor of benefits claimants.[21] They are often called committees and for good reason. Sometimes they are constituted as a subset of an elected local authority. They are differently constituted and apply different rules, but they all are responsible for administering case-level decisions and do not participate in explicitly reformulating or criticizing policy. Although tribunals did not fit into a law-policy division as well as courts might have liked, courts decided they ought to be more accountable through legal rules and appeals than ministers should be. Legal scholars also believed tribunals were held more accountable through law than other officials were; to those who emphasized the policy and administrative ends of tribunals, courts' judgments were an interference with policy.

In the postwar period case-level appellate committees, administrators, and tribunals fared less well in the courts than local or central governments did. Courts examined and overturned rent tribunals' decisions, for example. Rent tribunals adjudicate rent complaints between private landlords and tenants under a statute. In a 1949 case a local authority had referred all the tenancies in a block of apartments to the rent tribunal because there had been two complaints about rents by tenants.[22] In a suit by the landlords against the tribunal the King's Bench held that the local government could not refer all the tenancies without some evidence about the rents in each flat or without complaints from the tenants. The statute offered no standards for the court to use, and the court did not justify, criticize, or consider whether it had authority to decide the case. Instead, the court insisted that a tribunal must have evidence before it embarks on such a task. The case illustrates that judges considered tribunals to be entitled to less deference than were local and central governments. The tribunals applied law, while the elected governments set policy, and judges sometimes implicitly held that courts could apply law better than tribunals could. Tribunals lost in the 1950s in the courts about half the time (table 2.4). Their record, like that of local governments, is worse in the courts than that of central government. Both tribunals and local governments decided case-level decisions; indeed, the two were not always that distinct. Some tribunal-like committees have been simply subsets of local government. The tribunals' loss rate is consistent with courts' descriptions of the role of both courts and tribunals in administration. It is not consistent with an explanation that courts only prefer private property rights and will rule only in favor of those claims, as socialist commentators have argued from Jennings since the 1920s. Courts reviewed decisions from medical appeal tribunals and pension tribunals as well as rent tribunals. The loss rate and the victories against medical appeal tribunals are consistent with the underlying

TABLE 2.4. Cases Won by Individuals (by percent)

Against	1946–50	1951–55	1956–60	1961–65	1966–70
Tribunal	62	58	28	70	0
Ministr.	44	20	0	16	24

theme that some benefits are deserved and therefore are more easily assimilated to the model of legal rights under rules. Tribunals governing those programs in turn have operated in a more legal fashion, with legally qualified decision makers. While courts assimilated those cases to a model of property rights, they are not obviously property in the historical and common law sense since they were new programs. Therefore, noting how courts treated these cases does modify the argument that courts simply ruled in favor of property holders and ignored all other claimants.

Courts in the 1950s also established a ground for review of tribunals' decisions drawn from the practices of the writ system. A 1952 decision by the Court of Appeal overturned a tribunal's decision about the amount of unemployment compensation due to a complainant on the ground that the tribunal had made an error of law on the face of the record.[23] Another case only eight years before had held that there was no such ground for review.[24] Lord Denning, who appears erratically in administrative law as the champion of individuals against state administrators (or as the judge most committed to demolishing democratic governance), wrote the leading opinion in the 1952 case, distinguishing the earlier one. According to his version of review, tribunals ought to be applying rules to cases and courts could evaluate whether the tribunals had properly applied the rules. This decision was an important source of supervision; courts could ordinarily view tribunals' decisions as reviewable for error without reference to purpose or governance.[25]

All the officials who within British governance are not as closely accountable to Parliament or governed by political judgment as ministers or local authorities lost more frequently in the courts. Not only tribunals but tax officials, for example, lost. Similarly, in the few cases between central and local governments, local governments lost.

The cases just discussed review the substance of administrative decisions: whether the result is justifiable or whether it matches the statute. The other major ground of review in Britain is natural justice, which evaluates the process involved in reaching decisions: under natural justice courts decide whether the administration has provided a hearing to a citizen when it ought to have and whether the hearing was unbiased. Just as academic lawyers argue that courts imposed no substantive standards on administration in the 1940s and 1950s, they point to the lack of standards of natural justice. Hearings are usually required for quasi-judicial acts, which often meant the kinds of decisions tribunals made. Commentators cite a natural justice case the Privy Council decided in 1951 as the nadir of judicial review in postwar Britain. The case, which came to the Privy Council from India, challenged the Indian government's authority to deny a textile trader his license without a hearing. The Privy Council held, relying on British authorities, not only that the administration had given him a fair hearing but that it had never owed him one.[26]

Conclusion

Courts in the 1940s and 1950s reviewed tax cases; town and country planning decisions, including compulsory purchase order decisions; and decisions by tribunals. Most decisions fell into these categories. The courts did not review the policy-setting decisions of government in fields other than land use planning. But there were no statutes that would facilitate such cases coming before the courts. In the cases against central government that the courts did decide—cases that were most likely to raise questions of policy making, though even those were more commonly appeals from case-level administrative decisions—the courts held for the central government. And in some cases they deferred to administration in a deep constitutional sense: not because the administration had made the right decision, but because the courts held themselves not to be competent to judge, as in *Franklin*.

Where discretion seemed less essential to the scheme—with tribunals and local governments making case-level benefits decisions—the courts were willing to overturn administrative decisions. In case-level decisions, where so much of British policy actually emerges, courts were willing to overturn administrative judgments.[27] They did not develop standards of administration or new rules governing natural justice and they were reluctant to criticize explicitly central (often even local) governments' policies, but they did interpret case-level decisions as though they used rules and ordinary legal rights. The courts relied on a distinction between judicial and administrative acts; they could supervise the former while the latter could only be criticized through Parliament. The distinction is easy to criticize. It was frequently criticized as being too formalist, out of touch with administrative reality. But it was one the courts used and believed in, and for that reason it could be made to work. The few cases I have described in detail—*Franklin, Robinson, Wednesbury,* and *East Elloe*—are usually taken as representative of judicial review in the 1940s and 1950s. But such an approach mischaracterizes what the courts were doing. The question remains, why are these stories of the courts told when they do not fit what the courts were doing? The style of the decisions matters. *Franklin, Robinson,* and *Wednesbury* were cases that discussed, raised, or referred to the courts' place in governance, and they brought out the worst fears about the new administrative state. All legal rights would disappear. Second, people who watched the courts were either hoping for or nervously awaiting decisions that would impose wholly judge-made standards on the administration: decisions requiring hearings, requiring reasons from administrators, or holding that the need for planning was all well and good but that statutes set requirements. Courts did not provide these judgments regarding new programs. The ordinary decisions are easy to miss.

An analysis of land use planning shows that *East Elloe* hardly tells all of what the courts were doing: they were often willing to evaluate compulsory purchase orders to see if the local authority was justified in its decision. The outline of the caseload and outcomes in the courts helps to build a description of what the courts were doing during the 1950s: they seldom held against central government but held more frequently against local administrators. However, the perception of what the courts were doing is important. The common understanding of what the courts were doing is compatible with British lawyers' understanding of their constitution, outlined in the first chapter and the subject of a closer look in the next one. No less than the courts, they accepted a distinction between law and policy. If the courts were routinely applying law and reading legal rights in case-level decisions, it did not matter. Decisions imposing explicit restrictions on political judgment were what mattered. And the courts were not willing to judge the administration in that way.[28]

The courts found what they could readily perceive as a universal consensus on social programs and a hostility toward judicial ways of thinking about government, approaches that emphasized enforceable legal rights. The best strategy, some judges believed (as Lord Greene did), seemed to be to stay out of the new law. But, as this chapter has outlined, the courts never believed that parliamentary accountability extended to all the decisions administrators made: case-level decisions administrators made in land use planning and tax, and sometimes in benefits, were legitimate for the courts to hear. The courts translated political arguments in their own way; they did not abandon judging.

People have cared about what courts did for a reason; they want individuals to be treated well by administrators. But presuming that British administration was deplorable because the courts had little sense of the critical principles they could apply ignores the importance of administrative practices in bringing legality to administration. The courts were unwilling to create new rules of natural justice, but they often did not need to. Administration by tribunals was done by hearings. The courts were not the source of hearings, and they did little to expand them. Nor did they do much to criticize administrative practices. But where hearings or rules were provided for, and they were, the courts believed they could simply enforce the statutory rules and regulate the procedures tribunals used.[29] Where the courts believed statutes created standards, they used them to criticize administration.

Law and legality provide forms of administering, forms with their own principles and justifications of what makes for good decisions. It is less useful to see legality as a way of stopping administrators (Nonet 1969). From that point of view, it hardly matters what the courts themselves did but rather how open to criticism, participation, and justification the administrative programs were. While addressing that generally is beyond the scope of this study, the next two chapters will address reasons for the limited success of efforts to gain statutes that would open administration to legal justification.

One reminder in studying courts emerges from these cases: courts are often given far too much credit for what they do, as though they receive few clues or prompts from other institutions or as though the questions asked of them do not change. That is clearly insupportable. While the courts can and do choose how to interpret provisions in statutes, they find the job easier or more difficult with different statutes. A statute that only has as a guide for action "if the minister so directs" gives the courts little grip, and leads them to question the legitimacy of their finding critical standards. A statute that elaborates standards and regulations, though they may only be directions to administrators on how to tax or distribute benefits, gives the courts more to use. The fields in which they have heard most of their cases—tax and land use planning—are both those that concern traditional private property rights and ones that statutes have structured most. They are also fields of legal practice with a bar and interest groups organized around litigation as well as longstanding extensive internal administrative procedures.[30] Yet when legal scholars have wanted to argue that the courts have a role to play in administration these cases have been taken from their moorings in particular policies and used to argue for general powers of review (see, e.g., H.W.R. Wade 1961; deSmith 1959; and Griffith and Street 1951).

The theory of British governance drawn out of the reasons offered in the few cases I discussed—one that emphasized discretion for elected officials and some enforceable rules for administrators and tribunals—is the theory explicitly held to be the one Britain ought to and does work by, but it does not accurately capture practices in British courts, as the description of the caseload of the courts shows. (It does not capture the practices of any British institution as well as it once did.) While it is interesting that claimants have always won in British courts since World War II, the findings do not tell us enough. Conclusions drawn from comparisons of patterns of results must be tentative. Little more can be said than that individuals have won consistently since 1945, generally in appeals under statutes and in particular fields such as land use and tax. Without attending to the reasons courts give, the assumptions they make, and how they change the way they use decisions little can be drawn out of the different reversal rates against central and local government in the different fields.

The courts have changed in recent years but not in anything so straightforward as how often they overturn administrative actions. Instead, they hear a great many more cases now than they did in the late 1940s, particularly under the prerogative writs but also under statutes. They also hear appeals in new fields such as prisoners' rights, immigration, and race relations. These changes are, as we will see in the discussion of immigration, as much a result of changes in statutes and interest group organization and activity as they are a result of a change in approaches in the courts.

The findings do not get at one of the most significant issues: not only did tax and compulsory purchase order cases predominate but very little of gripping interest or importance in the regulatory state showed up routinely in the cases. Cases did not evaluate the standards of air pollution control, water pollution control, or workplace safety. They did not control the significance of sex or race discrimination law in Britain, though where they have had the opportunity they have often made it more difficult to bring cases and they have limited the investigatory powers of the agencies in charge (Kenney 1992; Commission for Racial Equality 1989). Taking what courts do—what they decide and how they reason—as the only thing worth studying about the courts takes the caseload as given, not allowing us to ask why only those cases are in court. Discovering why case-level decisions predominate requires looking outside both the courts' reasoning and their caseload to the reasons why statutes have been drawn as they have been and how the executive has controlled what issues may come to court. The burden of the next two chapters is to describe how the perceptions of what courts have been doing have shaped attempts to reform them through efforts to impose judicial review on British politics. Leading British judges in the 1950s grappled with the problem of how to fit courts and law into what they accepted as British constitutional doctrine; judges and others searched for a way to limit how deferential they had to be within the law-politics or policy divide (Denning 1949; Devlin 1956; Evershed 1956, 1961; Kilmuir 1959). Despite the affirmation in most of these discussions of the general irrelevance of the courts to most administration, civil servants in the Lord Chancellor's Department paid attention to these writings. Not only did they not want administrators to be criticized but they knew that criticisms of administrative state power could play on public anxiety. Immediately after the publication of his lectures in 1949, which criticized administrative tribunals, Lord Denning found himself subject to criticism from the Lord Chancellor's Department. Departmental officials thought this would be "controversial" (Stevens 1993, 93). The discussion about state administrative power and law accompanied a reform effort in the 1950s that enacted cultural anxiety about state power. How that reform condensed anxiety and the institutional limits to change are the topics of the next chapter.

CHAPTER 3

Imposing Legal Accountability, 1954–58

In 1938 the Air Ministry acquired Crichel Down for the purposes of a practice bombing range. The tract was poor land set in the countryside in Dorset. It provided the expanse that the Air Ministry needed for practice bombing. In 1949 the Ministry of Supply, by then in charge of the land, decided the state no longer needed the land and could let it out for agriculture. It took time to do that as they had to clear the land of bombs. In 1950 the Ministry of Agriculture gained control of the land, as the 1947 Agriculture Act had created the Agricultural Land Commission to manage state-owned agricultural land. The Agricultural Land Commission began to let out the land for farming; the postwar need for food lent a sense of urgency to letting the land, and developments in agriculture had made it more valuable for farming. The Agriculture Act also allowed the ministry to sell land should it choose to do so. In 1950 Lieutenant Commander George Marten, whose wife's family had owned the land before the Air Ministry acquired it, asked to buy it back. The Agricultural Land Commission refused. In 1952 Marten wrote his Conservative M.P., and the whole issue became the subject of major government inquiries, resulting in the resignation of the Minister of Agriculture in July of 1954 after more than six hours of debate in Parliament.[1] That signifies how much it was an issue to political elites who framed the issue for the broader public: a minister resigned, the national legislature debated the issue, and eventually the government sponsored a major inquiry into the problems of fairness in an administrative state.

Lieutenant Commander Marten was able to invoke all the concerns an administrative state could raise in Britain. The issues reached back to the 1930s discussions of state power. He found a bureaucratic run-around, contacting the Air Ministry only to be told to contact the Ministry of Supply and from there shunted to the Ministry of Agriculture. The land was not returned to agriculture as quickly as some local people thought it should have been, raising the specter of bureaucratic delay. Furthermore, the land was held in state ownership but no longer for a long-recognized state purpose, defense. And even a Conservative government, elected in 1951, seemed to prefer state ownership rather than, as Marten put it in his 1952 letter to his M.P., "offer[ing it] to the original owner or put[ting] it on the free market" (Nicolson 1986, 52). Marten's ability to address concerns about state power meant that his issue led to the major postwar public discussion of what fairness and legal accountability in an administrative state meant.

Governing elites, who by the 1950s were anxious about the capabilities of the British state, were concerned about administrative state power. Internationally, Britain was losing its empire. In 1956 it would suffer a humiliating defeat in Suez, directly challenging images governing elites had of Britain as a world power. Domestically elites worried about the place of the individual in mass society (Sinfield 1989); the administrative state provided evidence for that concern. Analysis of how to reconcile common law rights and bureaucratic power addressed it. While Robson had condemned an inquiry into accountability in the 1930s as doomed because the investigating committee began with "the dead hand of Dicey on its neck," the continuing recurrence of the issue is perhaps less an illustration of Dicey's grip than an illustration of the ongoing need for reassurance that the state is comprehensible and accountable yet capable of performing complex tasks quickly and efficiently.[2] Comprehensibility requires explanation, and accountability requires procedures; neither tend to fit well with working quickly. Polities want all three, and therefore struggles for reform recur.

Crichel Down provided an occasion to address these concerns publicly. In 1955 the government appointed the Franks Committee, an ad hoc committee charged with considering administrative accountability. Analyzing the Committee's explicit effort to enact a legality that would govern all of administration illuminates the concerns of British academics, lawyers, and politicians and the political alignments regarding the role of legality in administration. Despite the perception that Britain has been uninterested in legality and courts (Vogel 1986), the problem of legal accountability for administration has repeatedly appeared in political discussion. A focused consideration of specific postwar efforts to legalize administration provides insight. The Franks Committee provides an opportunity to explain choices about legality. Because the Franks Committee worked in a context of already existing concern about legality, the next two sections will establish the framework of debate that the Committee entered. This chapter will then turn to what the Franks Committee did and what the government's reaction was.

Legality: The Problem

In the introduction I referred to elements of legality—that there are rules, that they are known, that they are stated ahead of time, that they do not change too often or too quickly. These requirements can be imposed from without, perhaps through courts reviewing what administrators do. One political position is that for there to be legality in administration there must be an avenue for courts to review administrators. However, administrators could also or alternatively create legality within an organization. Review by courts might not be the only thing to discuss in discussing legality. When speaking of such internal developments, legality incorporates all efforts to borrow and institutionalize procedures from courts into administration. In addition to the issues already mentioned, that includes establishing a system of precedent, staffing administration with lawyers, and establishing courtroom-based standards of evidence and reasoning. While courts when judging administration can overturn the substance of administrative decisions or impose procedures, legality in administration can also be imposed by other institutions. Legislatures can institute internal appeal boards or administrative agencies can adopt strict rules governing their decision making.[3] Legality can be something that only happens within courts or it can be practice *within* administrative institutions. When American administration is condemned as "legalistic," people are as often referring to procedures within administrations as they are to review by courts (Mashaw 1983; Stewart 1975; Kelman 1981).

Lawyers in Britain in the 1950s split over whether legality would simply be a set of practices adopted internally to administration or whether it would mean easily available appeal to courts with courts' imposition of procedures and overturning of decisions. The division can be captured as a split between those who pursued internal administrative legality and those who were more concerned about supervision by courts, or external legality.

The structure of state institutions in Britain intersected with the legal profession's articulation of the right way to govern to shape the policy of administrative accountability. Lawyers built upon their cultural ideals and an assessment of what was wrong with the British administrative state. These concerns had found play in the wider culture; the Labour party discussed the importance of the individual in the new administrative state (Labour Party 1953). Lawyers' societies raised these issues around elections (Inns of Court Conservative and Unionist Society 1953). Lawyers' efforts for universal reform found a hook in the culture in Crichel Down. The reform that came out of the debate over Crichel Down was deeply shaped by the structure of institutions in Britain. The government's control over Parliament gave it substantial control over reform. The task for this chapter is to trace the debate and the reform. The first job is to discuss the rule-of-law ideal as it was articulated by the profession after World War II.

To do so I need to trace differences and similarities among lawyers in the reform proposals they made. Lawyers who seemed to differ about the value of the administrative state shared some perspectives about the importance of accountability through legal form. Some lawyers explicitly identified with a party. However, professional politics rests on a claim to expertise that transcends party affiliation. Not all the lawyers explicitly identified with a party: if they did, they did not make party affiliation a key to what they advocated to reform legal accountability. Since they did fall into rough groupings in terms of the forms of accountability they advocated, I need to divide them by some convenient term. No term works especially well, which illustrates the extent of shared perspectives. To call them conservative and reformist misstates the issue because all lawyers thought legal accountability needed reform. To call them anti- and pro-state misstates the issue because courts are a state institution and the conservative lawyers favored courts' participation in governance of private property rights.[4] I will therefore divide lawyers roughly into conservative and socialist-leaning; I mean both terms very loosely, to highlight differences in perspective relevant at the time rather than complete political ideologies. When lawyers spoke as representatives of party-affiliated organizations, such as the Society of Labour Lawyers or the Inns of Court Conservative and Unionist Society, I will identify them as such spokespeople.

Making the New Rule of Law

Lawyers elevated an ideal of the "rule of law" as the right mode of governing, and an appeal framed in those terms was attractive to the public. Rule of law, an important element of the common law ideology, meant that Parliament set standards while an independent judiciary judged whether those rules had been followed. It also required that state officials be subject to the same laws to which citizens were subject (Dicey 1920; Hamson 1954b). The rule of law required a distinction between law (the realm of courts) and politics and policy (the realm of legislatures and executives). The whole problem of dividing the realms that had been discussed in the legal polemical literature in the 1930s was revived in the 1950s. Conservative and socialist-leaning lawyers agreed that an executive was to follow law where it existed and make policy judgments where it did not (Denning 1949; Griffith and Street 1951; Wade 1947). These ideals are nearly impossible to achieve. Rules always must be interpreted, and they are interpreted strategically by litigants and administrators. We will therefore always find that legislatures have not been clear enough or it will always be possible to say that administrators did not follow someone's interpretation of the law (Moore 1978, 3–11). Next, officials and citizens may be subject to the same rules in tort law, but what of social security law? The rule-of-law concept has opened more questions than it has answered, and it has been used to support conflicting concrete proposals. That openness, which allowed people to appeal to it while making very different proposals, made it extremely useful in political debate. These concepts proved important in lawyers' efforts to find proposals for legality they believed they could legitimately recommend.

What proposals did lawyers offer? Conservatives believed that legality required externally imposed standards and review, while socialist-leaning lawyers argued for internal reforms through staffing and procedure.[5] They believed they were arguing across an impossible divide. Yet they substantially shared beliefs about the importance of administering through modes drawn from a model of courts. Legal scholars and judges all believed in the importance of a system of precedent, of giving reasons to people, of the publicity of decisions, and of requiring evidence for administrative decisions (Denning 1949; Griffith and Street 1951; Wade 1947; "Comment" 1954a, 1954b). But did precedent matter for courts or administrators? Should the giving of reasons be simply ordinary fair practice or a ground for appeal to courts? Lawyers differed on the valence given the concrete policy proposals but not on the importance of the ideals. The rule of law was a unifying legal principle; it allowed no variation by administrative programs. While socialist-leaning lawyers wanted to attend to what administrators actually did, they agreed with conservative lawyers that procedure was important enough that it may not need to vary program by program.

Procedure was important to address the issue of the individual against the state. By that no one ever meant that the new administrative programs served individuals by building hospitals, rehabilitating cities, or distributing benefits. They meant that individuals had to be attended to in spite of the need for collectivist social programs. To see the issue any other way was to deny what law was—the protection of existing common law rights.[6] An article in one of the new journals captures the flavor of the debate:

> [T]here is one school of thought which professes the view that England is rushing headlong to an anarchy in which there will be no law worthy of the name and in which the legal profession will either perish or be absorbed into the civil service—the latter fate, one gathers, being regarded as rather worse than death. (Gower 1946)

While polemical criticism might have been limited to the "lunatic fringe," as Gower put it, many lawyers thought Britain needed to respond quickly to the problem of bureaucracy (Gower 1946; Chorley 1946). This sense of the debate was common to all lawyers; in their concern with clients of state benefit programs such as national health or public housing socialist-leaning lawyers saw themselves as aligned with the power of the state. But the interests of the state controlled by the Labour party would be to protect the interests of claimants.

Class provided the basis of cleavage about the value of universal procedure and the kind of universal procedure worth having. The claim to universal and totalizing procedure was central to the insistence on the importance of legality in administration. Issues that would later disrupt party political agreements and that were very heavily based in administration were not at all on the elite political agenda. They went undiscussed. Immigration legislation and related race relations problems had not yet expanded dramatically. Sexual discrimination and environmentalism did not fit easily into these models and were not yet addressed in established state programs. These issues would later break open the dichotomy between individual freedom and state power more thoroughly than the issue of welfare benefits did. In the 1950s state benefits were not taken to have a race or gender dimension.

The perception that legality offered universal legal procedures came out of a limited model drawn from existing legal business, political debate, and social differentiation within the legal profession (Abel 1988b). The model of reform based on property rights and court processes fit well enough with the business of lawyers to seem to be a universal model of problems in state programs. Most of the business of solicitors was in conveyancing the transfer of land (Abel 1988b). When involved in civil suits against the state, barristers too found most of their business based in property, including tax. The state employed few solicitors, and legal aid had not yet been created (Abel 1988b). Thus common law rights meant property rights and provided an implicit background for discussions of reform (Sugarman 1994). Practitioners did not usually work on articulating principles of administrative governance or law's role in it. However, their business provided material for the part of the profession that *could* emphasize the coherence of principles rather than attend to problem solving—academia. Judges also participated in the conversation at times. Academics had an institutional position that allowed, even required, reflection (Freidson 1986).

Proposals for reform came out less through organized interest representation than through the legal academic literature. In turn the issues that the literature had raised came through in testimony before the Franks Committee in 1956. Proposals were of three types, not mutually exclusive. Lawyers could advocate a renewal of judicial review. They could advocate staffing administration with lawyers and encouraging the use of qualities of legality within the administration. They could advocate a new court or statute to implement either of the two approaches. Gower and other socialist-leaning lawyers emphasized training lawyers to work in the civil service, which would bring legality to administration internally, and developing administrative systems of precedent through the new journals. The Conservative lawyers, in their booklet *The Rule of Law,* proposed a new administrative court to impose law on administration (Inns of Court Conservative and Unionist Society 1953). Both sides were willing to consider a new statute that could change in any one of a number of ways the legal accountability of administration. Neither seemed to think that this was terribly likely.

Proposals for reform were built quite explicitly out of normative concerns rather than a detailed assessment of how the administration worked. Lawyers drew from an assessment of what was wrong with the workings of the state under normative constitutional theory—the different versions of the theory of accountability that were so hard fought with the rise of party government. Second, and part of that, proposals were drawn from analogies with lawyers' primary sphere—courts and the regulation of private property rights. Proposals for reform were based on interpretations of what the courts were doing, what they could be doing, and what both implied for what fair administrative procedure would be. Concrete solutions were formulated out of those assessments, in part by borrowing from other states, with attention paid to how much other states and their constitutional structures resembled those of Britain. Solutions were quite idealized. As March and Olsen argue in their "garbage can" model of problem solving, solutions are often available for adoption before a public problem is discovered. Available solutions have a greater chance of being adopted as problems appear. As we have seen, that point holds true for legality in administration in Britain. The concern for fairness had emerged in the legal literature after 1929 and again after the election of the Labour government in 1945. The Crichel Down inquiry brought out those same concerns and proposals in 1954, as though they were closely tied to the Crichel Down public problem. Recommendation of solutions preceded diagnosis of problems. Once a problem was identified publicly, the available solutions reshaped the problem. However, legal reformers' favored proposals were ultimately excluded for reaching too far. In order to understand how the British state deflected these ideas about structural change, it is important to know the range of choices considered available. Therefore the task of the rest of this chapter is twofold: to discuss how legal reformers saw their state and the solutions to its problems, and to analyze the statute adopted following this attention to reform.

Internal and External Legality

For the first time in the 1950s journals were created and textbooks written on administrative law as a British topic (Griffith and Street 1951; *British Journal of Administrative Law* 1954; *Public Law* 1956). Textbooks and articles urged upon the courts ways of reading the common law that would allow the courts to impose standards on administrators. Conservative lawyers even more than socialist-leaning lawyers tried to distinguish legal from political questions (deSmith 1955; Gower 1946; Wade 1947; Simon 1954; Friedmann 1946; Treves 1946; Hamson 1954b). The point of doing so was to delineate the sphere in which courts could not operate. At the same time, given the sense that courts were refusing to engage the administrative state, delineation would also determine where courts could feel free to judge. Roughly speaking, not even conservative lawyers thought courts should be deciding issues regarding collective goods rather than more focused private property rights—whether and how to consult in policy making. Indeed, conservative lawyers, like judges, perhaps surprisingly were more willing to concede than were socialist-leaning lawyers that legal skills were not useful to much of governance in an administrative state.

E. C. S. Wade, a leading constitutional scholar, analyzed this issue in 1947. He pointed to a statutory duty that public airway corporations consult with the appropriate organizations when concluding wage agreements. Courts could not enforce such standards, he argued. That could be for two reasons: that such a duty is intrinsically a matter of policy or that it was not specified clearly enough in the statute. Wade actually seemed to follow the latter track: if Parliament would state such duties more clearly, courts could enforce them (Wade 1947). Discerning law and policy was certainly tricky, yet lawyers remained concerned about such issues because of their concern for the legitimacy of parliamentary governance.

The political settlement reached as a matter of discussion and introspection rather than explicit choice was that courts might not be able to find or create ways of evaluating the substance of administrative decisions. But all lawyers could agree that judges could find ways of governing the *manner* of administrative decisions, through the doctrine of natural justice (Wade 1947; Griffith and Street 1951; deSmith 1955).

Even for conservative lawyers, the idiom of legalism required depoliticizing complaints. Professor E. C. S. Wade, for example, argued for revival of the common law. But that would not embody controversy or political choice.

> Just as Professor Winfield has shown that the independent tort of negligence sprang from the needs of the industrial age, so without the intervention of Parliament there is surely enough elasticity in the Common Law to extend the remedy to meet the needs of a free society in the age of rule by the discretionary power of the official. (E.C.S. Wade, 1947:172)

All lawyers shared the approach of appealing to growth and an understanding of uncontroversial "needs of a free society" to depoliticize and claim as within their area of expertise the restructuring of British policy making through legality. At the same time, they were careful *not* to claim that their expertise reached everywhere.

A new statute could provide guidance for the courts; drafting a new statute provided a second possible approach to imposing legality. Lawyers of all stripes in Britain looked wistfully to the U.S. Administrative Procedure Act (APA), enacted in 1946. The issue of legal accountability increased in importance to British lawyers who wrote after the new Labour government came into power, which was after the United States had enacted the APA. Lawyers reviewed American administrative law books, and Americans wrote about their administrative law for British journals (Heuston 1952; Jaffe 1956; Schwartz 1947, 1948, 1950; Wade 1950). Knowledge was shared, and the policy from the United States was readily adapted to existing concerns in Britain about the importance of rules, reasons, and fairness.

British lawyers thought a statute could impose legality and explicit standards for review in a way that would bring legality to administration. Even though British constitutional doctrine required deference to ministers, some believed that standards like the APA's "arbitrary and capricious" could be imposed on British administrators without giving courts the prominent position they seemed to have in American law. The standard would simply make such judgments a matter of law not policy (Wade 1950). In a review in 1950 of a book on American administrative law written for the British, one commentator wrote: "Cannot Marshall Plan Aid include 'administrative law'?" (Street 1950). That from a lawyer from the London School of Economics tradition, concerned that legal procedures and external review not disrupt administration too much. A new statute could require hearings in administrative decision making, and it could impose new standards of review by the courts on administration.

A third approach rested on getting administrators to change their approaches themselves and to bring legal training to administrators. In suggesting this, British socialist-leaning lawyers did not see themselves as suggesting anything that ought to be considered controversial or ideologically charged any more than conservative lawyers calling for the renewal of the common law did. Relying on their own "idiom of legalism," they implied they were only suggesting reforms that anyone with the right experience and time to reflect would accept (Halliday 1987). The lawyers believed they could and needed to change administration, bringing internal legality, and that they could do that by pointing out problems and educating administrators. The new administrative law journals meant to do just that. Their editors designed them as much for administrators as for legal scholars. Journals would publish administrative decisions; the knowledge of how others did their job and how to do it right would encourage administrators to develop uniform, fair procedures—a system of precedent within administration, yet nonbinding and therefore flexible. In addition, lawyers believed they needed to reorient the profession: if it could learn to work within the civil service and attend to administrative problems, legality could also be brought to administration without dramatic changes, external review, or a new statute imposing irrelevant standards. Lawyers would bring to the job their professional practices. British socialist-leaning lawyers had as apolitical an approach to reform as the American New Deal lawyers did ("Comment" 1954b; "Comment" 1956; Gower 1946). Finally, reformers could encourage judges to read precedent differently. For example, a standard holding that administrators could not decide without evidence was constructed out of court dicta, or unnecessary statements outside the holding in the case, in the first textbook on administrative law (Griffith and Street 1951, 152).

These latter reforms imply nothing about changing political structure or forms of accountability. They do not require explicit consideration by any major institution—Parliament need not legislate. The administration could simply decide that legal training was relevant to administrators and either hire law graduates or train their administrators. Such internal reforms did not require major restructuring. Internal reforms relied on politics within expertise.

One final method of reform drew the attention of all lawyers, though for different reasons. It borrowed from the French system of legal accountability for administration, or the British perception of it. France, at least since Dicey, had been held up as having a system that did have administrative law. British lawyers discussed it in a way that molded the system to British lawyers' perceptions of British problems. That is, is there an institutional way to reconcile the interests of the state with those of individuals subject to state regulation? The French system seemed to offer an innovative "yes." The alarm and the need for a new approach, as the British perceived it, is best summed up by Professor C. J. Hamson, who in 1954 published a series of talks entitled *Executive Discretion and the Rule of Law*.

> There is a most important, an increasingly important territory into which the writs of the High Court no longer *effectively* run, if ever they did: a domain which in England the executive has made its own, in which its own will is paramount and unsubjected to any kind of judicial supervision, or interference as it is called. This domain is in France the province of the Conseil d'État; and in its province the Conseil d'État has introduced a rule of law which deserves the admiration of any observer. The extent of the French achievement is not at all sufficiently appreciated in England. It ought to be the object of our keenest study. It is *not* impracticable, as in England it is by some supposed, that the executive should be effectively subjected to a rule of law: the French have succeeded in the undertaking. It seems to me essential to the survival of any rule of law in England that the executive should speedily be subjected to *some* rule of law. (1954b, 6)

Two facets of French administrative law were most attractive. First, judges on the Conseil d'État had training and experience as administrators. Yet they judged complaints against administration. Surely this system united administrative purpose with concern for the individual. Second, the Conseil d'État developed judge-made principles for evaluating administration. They were not clearly tied to the statute alone.

According to all lawyers the courts in Britain were in sad shape. They had abandoned their responsibility and refused to protect individuals as they should, whether they were individuals holding private property rights or individuals claiming benefits from the state (Wade 1947; Griffith 1954; Hamson 1954b). Lawyers therefore suggested that an effective administrative law required a new court to judge disputes arising from administration. Socialist-oriented lawyers favored a new court because it could be staffed and designed so as to take into account the needs of administration, the general welfare, and the state interest—

terms used interchangeably. Most conservative lawyers favored a new court because the old court was so entrapped in precedent and concern for not disrupting administration that it would never create a protective administrative law (Wade 1947; Hamson 1954b).

The creation of a new court was the last of the solutions discussed to alleviate the lawyers' anxiety over individuals in an administrative state. To sum up, the proposals ranged from properly training administrators in law and developing internal staffing to asking the courts to change their interpretation of the law so as to increase legal accountability of administrators, writing a new statute with new standards for administrative practice, and creating a new administrative court. The changes that required no substantial institutional revision, rather just a changed perspective, would threaten administrative control least. The government had the least control over the possibility of judges revising their readings of the law. The government had the most control over a new statute, creation of a new court, and the relevant training of administrators. The latter probably threatened administrative discretion the least.

Conservative British lawyers were never able to persuade Parliament to consider legislation that would comprehensively reform administrative law. A standard cultural explanation would imply either that lawyers deferred to administration or that they could gain no support in the wider culture. Neither was true. For parliamentary—even administrative—opinion was easy to mobilize around criticism of administrative oppression, as the next section will show. Instead the division of responsibility and interests between the American administration and Congress, which allowed Congress to seriously consider proposals the administration did not favor, simply did not exist in Britain. The central administration controled the agenda from the beginning and could "veto" reform proposals simply by never sponsoring them rather than waiting until they were enacted (Shepsle and Weingast 1987).

Crichel Down and the Committee on Tribunals and Inquiries

All these proposals—the expansion of hearings and legal training, attention to rules, and a new administrative court—were already being discussed in the legal literature when a public issue emerged that fit all the existing categories. Lieutenant Marten's complaints about Crichel Down, which led to an inquiry between 1955 and 1957, raised the specter of the problem of the individual in the administrative state. The role of the opposition in the structure of parliamentary government rewards scandals that can be placed on ministers' heads. Debate is almost all that Parliament can do. But anxiety about British governing institutions was waiting for a public problem to bring it into public debate in the mid-1950s. Crichel Down can be seen as one part of that collective concern. Once a problem was found, legal academics could place their concerns on it.

Both politicians and the press played up what they saw as the agriculture ministry's mishandling of the situation, framing the issue in terms of bureaucratic menace to individuals (*The Times,* 20 July 1954, 9; *The Economist,* 19 June 1954, 951; Brown 1955). *The Times* denounced the "arrogant temper . . . among those who are meant to be public servants." *The New Statesman and Nation*, cautious about joining the Conservative denunciation of planning generally, deplored the "improprieties and abuses of public officials" (19 June 1954). Academics immediately addressed the issue as raising reform questions (Chester 1954; Hamson 1954b). Thirty years later a book attempting to correct what it called the myth of Crichel Down was published, arguing that bureaucrats had not mishandled things as much as had been understood at the time (Nicolson 1986). But that "myth," not its subsequent correction, is the significant part of the story for our purposes. It was the myth that gave the issue its shape and gave the public its perception. That it could be shaped as it was when a later account argued it was wrong suggests the power of the image of out-of-control bureaucrats.

Though much of administration distributes benefits and industrial subsidies and sets housing, finance, and pollution policy (to name only a few fields), Crichel Down fit what many considered to be the exemplar of the problem with bureaucracies: they did not exhibit adequate concern for people's private property interests. No other field fit that model of state power as well as the government's purchase and use of land. Lawyers who emphasized it universalized the problem of being a property holder subject to government decisions, so that it became representative of all problems of administration. "Fairness" for the private property holder whose property had been used for some collective good linked the administrative state to the problem of individuals in mass society.

The Crichel Down issue was somewhat quirky; it is difficult to see how institutional reform could solve the problem, if it was one.[7] For the ministry had initially just not agreed with Lieutenant Marten that he should regain what had been his family's land. Indeed, the ministries had an ongoing debate over whether they should presume in favor of renting or selling land back to former owners when the state no longer needed it (Nicolson 1986). But the case provided a good opportunity for more general consideration of reform.

On 1 November 1955, still in response to Crichel Down, the government appointed an ad hoc committee, the Committee on Tribunals and Inquiries (the Franks Committee), to investigate the conduct of administration in the British state. This Committee was similar to the U.S. Attorney General's Committee that considered administrative legality in the 1940s. However it followed the British practice of not including those who had actually been responsible for administration (Ashford 1981; Weir and Skocpol 1985, 128; Heclo 1974, 44–46). The central government wanted a reformist committee that would also avoid disrupting administrative practice. Concrete proposals for reform, drawing on the themes outlined above, proliferated in the investigation.

Although Crichel Down became a symbol of every problem with bureaucracies in their treatment of individuals, the Lord Chancellor—the minister in charge of the department commissioning the committee—gave the committee very narrow terms of reference. He charged the committee with investigating statutory tribunals and enquiries held "by or on behalf of a Minister on an appeal" (Cmnd. 218, 1957, iii). The Committee interpreted that to mean only enquiries that statutes *required* ministers to hold (106). Ironically, the terms of reference and the Committee's interpretation of them excluded the Crichel Down problem. The terms of reference also excluded most of administrative policy making by focusing only on proceedings required by statute. Before even beginning it was clear the Committee would not reconsider administrative authority in Britain. The central government controlled the design of the Committee and faced no important challenge from outside. Nor could Parliament effectively challenge the government's definition of problems, had anyone wanted to do so. Therefore, the central government could veto substantial reforms at the beginning of the proceedings rather than at the end.

Even with those limits, Crichel Down was used as a hook on which to hang existing concerns. People testified about much more than was included in the Committee's commission. Regulation of property was central, but unions did testify about social welfare and labor issues.

Wide-ranging legal reform was discussed. But the Committee had no reason to go against the central government. The Committee had few resources that would allow it to impose an alternative point of view anyway. It could not build alliances with any departments within the executive. Members of central government departments testified before the committee and it was very clear that they were reluctant to impose legality on administrative programs. Departmental officials testified, and unions and industry agreed, that they were reluctant to allow legal representation before tribunals or to make hearings more formal because that would make administration more time consuming and more intimidating for claimants. Similarly, courts ought not to substitute for tribunals (*Minutes of Evidence*, 1957, 310–20, 434–48). But that did not address the question of appeal to courts after administrative decisions were made, something to which no one objected. It also did not address the structure of internal proceedings.

The major institutional reform that drew the Committee's interest was a proposal for a new council. It would at least advise tribunals on their procedure, and some lawyers interpreted the proposed council as a new court. Lawyers on both sides of the partisan divide had advocated a new court, one that implicitly borrowed from French models. For socialist-leaning lawyers, a new court, differently constituted from the existing courts, could reach further into administration. The problem with the existing courts was that they were unsympathetic to administration. If some institutional solution could be accomplished, whereby concern for policy and administration could be united in one place, socialist-leaning lawyers did not necessarily object to the extension of courts and what they did. Indeed, they were less concerned than were the Conservative lawyers to keep courts out of "policy." The problem was more how the current courts were constituted. If a court could be staffed on the French model, with trained administrators, there would be little objection to the *form* of law and legal right. Professor Robson, an eminent British constitutional scholar, implicitly suggested what a new court could do in the course of his critique of the existing courts:

> [T]he Courts usually apply to disputes arising from public administration the rules, doctrines, standards and precedents which have been evolved for dealing with disputes between private persons. . . . [T]he increasing complexity and technicality of public administration appear to have made the Courts encounter increasing difficulty in attempting to control or even inquire into the substance of Executive action, and have led them to concentrate on the purely formal aspects of legality. . . . Lastly, the notion of a unified system of justice has inhibited the courts from devising new doctrines, new remedies, and new standards of conduct which are needed to meet the problems created by the Administrative State of the mid-twentieth century.[8] (*Minutes of Evidence,* 1956, 486)

Most of the other lawyers testifying—the Society of Labour Lawyers, the Inns of Court Conservative and Unionist Society, the conservative Professor H. W. R. Wade—all agreed on the need for a new court, along with Robson. The committee itself also heard testimony from a member of the Conseil d'État to explain how that body reconciled administrative purposes and individual claims. The conservative and socialist-leaning lawyers were concerned about different clienteles. Professor Wade wanted to protect private property holders. On the other hand, a representative from the Society of Labour Lawyers explained what he meant by arguing for a liberal and purposive interpretation of a statute: he meant an interpretation favorable to a claimant, presumably a benefits claimant.

Clearly legal ideology takes procedures seriously enough to accept these concerns about fair courts at face value. That is, those arguing for them really believed the form of decision making was important. However, lawyers were also arguing for freezing into place their version of what had been won or lost in the substance of statutes. Legally structured administrative procedures in policy making were not widespread and not the core concern; individual claims under statutes were. But within that limit the dispute over legal procedure was a dispute over protecting the substance of policy that was currently in place. Perhaps, in part, for that reason it seemed useful to think of generous grants on appeal by courts as important; administrators under a Conservative government might seem to be less likely to be generous.[9] However, local governments were also likely to be sued regarding the administration of some of the benefits for which they were responsible, and these might be Labour governments.

Note how much the lawyers agreed. First, they agreed on what the courts could offer: decisions in favor of individuals subject to administrative state programs. They were not discussing requirements of consultation with unions, nor were they discussing legal rights as structuring the relations between central and local governments. Second, they agreed in part on the problems: the courts were not doing enough to revise the law to "fit" administrative state programs. Third, they agreed on specific remedies—new courts, new common law standards, and new procedures and staffing within administration. They were concerned with different claimants—benefits as against private property holders, to use the conventional distinction—but they shared a sense of problems and remedies. Legal ideology provides a powerful glue that works partly across partisan lines. An idiom of legalism, a way of talking about law that deemphasized the political choice and instead appealed to constitutional norms and modern needs, dominated. Disagreement was stronger between the government and outsiders, as attention to the threat actually posed by a new court and expanded hearings would suggest it should. That division is illuminated by the testimony over which department should control the new council, which is what the proposed court became.

The rather formal question of whether the Treasury or the Lord Chancellor's Department should control the proposed new council contained the question of whether "law" was independent of "policy." The division between the Treasury and the Lord Chancellor's Department mapped onto the division between policy and law that the lawyers used. The Treasury was formally in charge of coordinating policy between departments. The Lord Chancellor's Department was the courts-and-lawyers department. If any department would have been interested in "legalizing" administration, the Lord Chancellor's would have been, if we take administrative interests to be defined by administrative position. The formal question of what department would house the new council focused the debate over what the new council would be and how far legality would run in administration. And in their testimony both departments were very clear. The Lord Chancellor's Department did not want to be in charge of this new council because the Department was naturally too law-oriented (legality-oriented) and legality was inflexible and not appropriate to administration. The Treasury, on the other hand, was already responsible for coordinating policy. It could be flexible and trade administrative priorities off against the values of standards and external review in ways the Lord Chancellor's Department could not (*Minutes of Evidence*, 1956, 1099–1100). Conservative lawyers found the prospect of the Treasury having charge of legality discouraging. Legality ought not to be a policy to be traded off against others but the right way to govern (551). After hearing testimony on what legality should mean in Britain's administrative state, the Committee issued a report.

In the opening pages of its report the Committee endorsed "openness, fairness and impartiality"—surely the legal British equivalent of baseball and apple pie (Cmnd. 218, 1957, 5). The Committee focused on tribunals that heard case-level appeals. The committee, commissioned by the government, also largely took up the interest in internal reforms rather than external review. Indeed, it did not even prescribe many standards for administrative operation; instead, it relied on giving supervision of tribunals to the Lord Chancellor's Department and on the professional perspective lawyers would bring (Cmnd. 218, 1957, 91–99).

Deference to its limited terms of reference kept the Franks Committee from recommending an administrative court, popular with lawyers on both sides of the partisan divide. While the committee wanted to retain appeals to the ordinary courts from tribunals, it recommended that appeals be concentrated in the Queen's Bench Division. Concentrating the appeals in one court would promote uniformity in law, which seemed necessary for creating a system of administrative law with comprehensive principles (Cmnd. 218, 1957, 27). But the committee only suggested concentration.

The committee actually did recommend opening up review by the courts, even given its circumscribed commission. However, it did so by incorporating a Court of Appeal decision. That court decision, which fit well within legal ideology, required that tribunals give reasons for decisions so as to facilitate judicial review (*R. v. Northumberland Compensation Appeal Tribunal ex p. Shaw* [1952] 1 K.B. 338). Following that decision the Committee recommended that all tribunals give reasons for their decisions. Courts, the Committee urged, should then be able to provide both appeal and review (Cmnd. 218, 1957; 25–26). After all, judges could not evaluate whether a decision was correct under a statute unless they knew *why* a tribunal had made it. In turn, that could encourage appellate courts to overturn decisions made for bad reasons. The Committee also recommended allowing appeal on fact, law, or merits (Cmnd. 218, 1957: 25).

The main recommendation of the Committee drew on proposals for an administrative council: it suggested an advisory Council on Tribunals. The Committee, based on its perceptions of the strengths of British institutions and its terms of reference, drew up its own proposal, which was only loosely based on the ideas of legal scholars who had wanted a combined council and court. The committee's council would design procedure for tribunals (Cmnd. 218, 1957, 30). The new Council would be the responsibility of the Lord Chancellor's Department—again a decision that probably meant very little substantively but symbolically put law out of the reach of policy trade-offs.

The Council on Tribunals became the centerpiece of the Tribunals and Inquiries Bill. But the government weakened the Committee's proposal by making the Council only an advisory body. Tribunals were to consult it when making their procedural rules (cl. 1, 8). The bill also adopted the Franks proposals that there be appeal to the courts on points of law (it excluded appeals on fact or merits) and that finality clauses excluding review be repealed (cl. 9, 11, 13). The government's bill did not initially require tribunals to state reasons for their decisions, but an amendment in the House of Lords reinstated that provision. Finally, the bill also provided for appointments of lawyers to tribunals, legal representation, and some of the other changes in staff the committee had recommended (cl. 3–7). The government relied on a strategy of bringing legality to bear that had been discussed by Gower and other socialist-leaning lawyers: staffing, that is, relying on the legal ideologies particular lawyers brought to the job as a substitute for structural changes.

As outlined in the preceding section, the division between lawyers who favored internal reforms and those who favored external review was roughly a division between Labour and Conservative lawyers. Had the divide over the importance of legality been simply one of partisan politics, we would expect that a Conservative government would implement Conservative lawyers' proposals. That was cast into doubt by the commission given to the Committee, which substantially limited investigation. It was belied by the Committee's report and, even more, the bill that came out of it. The difference between what lawyers, conservative or socialist-leaning, proposed and what the Committee believed it could endorse or what the government was willing to do highlights the importance of the distinction between lawyers who were not responsible for administration and government ministers and civil servants, who were. The party in power emphasized the importance of flexibility and purpose, just as the American administration when considering administrative legality had and any administration does (Ashford 1981; Offe 1985).

In the second reading debate in Parliament lawyers of both parties in the House of Commons competed to endorse the Franks report, but they did so within the framework of parliamentary ritual—that is, partisan competition. The Labour party wondered why the Conservatives had not done anything to limit bureaucratic discretion earlier and criticized them for not implementing all the Franks recommendations and for ignoring the problem of decisions not governed by statute (*Parl. Deb.*, Commons, 5th ser., 590 [1958]: 1619–20, 1629–30, 1639–40).

One speech proved to be an exception to the practice of partisan competition. The Conservative M.P. Charles Fletcher Cooke said that the two parties were united on the issue and that the civil service should be sitting on the opposition benches "with the permanent secretaries on the front benches," for the civil service posed the only possible opposition to the bill (1655). Attacking bureaucracy was politically popular in Britain, just as it was in the United States. The very existence of the Franks Committee had shown that, and the debate in Parliament was no different. However, the bill did very little to reconstitute administrative decision making. The proposals did nothing to open up policy making in Britain, the area of decisions purposely excluded from the Committee's consideration. The debate and the bill represented a disjuncture in British politics: the popularity of criticizing bureaucrats alongside the unwillingness of any central government to bring rules, general standards of review, or procedure to administration.

The Tribunals and Inquiries Act consolidated decisions the High Court had made. It did not provide for standards of review for the "merits" of administrative decisions. But it is important to note that this was not because the British culture did not support legalizing administration. The lawyers who favored such provisions simply had no place to take them; Parliament and the ad hoc Franks Committee had no independent power. Indeed, at least some of the English lawyers knew that, which shaped the proposals they were willing to offer (Wade 1947). Preferences were not a deeply embedded part of the culture, separate from the institutions themselves. The common law told lawyers how their state should operate; their reading of recent court decisions and statutes told them how it did operate. The institutions had some causal force in forming preferences about legality.

Scholarship on administrative law treats the Tribunals and Inquiries Act as a significant achievement, a triumph of legality over bureaucratic discretion (McAuslan 1980, 46). However, what started as a potential reconsideration of the powers of the judiciary and the executive in administration ended with some tinkering with the tribunals' procedures and the creation of the advisory Council on Tribunals. The Tribunals and Inquiries Act does not mark a turning point by itself or because of its subsequent use.

The Tribunals and Inquiries Act does not exhaust the structuring of administration in postwar Britain. It was significant as a prominent effort to get uniform procedures structuring all of administration. Changes in procedure in Britain have since then largely been fragmentary, working program by program. Many of the changes that have occurred in the United States, facilitating an expansion in legality, have not occurred in Britain. While legality can matter in social welfare claims, which come up in both countries, the policy-making cases have been rarer in Britain partly because Parliament could so readily revise judicial decisions (Prosser 1982). Even so, the consolidation of central control by the Thatcher administration has made litigation more attractive as a way of gaining access to state benefits or policy making (Cooper and Dhavan 1986).

The approach taken here suggests the hypothesis that if legality were to be extended in Britain it would not come through statutes unless the central state became much more fragmented, allowing some independent power for committees in Parliament. Nor would change come about as a universal set of procedures across administrative programs. Instead, legality would be more likely to come about through what would seem to be minor changes in legal procedure, fitting easily into the law end of a law-politics divide. Change would occur through institutions not completely allied with the central administration or through specific programmatic departments that can see advantages to expanding legality in a particular field. The expanded use and availability of appeal to courts in Britain came about in just that way: the procedure for applying to court was loosened and streamlined (Sterett 1990). The most noticeable change in legality in recent years has been in the expansion in the number and types of cases in court in part as a result of procedural change (Sunkin 1987a), a change that did not initially seem that important. Appeal in programs such as immigration (an area of rapidly expanding appeal in the 1970s and since) has looked attractive because the courts have sometimes given more generous interpretations of the law for applicants than the administrative tribunals have (Harlow and Rawlings 1984; Martin 1986). Privatization and its attendant regulation (Swann 1990) have also contributed to opportunities to challenge administrative action program by program. In the context of these changes and the continuing control by the central state over proposals for more explicit change, some lawyers' continuing interest in uniform procedural reform (JUSTICE/All Souls 1988) has looked out of touch (McAuslan 1989). But that interest clearly persists. That it does so in the face of indifference on the part of the central administration attests to the power of legal theory's emphasis on fair, uniform procedures and the availability of review.

Conclusion: Explaining Legality through Institutions and Ideology

To the extent that there are different and conflicting beliefs and practices in a society, as there have been about legality, we need to explain why one set of practices becomes more integrated into political practice than another. Analyzing the framework within which disagreement about the particular proposals for legality occurs shows the deeper set of shared concerns. To frame the questions about legality as liberal versus conservative is to miss how much lawyers shared and what a narrow range of policies was considered. Power in policy is not, as studies of agenda setting show, just a matter of whose solution wins but of how the question is posed. Studying the cognitive frameworks deployed provides a way of understanding how questions are posed (March and Olsen 1989). Effective cognitive frameworks shape an issue as most people see it, not as some small group sees it. Legality has satisfied that requirement; the media and politicians in Britain stated the same kinds of concerns that the professionals did. They differed on the kinds of proposals worth supporting, not on the abstract, antibureaucracy value. The lawyers did the more detailed work of actually offering and justifying proposals.

From this perspective it is clear that this account attends to the interests of regulated businesses or unions, though they were not central to the discussion. While business trade unions testified before the Franks Committee, lawyers outside those associations were the primary source for specific policy proposals. Business representatives saw little of relevance to their interests in the proposals and did not participate aggressively. The unions were clearly concerned about preempting union assistance and making it difficult to make welfare state claims. The lawyers and ministries tended to be the most concerned. Furthermore, the Franks Committee also spent much of its energy soliciting testimony and evidence from a range of state tribunals and agencies. Business associations and unions were not the primary organizations offering testimony and proposals.

But business interests were tightly integrated into the very concept of legality as a policy choice in the first place. The lawyers testifying before the Franks Committee were concerned with protecting those who held legal rights—private property rights—which meant regulated businesses and property holding individuals. To emphasize the significance of lawyers, administrative agencies, and ministers in settling on an administrative procedure bill is both true to the story and accounts for business interests, the more traditional place to look in explaining policy outcomes.

The organization of British governance shaped the outcome of policy in a way that is part of policy-making patterns but at the same time is somewhat distinctive to the issue of legality. That illustrates the importance of disaggregating and analyzing particular state-society configurations in issues (Caporaso 1989b; Suleiman 1987).

The explanation of efforts to change legality in administration in this period is suggestive for explanations of administrative practices today. In explaining legality in administration we need to explain the policies that are put in place, not just litigation rates or decisions by judges. To do that we need to attend to articulated preferences and state organization and selection. That would mean that in Britain the advantage taken of the expanded availability of review in England and Wales in recent years, made possible through both procedural changes and the expansion of privatization and regulation, should be approached from the perspective of changes in state organization and opportunity (Sterett 1990).

Approaching administrative procedure as though its meaning is static—as though increasing formality always threatens the control of the government or as though it always does or does not fit with a political culture—would suggest that none of the proposed reforms would ever be implemented. For example,

Terry Moe, in pointing out that structural administrative choice has a politics to it, has suggested that a parliamentary system such as Britain's will seldom institute administrative accountability to outsiders. Why should it? The unity of executive and legislature allows administration to avoid public pressure. The legislature either has little reason to want to impose accountability or has little power to do so (Moe 1987). However, there is another way to think about it. The ministries controlled this issue, so that changes in administrative accountability were most likely to come about when and if it was ever advantageous to them. The ideas—an administrative court, increasing the availability of judicial review—were available. If they ever seemed to fit an executive-defined problem, they could prove useful. But in the 1950s they did not, nor did they fit with the central concerns of union and producer groups. Therefore, despite the interest by prominent legal academics, and despite a public problem to dramatize the concerns, most reforms were not adopted.

If pressure for change were institutionalized the advantage of the ministries could change. Indeed, in the 1960s the government created a Law Commission to reform the law. With that, pressure for legal reform could be kept on a priority list and could be used in partisan debate in Parliament should a government ignore its "experts" and avoid administrative law reform. As we shall see, reform in administrative law came about for almost precisely that reason—a minimal reform was permitted in part out of a sense of need and in part as a way to preempt partisan debate. A Law Commission, like the Franks Committee, could gain enough attention that it could in part force the government's hand and gain a concession. Like the Franks Committee, it could not gain all that legal academics might hope for, despite a lack of serious sectoral opposition.

CHAPTER 4

Rethinking Accountability: The Law Commission and Professional Politics

By the mid-1960s British elites were expressing extensive discontent with their government (Beer 1983). The government was not democratic enough to attend to the polity between elections. The rule of law was under attack as a disguise for class interest, as no longer existent under social welfare governments, or both. Beyond the elites, the rise of feminist and environmental advocacy provided in Britain profoundly antistatist critiques of state power, ones that often refused to engage state reform questions. The state's ability to exclude particularly disruptive perspectives made sense of some social movements' choices to absent themselves from reformist discussions (Gelb 1989; Kenney 1992; Vogel 1986).

However, the British state's willingness to incorporate organizations advocating more marginal change provided a way for professionals to frame discontent with British governance in a technical way that could gain attention. Advocates offered a variety of solutions to the rather broadly defined problem; those within professions offered solutions that made sense from within their own professional frameworks. From within law, legal strategies for improving state accountability made sense. Others advocated ombudsmen, new parliamentary committees, and new regional divisions of power (e.g., Stankiewicz 1967; Stacey 1975, 1976).

The European Convention on Human Rights provided a context for legal strategies of accountability and reform. A rights-based strategy that included fundamental rights, while not part of recent British political tradition, looked more plausible in light of the Convention. By the late 1970s a discussion of the possibility of a bill of rights for Britain was receiving attention among academics and lawyers (Zander 1975; Campbell 1980). The diagnosis of what was wrong with British governance was wide and broad, but it could receive technical-seeming and narrow consideration within a professional framework. Legal accountability provided an issue with already existing experts and diagnosis to hitch onto a concern with British governance. The creation of the Law Commission in 1965 provided an institutional home for just such concern.

In the Tribunals and Inquiries Act professional organizations participated in the discussion of law reform, as did individual lawyers and academics.

However, none had been institutionalized as advice-giving organizations with ongoing responsibility for that function to the state. The Law Commission provided an ongoing commitment to framing issues according to how legal advocates saw things.

The Law Commission's conception of the problem with English governance came out of its more general mandate. Therefore, I will first discuss the creation of the Law Commission. It immediately chose to work on administrative law. Its efforts toward general reform in administrative law resulted in two changes. The first was in the writ system, or judicial remedies, and the second was in specialization among judges in administrative law. Those more particular reforms emerged from the interaction of the Law Commission with the central administration.

Law Reform and the Law Commission

Before 1965 law reform was managed within the administration on a part-time, ad hoc basis (E.C.S. Wade 1961, 1). Gerald Gardiner and Andrew Martin, both Labour Queen's Counsel (elite barristers), deplored this situation. They edited a collection of essays in 1963 entitled *Law Reform NOW* (1963). The book included essays from leading academic lawyers on what needed reform in a variety of areas of law, including administrative law. Written from a Labour perspective, J. A. G. Griffith's essay in that volume argued for reform in procedures and representation internal to the administration, but he did not favor expanded review to the courts (1963). In the introductory essay Gardiner argued for a Law Commission to "keep [the law] up to date" (Gardiner and Martin 1963, 9). That stated the lawyers' perspective on the political nature of legal expertise in Britain, similar to that of the United States. It implied that expertise was neutral, without implications for redistribution of rights or resources.[1] Such a claim formed part of the language of experts in the effort to persuade a public that they were making technical, social tuning recommendations (Brint 1990, 35–36; Halliday 1987, 365–68). Yet providing for rights and hearings within administration certainly carried implications about the power of administration to choose policy and decide individual cases.

The Labour government elected in 1964 established the Law Commission under Gerald Gardiner as Lord Chancellor, the government's highest legal officer. The expertise the Commission embodied was part of the Wilson government's program to bring the "white heat of technology" to the work of governing. The Commission fit in with a general approval of expertise, with a pervasive sense that expertise could solve a variety of ills. The second reading debate in the House of Commons illustrated the tasks that would be set before the Commission: it would clear out obsolete statutes, simplify the law, and bring it "into line with modern requirements" (Parl. Deb., Commons, 5th ser., [1965]: 48–50). In response to Conservative concerns that the Commission would reach into areas that would affect people and therefore ought not to be left just to lawyers, the insistent response was that the Commission would be updating the law. Clearly the Commission's venture into expertise and advice would be constrained; political officials in that particular debate saw that the public justification of expertise went alongside a narrow presentation of it. The example used in the debate illustrates the rather narrow reach initially intended for the Commission, alongside the assumption that such changes raised no legitimately controversial issues.

> Much of the law relating to landlord and tenant is still largely based on conceptions dating from a feudal or semi-feudal organisation of society. . . . Hire purchase law is surely due for a complete overhaul now that this method of acquisition of goods has become the rule rather than the exception. . . . The law relating to accidents caused by animals on the highways dates from a time when the motor car was unknown. (49–50)

The Law Commission Bill received the Royal Assent in 1965. The Lord Chancellor was responsible for appointing the five members of the Commission. Members included leading academics and Queen's Counsel. The first ones were Mr. Justice Leslie Scarman, a High Court judge who later became a Law Lord (a judge on Britain's highest court of appeal), a law professor (L. C. B. Gower, a Labour lawyer who had practiced as a solicitor), and three Queen's Counsel, one of whom was an academic lawyer.[2] Membership and activity were not tied to the professional organizations, although the commission has since used such organizations for support and advice (Diamond 1977, 397). "Representation" worked through functional representation by leading members of the profession in line with the ordinary practice of British commissions and inquiries (Ashford 1981; Griffith 1991).

An implicit claim to representativeness rested not only on functional representation but probably on the limited social background of the legal profession. In 1965 and even as late as the administrative law reforms that emerged in the late 1970s the profession was almost exclusively white and male (Abel 1988b, 70–72, 80, 172–73). Certainly the elite and academic segments were. While there were substantial political differences among members, they revolved around a Labour-Conservative split. That did not include race and gender. Race, gender, and even class created little of the centripetal tension occupying the legal profession in the United States. Women and racialized minorities were not just excluded from elite policy articulating groups such as the Law Commission. They were not even in the profession. Such homogeneity, within which different ways of viewing the world were not raised, facilitated the consensus that is part of expertise. Furthermore, the 1960s were a period in which race and immigration issues were suppressed from parliamentary debate and therefore from public politics. They just didn't seem relevant (Messina 1989).

The Commission was to keep all the law under review. If the Lord Chancellor approved, the Commission could undertake a study of an area of law. It could plan programs for reform on its own initiative in this way; it was also to accept recommendations from the Lord Chancellor for studies of reform. The Commission could not enact anything on its own. Its recommendations for change would be considered by the Lord Chancellor's and other relevant departments. They could be acted upon by administrative action or statute. The Law Commission could bring legal ideology to the administrative agenda, but it could not act on its own.

The Law Commission provided a new opportunity for addressing the concerns about the administrative state that have continued to reappear during the twentieth century. In creating the Law Commission the state was creating an organization that could mobilize and articulate concerns that members already had. The connections between the central administration and the Law Commission point out the importance of disaggregating the state, if "state" is to be at all a useful concept in explaining political choice. Connections, divisions, and strengths of different organizational players need to be noted; it is less important to decide what is and is not the state (Rockman 1989, 193–95). In this case, the Law Commission, while state sponsored, did not have to agree with the Lord Chancellor's or other central administrative departments. It had some independence based on its expertise. Yet divisions between the two would be resolved in line with the priorities of the central administration.

The Commission has comprised the primary body representing professional legal advice to the state. It does not represent a Labour-Conservative split; a Labour government began it but subsequent governments have continued it. A state-created organization, it did not otherwise fit within corporatist policy-making paradigms. It could not make and enforce policy, and it was not a peak organization the decisions of which would be binding for the whole profession.[3] As a formally constituted, advice-giving group, it highlights the ambiguous status of legal expertise in Britain's quasi-corporatist politics.

In its composition the Commission represented both standard practices in British commissions and a change for academics. High Court judges are often chosen to lend prestige to investigatory commissions and inquiries (Stevens 1993). The status was not exclusive to the commission as a body of legal experts. Rather, judges comprise part of Britain's "generalist" elite. Next, academics had been largely peripheral to the practicing profession. In appointing academics the commission brought them more into practice. The Commission was also criticized by the Law Society, or solicitors' association, for including only one solicitor.

In its *First Programme,* the Law Commission mentioned the rule of law in an administrative state as an important concern.[4] The first annual report also announced that the Commission intended to review administrative law (Law Commission 1967b, 27). It thought a comprehensive review of "that important branch of law which regulates the exercise of powers and the discharge of duties assigned to public authorities and which determines the institutions, procedures and remedies incidental thereto" was in order (Law Commission, 1966b, 27). The Commission was drawing on the problems professional ideology had long stated; no indicators of some more generally definable problem existed. Litigation rates had not changed. There had been no recent public denunciations of administration and its inability to meet demands. Instead, legal critiques of fairness within bureaucracy provided a framework for a problem. The Law Commission provided an organizational home for it.

From within the Law Commission's perspective, it was addressing long-standing problems. But that is not the best way to understand policy making in that field. Instead, lawyers took reforms that were attractive from the perspective of their ideology of due process and legal accountability and applied them to the British state. Solutions were much better defined than the problems they were to solve, just as they had been in the 1950s (March and Olsen 1989, 62). The solutions had been available in the legal academy since the 1950s, as we saw in the last chapter. But the problems themselves change over that length of time.[5] Indeed, many "solutions" were borrowed from France and the United States; only from a very abstract point of view could one conclude that the problems with policy making and bureaucracy were the same in the three states.

The Law Commission argued that it could help rationalize the law; Terence Halliday has argued that rationalization is the task legal experts undertake (1987). However, the politics of administrative law illustrate difficulties with the Weberian concept of legal rationality and its tension with bureaucratic rationality—two concepts that are sometimes taken as at least mutually supportive.[6] Rationality is a messy concept; exploring it before evaluating the profession's activity in England and Wales will illuminate the way the state can contest expansion of rationality. Legal procedural rationality is not welcome by administrators to the extent that it means supervision through appeals initiated by outsiders. While the English legal profession has been notorious for not contributing to rationality in the past, its proposals for administrative law have been similar to both American and French administrative law reforms. They have included stricter adherence to rules, the possibility of hierarchical review via courts, and hearings so that decisions are based on evidence.[7] These proposals should be related to what Claus Offe has called Weber's legal rationality—that of adhering to norms (1985, 301–2). Yet the bureaucracy has resisted them. That is not only true because bureaucracies support irrationality (though universal rules are often not followed and procedures are followed though they are not related to goals).[8] Rather, proposals for legal rationality limit flexibility and disrupt administration somewhat unpredictably. If rules and adherence to them are useful in a bureaucracy, it is largely for internal supervision, not external review (Weber 1978; Mashaw 1983). As Offe argues, legality-based procedures do not support a type of rationality bureaucracies value: the rationality of "satisfying functional requirements"—that is, meeting whatever goals are set—something entirely inimical to the idea of rules, hearings, and appeals to courts to interpret those rules (1985, 301–8). The tension between those two types of rationality has been the central conflict around the development of uniform procedures in administrative law in Britain.

That tension highlights a problem with expecting the legal profession to contribute to rationality. Even if an organization wants to contribute to rationality organization, the profession's understanding of rationality can diverge from administrators' sense of it. Rationality has become a universal Western institutional norm, but that very universality suggests that it carries multiple meanings. It can be more important as a symbol of legitimacy than as a description of how work gets done (Meyer, Boli, and Thomas 1987, 24–27; Meyer and Rowan 1983, 24–25). This tension between forms of rationality defines the tension between the Law Commission's concerns and the central government's resistance.

The Law Commission and Administrative Law

The solutions brought up in the 1950s and since were still available—a new administrative court, more extensive judicial review, and simplified access to judicial remedies. As March and Olsen (1989) have argued with regard to organizational change generally, solutions that are persistently available have a higher probability of being adopted than those that are not, no matter how well they do or do not accord with problems. However, the persistence of the Law Commission and the legal community it mobilized did not mean that all its proposals were simply adopted. The Law Commission ran into the resistance of the central government. Proposals were adopted that the Law Commission advocated and that fit with some concerns of some part of the central government. No proposal was adopted out of a straightforward response to a clearly defined social need.

The Law Commission held a seminar on administrative law at All Souls College, Oxford, in December 1966.[9] Lawyers and administrators participated. One lawyer called All Souls seminars a "universal poultice for difficult problems"; certainly affiliation with All Souls College has symbolized prestige within educated elites. Six months later and on its own initiative the Law Commission published a working paper expressing the criticisms of administrative law that the Commission considered important (Law Commission 1967a). First, it claimed that the system of prerogative writs (judicial remedies), which regulated access to the courts, was too complex. They made it too difficult to get to court (par. 6). Second, the commission argued that British administrative law focused too much on predecision safeguards such as hearings. These were costly and imposed no great control on the administration. No standards of fact-finding or requirements of support by evidence were imposed on the administration, and such standards might provide a better check on administration than hearings did (par. 7). Third, Britain had no principles designed specifically for administrative law—for example, special rules of negligence, malice, and fraud (par. 8). Finally, courts did not evaluate administrative decisions well, perhaps because they had no expertise in the field. They could not "get near enough to the administrative decision," as the commission put it (par. 9). (Such a diagnosis hardly makes clear what the problem was.) Each of these issues had been discussed in legal scholarship since the 1950s.[10] The Commission's diagnoses of the problems with judicial review led it to suggest reforms along the lines of the French Conseil d'Etat (Law Commission 1967b, par. 9). To English lawyers that implied general judge-created principles for review of administration as well as a specialized administrative court.

In its Working Paper the Law Commission put forward five questions about necessary changes in administrative law addressing these issues (par. 10). It then sent out the working paper for comments to judges, including some of the leading appellate judges, academic and practicing lawyers, government departments, and a few pressure groups (Law Commission 1969, 9, app. B). It mobilized support for its investigation. That support becomes especially important in light of a later statement by a commissioner that it had expected its request to study administrative law to be turned down by the Lord Chancellor (Gower 1973, 260).

In a 1969 working paper the Law Commission summarized the comments it had received in response to its specific questions about areas of law. The commission also took into account the views about administrative law expressed in writings by academics and interested lawyers' groups (Law Commission 1969, 13). It claimed that virtually all legal and administrative officials favored an inquiry into administrative law. Respondents were divided by their responsibility for state administration; state officials wanted the least expansive investigation while lawyers without any such responsibility wanted the most. The officials put top priority on changing the existing judicial remedies, or writs. A review of remedies had received the most support. It fit well into a law-policy divide, and it is worth outlining here.

The remedies system governed the availability of judicial review. Academic lawyers had long criticized the remedies system (deSmith 1959; Davis 1961, 1962; H. W. R. Wade 1961). It regulated what relief was available against government actions. Different orders applied to different sorts of actions, they had different restrictions on the interests they would protect, and different time limits for suing. People applying for the wrong prerogative order could be denied relief even though the government action they were challenging was illegal. For example, certiorari only seemed to apply when the government had a duty to act judicially or to decide specific cases neutrally. A complainant could lose simply for suing under the wrong writ. The point of reviewing the remedies system was to suggest reforms that would simplify it. Changes in the remedies available would mean that it would be easier to take the government to court. Such changes clearly fit within a model of legal rationalization in which law becomes more uniform and predictable rather than dependent on technicalities only the profession could possibly understand. Simplification would not change the substantive law or the complaints that people had about administration.

Many officials also thought important an investigation into the possibility of reorganizing the courts that heard complaints against the administration; this also fits readily into procedural reform not touching "politics" or "policy," the substance of legal claims. Lesser priorities were expanding judicial control to new areas and investigating the right to damages and the principles governing contracts and torts for the administration. Some lawyers favored a comprehensive inquiry into administrative law (Law Commission 1969, 3–4, 10–11, app. C). All those possibilities drew directly from the five questions in the Commission's working paper. The Law Commission then provided a summary of the comments it had received.

Central and local government organizations that responded to the Law Commission's questions, such as the County Councils' Association and the Association of Municipal Corporations, approved of an inquiry into judicial remedies. As the Law Commission put it, they approved of reforms designed to "eliminate existing procedural complexities and anomalies" (10, app. C). The government made a jurisdictional point regarding the more far-reaching proposals about judicial review and the "quality" of administrative decisions: the ombudsmen took care of those problems of review. The distinction made earlier between legal and bureaucratic rationality is useful here: it makes sense of the bureaucratic resistance to external review that the government offered.

The perception of the courts as favoring individuals against administration held sway for the government and the civil service. In supporting an inquiry into remedies, administrators used a very circumscribed law-policy divide. They did not mind making it easier to get into court under existing substantive rules, while they were quite wary of changes in standards of review. In a system with few rules governing policy—whether concerned with social security benefits or environmental regulation (Vogel 1986; Hawkins 1984)—administrators had little reason to ask for something that would make it more difficult to pursue and evaluate goals.

Of the groups consulted, only lawyers not within the civil service approved of a full-scale inquiry into administrative law (Law Commission 1969, 10–11). There was no direct summary in the working paper of the thoughts of *lawyers* in administration, only those of the officials in central administration who opposed a general inquiry. A few importantly placed, legally trained officials have not supported later efforts generally to revise administrative law; some remember a lack of support for it when the Law Commission suggested it. The lawyers' ideology did not necessarily build bridges between career civil servants and outsiders.

Despite the opposition to a full-scale review, the Law Commission proposed one. The Commission did not claim the inquiry for itself, saying that such an investigation would be too politically sensitive for it to pursue. So, while the Commission hoped to reach into all of administrative law and shaped its claim through an idiom of legalism, it simultaneously retracted its reach. It claimed the knowledge to ask questions but not the cultural authority to answer them. It suggested that a royal commission be appointed specifically to conduct the inquiry. A royal commission would not just include lawyers.

The Law Commission had initiated the discussion on administrative law and had sought support from leading judges and academics. It reversed this sequence in putting its case for a comprehensive inquiry to the Lord Chancellor in 1969: "The large response to our Paper and the other evidence of public concern with the problems which it raised clearly favoured the initiation of a study of administrative law as an undertaking of considerable importance and even of some urgency" (Law Commission 1969, 1). The solution defined the problems, and those who designed them searched out a constituency. The Law Commission, however, framed the issues as required for legitimacy: the problems, and pressure from the public, required a solution. In setting the agenda for reform the Commission controlled quite a lot. Despite the efforts to mobilize support, the commission had not found widespread enthusiasm for a full-scale investigation into judicial review. Yet it reached beyond what it had found in its survey in recommending a wide investigation.

The circumscribed approach the Commission followed relied on depoliticizing as part of claiming expertise. That meant presenting its claims to knowledge as though it were simply offering technical expertise rather than doing what it would have seen as illegitimately treading in "political" realms.[11] This strategy also required accepting that some suggestions were too controversial for such claims; the profession could not use the "idiom of legalism" to expand its jurisdiction without limits. Where it was reaching rather broadly in recommending review of all of administrative law, the commission immediately suggested that some other more broadly constituted group undertake the task. Maintaining a claim to expertise depended on withdrawing once the commission had found divisions.

A sense of the importance of circumscription was not exclusive to administrative law. For example, Mr. Justice Leslie Scarman, the chair of the Law Commission, said the Commission was unlikely either to suggest that it study labor relations law or to be requested to do so by the Lord Chancellor's Department. Labor relations law was too politically charged (Scarman 1971, 867–70, 868). Mr. Gower, in surveying the work of the Commission, said that it had known it must be most careful in areas of procedural reform. What he meant by that was reform affecting the practices and business volume of the profession (Gower 1973, 265–66).

Where the Commission did have an expansive understanding of its role, framing questions as ones of proceduralism and institutional choice also depoliticized and circumscribed administrative law reform. For example, creating judicial principles through a Conseil d'État could be a substantial institutional change, yet it said nothing about the substantive choices that could be made. Instead, it abstracted what accountability should look like by giving the problem to a court.

The Law Commission had not encountered any opposition to an investigation into administrative law from interest associations, but it did not threaten them. Each of the issues it wanted to investigate threatened instead to expand the availability of claims against the administration, disrupting (as officials saw it) the structure of bureaucratic controls by making judicial control more available. Consent of the central administration was essential before a new commission could conduct an investigation. That would be likely to occur only when the issue seemed insignificant, when political embarrassment and mobilization threatened, or when the Law Commission was addressing a problem in a way that could help the administration. Developing a uniform administrative law with supervision by courts did not coincide with any goal-rationality administrative officials would favor.

The next section addresses the central administration's response to the Law Commission's request. The reform that was approved articulates very concretely the proceduralism and limits that the idiom of legalism supported.

Reform of the Prerogative Writ System

Two Lord Chancellors turned down the Law Commission's recommendation for a general review of administrative law. Lord Gardiner for the Labour government said in response to a question in the House of Lords in 1969 that the time was not ripe for a comprehensive review, but that the Law Commission had been asked to review the system of remedies (*Parl. Deb.,* Lords, 5th ser., 306 [1969]: 189–90). Four days later the Law Commission was formally requested to review the remedies. Lord Hailsham, Lord Chancellor for the subsequent Conservative government, confirmed that decision a year later. Neither government was interested in restructuring administrative procedures so as to expand judicial control of discretionary procedures or to allow courts to judge the adequacy of evidence on which the administration relied in its policy making. They did not turn the recommendation down because there was partisan dissent in the profession about the worth of the project; the proposal had been general enough that it could command the agreement of both Labour and Conservative lawyers. While the formal lawyers' associations—the Law Society and the Inns of Court—were not that involved in the proposal, they had offered support in their comments. Instead, dissent came out of the administration. Or, as one senior civil servant said, "every permanent secretary in the land was against [the investigation]" (interview, 1990).

Once created, the Law Commission took administrative law upon itself, creating an issue to which the administration could react. In turn, the administration reacted to the substance of the issue, not just to its proposal by an "expert" body: central administration was reluctant to allow increased judicial supervision of administration out of a concern for the disruption it could bring. In shaping the terms of investigations rather than just saying "yes" or "no" to final policy recommendations, the central state has been deeply involved in policy making regarding administrative law.[12]

Though the Law Commission was formally part of the Lord Chancellor's Department it did not in this case share the central state's perspective. It had no reason to: it had no programmatic administrative responsibilities, as the departments did, so it had no strong grounds for wishing to limit checks on government's action. The Lord Chancellor's Department, however, did have to coordinate its actions with other departments and gain their consent to policies affecting them, which a systematic review of administrative law would surely do.[13] State power was important in halting the administrative law project. But it was nothing so simple as state against interest associations or, conversely, the profession allied with the state to extend rationality. Rather, departments had concerns separate from the state-sponsored Law Commission. Indeed, the issue illustrates the importance of disaggregating the state in different policy sectors (Suleiman 1987; Atkinson and Coleman 1989).

Instead of a general investigation the Lord Chancellor's Department authorized the Commission to investigate and suggest reforms for the system of remedies. A reform of remedies would ease access to the courts. That might influence the number of cases, but it would not change the grounds of review available. More concretely, while the change might make it easier to bring a claim under, say, a town and country planning act, it would not encourage the courts to develop general principles of fairness for decisions reached under that statute. That procedural change fit well within the "law" part of a law-policy divide. The courts could still primarily hear compulsory purchase orders and some individual social welfare claims, refusing to consider the policy-setting questions that arise in administration. That was the point.

The Law Commission set up a consultative panel to address the problems of remedies in administrative law. The members included a Law Lord, two of Britain's more prominent academic administrative lawyers, barristers, and solicitors from within the administration (Law Commission 1976, app. B). It was an opportunity for judges, lawyers within administration and academics to develop together policies regarding judicial remedies. Once again, representation of the profession, to the extent that it was accomplished, was done not through collective choice but through the role representativeness of the committee members.

As the Law Commission saw it, there were several problems with the existing set of orders available against administrative authorities.[14] It was not possible to apply for a prerogative remedy and a private law one—certiorari and declaration, for example—in one case. Such an application could be useful to get an order quashed and get the court's declaration of the law. Second, under prerogative orders the court could not order discovery of relevant documents, nor could it serve interrogatories or mandatory questions about the case. What this in practice meant was that if a case turned on a conflict of evidence the court could not judge it. Finally, the time limits varied for the different orders. The Law Commission believed that the system of prerogative orders was unfair because whether a claimant won in court could depend on what writ he or she had sued under, rather than on the substantive legal merits of the case.[15] The point of reform of the writ system would be to ensure that people would not be denied a remedy under existing substantive law because they applied under the wrong writ.

The Law Commission published a working paper on the subject in October of 1971 (Law Commission 1971) and once again sent it to groups that might be interested, including judges, academics, lawyers, government associations, and a few pressure groups, primarily ones interested in town and country (land use) planning (Law Commission 1976, app. C). The Commission issued its final report in 1976 recommending changes in the prerogative orders to address the problems it saw. The Commission proposed as a solution a single application for judicial review, which would consolidate and simplify all the existing remedies (Law Commission 1976, 27). One source for this proposal was the American statutory provision for review, which was the primary way of challenging agency action in court.[16] The Commission proposed that with this one procedure an applicant could apply for any relief available in the High Court. An appli-cant would not have to choose between the remedies. Under the application for judicial review a complainant could obtain whichever of the old remedies—mandamus, prohibition, or certiorari—was most appropriate without applying for any particular one. An applicant could also obtain the private law remedies of declaration or injunction through the same application (19–23). The purpose would be to make it easier to restrict government action but only under existing substantive law. The procedural change was intended to be a minor alteration, one that would not change the existing system of checks on administrative action substantially. At the same time reform of remedies addressed the real problems lawyers saw. Certainly the central ministries had not wanted to enhance judicial review very much; the Law Commission had been offered the job partly as a consolation for not being allowed to do a comprehensive review of administrative law. The government might also avoid an outraged debate in Parliament accusing it of trusting civil servants too much (Law Commission 1971, 1). A recommendation for procedural reform fit lawyers' longstanding constrained image of judicial remedies in Britain: if courts could be given power without changing substantive rules, they would not be given greater *illegitimate* power. Courts would still be limited to law and kept from policy, as lawyers formulated that dichotomy. The commission relied on an idiom of legalism, and it was easy to play to that sense of the issue with the talk of certiorari and mandamus—procedural issues that hardly explain themselves to laypeople. At the same time, while those terms themselves were meaningless in public discussion, the general issue could be used to show that the government had permitted the Commission to address law and issues of fairness, not politics. It just seemed unfair, not political in any partisan sense, to be shut out of court because one had sued under the wrong writ rather than because one didn't deserve public housing under the housing laws.

The commission proposed a bill, but the changes were made instead by an administrative order in 1977 through the Lord Chancellor's Department, changing the Rules of Supreme Court Order 53 (Supplt. 29 [1978]). One advantage of that form is that the issue is not debated in Parliament, and the government would not be questioned on why it did not undertake a more comprehensive review of administrative law as the Law Commission had recommended. In addition, time in Parliament is always a scarce resource; conserving its use is a concern administrators address in choosing how to frame policies. Order 53 was enacted again and changed slightly in 1981 by a consolidating statute. Consolidating statutes are also seldom debated in Parliament.

The rules were changed through the profession's branch of the state—the Lord Chancellor's Department. While not managed through the profession's peak organizations, which as a matter of longstanding historical settlement have not been tightly integrated into subservience to the state in Britain (Rueschemeyer 1986, 123–24), the issue was one of expertise politics.

Academic lawyers in Britain have also not been well integrated into the rest of the profession in comparison with the United States. They did not become judges (Tate 1975, 108–29), and their work was less often cited by courts than was that of American legal academics in American courts.[17] They did not routinely work with law associations on reform. But academic lawyers were brought into the Law Commission, and the principles they had developed borrowing both from French administrative law and their interpretations of English common law fairness provided the most readily available ways to think about whatever problems administrative law posed.

The point of limiting reform to remedies had not been to change administrative law very much, as I have argued. But motives of actors hardly determine the importance of the change. The simplification came when there were many immigrants who wanted to stay in Britain. In addition, statutory change regarding the homeless and rights of school choice also made it possible for more cases to come to court. Between 1978 and 1983 the number of applications for judicial review tripled (Sunkin 1987a, 432–66). Some practicing lawyers believe the order has had an effect on judicial review and more importantly on the administration just through the large increase in the numbers of cases that come before the High Court. Indeed, while legal commentators wanted to discuss "activism" in the appellate courts in the 1960s and 1970s based on a few unusual cases, some administrators have seen Order 53 as being the more important legal change of the 1970s.

Analysis of the politics of professional expertise suggests that it is the restraint professions exercise in defining problems that makes professional politics persuasive. By staying within their technical language a profession persuades a public that their expertise is relevant. But this is a comparative question; persuasiveness can depend as much on the audience as on the profession. For example, administrative law reform was very much a procedural issue, framed as only protecting claims people already had under the law. The Law Commission claimed to be doing that by proposing new procedures. However, no matter how technically framed, the commission's work attacked the administration and expanded the availability of review. The technical language of administrative law—certiorari, mandamus, natural justice, even reasonableness—fits into an idiom of legalism if that is broadly construed as the profession's esoteric language. Yet it was not the framing of the issue in the profession's terms that determined its effectiveness. Rather, the fit between the concerns of the profession and the concerns of the central administration shaped the reforms.

The reform of remedies was not the only piecemeal reform in administrative law. The Law Commission, in line with longstanding academic concerns, had also mentioned the possibility of an administrative court. That issue provides the topic for the next section. The explanation of the result is similar: the policy is the result of an interaction between the Law Commission's conception of its job and the concerns of the central administration. Only when something like an administrative court fit the concerns of the Lord Chancellor's Department did a version of academic proposals get adopted.

An Administrative Court

In its first report on administrative law in 1967 the Law Commission also recommended moving toward a special administrative court (Law Commission

1967b, 7). Separate and special principles could better develop in a separate court. Academic lawyers had also suggested that judicial review would work more quickly and consistently if a court specialized in it. Instead of having a three-judge court deciding administrative appeals, there could be just one High Court judge hearing each case. To ensure some consistency in the law, the Law Commission advocated establishing a limited group of judges, called a list, to hear administrative law cases. The 1957 Committee on Tribunals and Inquiries had considered a similar plan (Cmnd. 218, 1957). Judges would be chosen for their expertise in administrative law. The Law Commission was never authorized to investigate and issue a report on such a court, and this proposal did not go through at the same time as the reform of Order 53. However, England and Wales now have a list system of administrative law judges, which came about a few years later. That court was a solution defining the problem that the Law Commission had called the courts' "inability to get near enough to the administrative decision." However, the list system was not adopted until it also solved a practical problem faced by administrators and practicing lawyers.

By the 1970s applications to the courts for review of administrative action had increased considerably, even before Order 53 was changed. At least part of the reason was the courts' decisions against the administration in the 1960s (Blom-Cooper 1982, 252). A few decisions in favor of applicants encouraged other similar cases to come to court. Furthermore, restrictions on immigration introduced in 1971 coupled with the development of an immigrants' advocacy group provoked more immigration complaints before the courts. One barrister active in suing the government said that "applications under the Immigration Act 1971 alone was a growth industry, sufficient to swamp the courts" (ibid.). Controlling immigration was a pressing problem to national politicians, though courts and administrative law themselves were not. The new immigrants were seen as the key to Britain's race problems: there were too many New Commonwealth (or "black") immigrants to allow for good race relations (Bulpitt 1986). Finally, the presiding judge was taking a long time to hear cases. By late 1979 seven hundred cases were waiting for the Queen's Bench Division to hear them; that affected many practitioners because the backlog delayed all cases before that court (Blom-Cooper 1982, 253). The Home Office, trying to clamp down on immigration, found the standard two-year delay for hearing immigration cases frustrating, for immigrants could stay in the country that much longer. Facing these problems, the Lord Chancellor's Department and the High Court were attracted to the academic administrative lawyers' vision of a specialist administrative court—it seemed to offer speed, coherence, and an understanding of administration.[18]

As it stood, internal coherence was supposed to be protected by having one judge sit on all administrative law cases. The Lord Chief Justice sat on all cases with two other judges, who changed from case to case. But this was a slow and intensive use of judges. The executive's and lawyers' frustrations with the system of deciding appeals from administrative action led to an administrative court.

In mid-1980 Lord Lane (Geoffrey Dawson Lane) was appointed Lord Chief Justice; he wanted to rid the court of the backlog of applications for review. Mr. Justice Donaldson of the High Court was appointed to preside over a special two-judge court to clear the cases. Mr. Justice Donaldson had practiced in administrative law when he was a barrister, and he had chaired an administrative tribunal for three years; that experience was supposed to give him the expertise in administrative law necessary to settle the cases quickly. Within six months the work was done (Blom-Cooper 1982, 257). This accomplishment gave impetus to the idea for an administrative court.

The High Court, the profession practicing before it, and the Home Office comprised the primary support for the court, and there was no real opposition. Most often, lawyers and the Law Commission had proposed that an administrative court be established as a division of the High Court.[19] Such a proposal would have required a statute, opening the issue to debate in Parliament. In addition, an administrative committee was already tinkering with applications for review to the courts; adding to that task seemed the most straightforward way of gaining an administrative court. So in 1981 the Supreme Court Rules Committee established by administrative rules a list system of judges ([1981] 1 W.L.R. 1296). Nine judges chosen for their previous experience in administrative law would hear all appeals against administrative action. Only one judge would sit on each case, unlike the earlier system of three-judge courts. Such a system would promote uniformity in administrative law by limiting the numbers of judges hearing the cases. It would also save personnel and provide for speedier decisions. Some of the judges had worked for the administration: three had been counsel for departments, two had conducted major policy inquiries, and two had been members of the Employment Appeal Tribunal. These backgrounds give a sense of what administrators wanted in administrative judges.

England and Wales have established a specialized administrative court, a proposal that had been discussed for years. However, it was created as a reaction to a concrete problem in the administration of courts rather than an innovation based on ongoing lawyers' debates about balancing individual rights and collective welfare.

The Law Commission and lawyers practicing in administrative law and the central state administration have comprised an important working group on administrative law. But the courts have also participated in creating a separate public law, extending what the Law Commission and Lord Chancellor's Department did. They too implicitly drew on a longstanding debate (beginning with Dicey) about whether Britain had or should have a separate public law. On the one hand, a separate public law implied a special sense of public purpose; on the other, it suggested executive privilege. The courts have addressed this problem through interpretations holding that Order 53 and the administrative list created a separate and *circumscribed* public law (*O'Reilly v. Mackman* [1983] 2 A.C. 237 *Cocks v. Thanet U.D.C.* [1983] A.C. 286).

The Law Commission's understanding when it had recommended the application for judicial review was not that it had created an exclusive remedy against officials. Ordinary actions raising "public law" issues would still be available (Law Commission 1976, 16). While ordinary actions had some inconveniences, they offered some advantages as well: suit could be brought in the local county court rather than only in the court in London, discovery was automatic rather than discretionary, and the plaintiff did not need the court's permission, or leave, to sue. The time limits for bringing suit were also longer. *O'Reilly* and *Cocks* consolidated judicial review as a separate and exclusive public law, concentrated in London; the next chapter will address these cases further.

Conclusion: The Legal Profession in State Policy Making

The meaning of court decisions has been conflicted. To the extent judges do not defer to central administrators and policy, judges and the availability of review frustrate consolidation of power in the central government in a way that varies across programs. Yet the courts have limited the availability of review, and the courts have also interpreted Order 53 so as to limit review in immigration and for homeless people.[20] On the other hand, the availability of appeal to independent courts is an important symbol, particularly to a Conservative government (Meyer and Rowan 1983, 30–31). The courts and policies governing their use constitute an effort to limit the reach of legal rationality while acknowledging the importance of review.

The interest in a wholesale reform of administrative law has not faded. The Law Commission has not submitted a proposal for a comprehensive inquiry since the government turned it down in 1969 and 1970. However in 1978, shortly after the changes in Order 53, the lawyers' reform group JUSTICE organized a discussion group on administrative law in conjunction with All Souls College, Oxford. This was part of the strategy of expertise in which the profession is represented not through internal democratic mechanisms but through the prestige of leading members. Some within the Law Commission hoped that a good report from an interested group of lawyers would be the catalyst for a systematic change in control of administrative action, though that would be unlikely given the way law reform had worked in the past.

The JUSTICE/All Souls Group issued its report in 1988. It included a detailed discussion of the operation of the administrative system and specific suggestions for change. It was based in an academic (and rationalizing) perspective on law: it proposed a comprehensive code that would rely on good clear principles of administration, promoting uniformity and the possibility of judicial critique of administration.[21] It entirely ignored political choices in administration, including changes the Thatcher administration wrought, and it has been criticized for that (McAuslan 1989, 402–12). The consent and interest of the programmatic departments would be necessary, of course, for any substantial change based on a report. Acknowledging that, the other hope for reformers was that a comprehensive code of procedure would have become more attractive to the central administration in comparison with the piecemeal, unpredictable reforms the courts had imposed on the administration in recent years through some of their decisions. That hope has not been realized. The courts have required much less change of the administration than a code of procedure that the courts could interpret in any way might; adaptation is easier. Even after the JUSTICE/All Souls report was issued in 1988, the Commission expected to get no request to study administrative law. Lawyers in administration showed little interest in the central recommendations of the report, and there has been no expectation it would be acted on.

The Law Commission once again received a request to study remedies in administrative law. It issued a consultation paper in 1993. In doing so it worked within its limited commission; one commentator interested in more sweeping changes accepted the limited investigation but noted that all the work was "for others to do if they can" (Cane 1993, 887). It is hard to see how anyone could effectively find a way of gaining the consent of the government required for comprehensive change.

The story of changes in remedies and the list system of judges highlights the interaction, mobilization, and contingency of "technical" legal reform. Success (and lack of it) rested in part on how well proposals fit with the central administration's concerns. The Commission also illustrates the overlap between expertise, support, and representation. Commissioners were chosen for their knowledge, and they worked to gain support from the profession and interest associations most concerned. In an environment in which constituent support legitimates policy, an organization however constituted will see advantages in mobilizing support. That the Commission was not a peak association might not have mattered given its mobilizing efforts.

Such management did not ensure success. Even in areas that might be considered the profession's primary sphere—esoteric issues of court management in administrative law—the part of the profession that focuses on law reform largely lost in Britain. State organizations have concerns that diverge from those of the legal profession or of any body of experts. The deployment of expertise in state policy making depends on the usefulness of expertise to state administrative apparatuses within existing divisions of power (Stryker 1989). The report that the Law Commission produced in 1994 focused on remedies, to the frustration of those within the profession who see administrative law as raising the opportunity to reconsider administrative state power (Law Commission Report #226, 1994). While the legal perspective has not prevailed, the Commission and the profession did have the power to set the terms of discussion and offer the list of "solutions" from which administrative officials would select when court-related issues arose.[22]

The Law Commission is an example of professional politics—that is, a profession advocating a position in public policy by relying on its special claims to knowledge. It illustates the limits of the dominance of politics by the discourse of the professions. Analysis of professions in politics has most often attended to the undeniable efforts professions have made to consolidate a monopoly on providing services (Abel 1988b; Larson 1977). Professions have, however, also acted in more than that capacity. Reform of administrative law is an important illustration: while the cynical might say that is was simply an effort to expand professional jurisdiction into a new field, it had wider implications than that for public policy. Furthermore, by addressing concerns about bureaucracy lawyers were addressing concerns easily mobilized in the wider polity rather than simply playing for a putative interest in expanding business. Terence Halliday has argued that the effectiveness of a profession in public policy depends on its having consolidated a monopoly (Halliday 1987); given the English profession's control over conveyancing property and representation in court it would seem the profession would have met that condition. Professional politics often seem to be most effective when they work through a peak organization—an organization that can claim to represent the entire profession because all professionals are members of the organization. However, the Law Commission's effectiveness or its lack did not hinge on internal dynamics. Representation of the profession through respected elites allowed the organization to claim to represent the profession's position. If professions base their claim to expertise on their special knowledge, it would seem that the legal profession would claim a very wide basis for its authority since its knowledge claims are strongly normative and can touch on any part of the world the legal system touches (Halliday 1987). However, a claim to expertise can also depend on narrowing the framework, to emphasize that the profession is not reaching too far. The Law Commission circumscribed its reach from a realistic appraisal of likelihood of success in a political system that administrators controlled and in which concerns about breaching the law/politics divide were common.

What relation does the profession's advisory efforts have with its market control? Halliday has suggested that professions work in state crises when they are *beyond* monopoly—that is, when they have consolidated their economic power, which frees them for their ideological work (1987, 99–100, 351). Could the limited effectiveness of the Law Commission be related to the market control status of the profession? The English solicitors did not have a monopoly on legal advice, and neither part of the profession had a monopoly on representations before administrators or within administration. However, solicitors had a public jurisdiction over legal advice, and barristers had a monopoly on representations before courts.[23] Michael Burrage (1989) has argued that the market control of the English profession was quite strong. The judge heading the Commission represented the elite part of the profession. Barristers, who had the most market control, were also involved in the JUSTICE/All Souls Group, which was unsuccessful as a lobbying organization. The profession had some kind of market control when the Law Commission and JUSTICE/All Souls were working on administrative law.

In addition, the Law Commission was not always so constrained. Its work on change in divorce law in the 1960s was much more successful.[24] (That reform also went on without reconsidering the place of women in society, which was not true of divorce reform in the United States.) Instead of focusing on sequencing between market control and advising, two issues deserve attention.

First, the fit with state interests does seem to matter, as has been discussed. Second, the public ideological work can be a task alongside market control. Indeed, the two can be mutually reinforcing: articulating important law reform can provide an indirect justification for expertise-based market control (Larson 1977). Furthermore, as Halliday has argued (1987), the expansion or consolidation of a monopoly can be a spillover from legal advising. The changes in Order 53, for example, have been one part of the reason the variety and numbers of cases challenging administration have expanded in the last ten years. Finally, in the United States and now in England legal reform was working at the same time that the profession's market control was undergoing challenge and change. In the United States, bar associations have had to defend their economic turf while they have been working on issues of judicial selection, civil liberties, and reform of court procedures. Market control is not one clear thing, achieved once and for all; recent changes in the American profession illustrate that, as do the problems the British profession has faced (Powell 1985). The power of the profession has depended on how its expertise fit with concerns of other powerful and significant actors—the central state in the case of administrative law in England. Market control was an issue deeply enmeshed with the ideological work of the profession, but it did not have to precede and it does not explain limits to success (Abel and Lewis 1989d, 502–4; Stryker 1989).

Administrative reform in Britain offers a way of reconsidering the politics of legal expertise in state policy making. Halliday (1987) argues that the profession can help manage problems of governability when the state devolves problems to the profession. Instead the Law Commission, drawing on longstanding debates in academia, created and insisted upon the administrative law problem, using its resources to mobilize support. It was insisting on rationalizing bureaucracy according to legal rationality, while the central administration insisted on its own flexible sense of rationality. The ideological commitments and the different tasks faced by the actors are useful in unpacking the difficult idea of rationality within organizations.

The English profession's shaping of administrative law took a different form from that of the American bar associations in issues they have addressed. However, it was framed through an idiom of legalism, if that idiom means the technical language the profession uses. It did not in Britain rest largely on explicit reference to a constitution, as it does in the United States. In its reliance on proceduralism and the focus on who should decide it did share a conception of legal expertise with the American profession (Halliday 1987, 254, 256). That conception has been both expansive and circumscribed. It would give more authority to courts.

The way reform happened fit with a garbage can model of solutions looking for problems. The state was not coping with problems of overload or devolving particular issues on the profession.[25] If anything, reform added to rather than helped to resolve a legitimation crisis, for it facilitated increasing demands. Yet it would seem to be *exactly* in administration, where the state has been taking on the demands that lead to a legitimation crisis, that one would think the profession would alleviate a state crisis.

Administrative law in England and Wales highlights the importance of an idiom of legalism and the knowledge on which it is based. Problems were in part created by the existing complicated system of remedies, while both problems and solutions were created by the professional interpretation of what was wrong with that complexity.

A study of the English Law Commission's efforts in administrative law provides an opportunity to elaborate the relationship between knowledge base and political claims. A strongly normative framework did not imply a broad claim to expertise. The Law Commission concerned itself with whether it was overreaching. That was based both on its sense of legitimacy and on an assessment of the likelihood of success with the central state. If the U.S. legal profession has a broader definition of its expertise when recommending policies, that may rest on a wider scope of client service it has already won as well as on an understanding of the broader scope for successfully pressing claims to state authorities. Those two factors can work through the profession's epistemology, making the power of an epistemology variable across societies.

The central concern legal elites had articulated regarding administration throughout the twentieth century had been that of the individual against the state; that concern had justified the attention the Law Commission paid to remedies. By the 1980s political concerns about governance had shifted to include an interest in participatory policymaking—that is, for example, consultation as a matter of legal right rather than corporatist practice. Those concerns had appeared in judicial review of administration in the United States by the 1970s. As litigants used the new remedy for judicial review, once again legal commentators almost ignored the ordinary caseload and instead emphasized new cases they could fit into a framework of concern about the structure of policymaking in Britain. The framework not only relied upon new concerns about participation; it drew on the ideology of the rule of law. In contested cases over statutory interpretation the rule of law framework focused political debate on whether central or local governments were law-abiding. Duties of consultation that legalist commentators had asumed could not be legally enforceable in the 1940s became part of the new debate over accountability in governance.

As we have seen, administrative law has sporadically been of concern to publics in Britain in this century, while it has been a topic of almost continuous concern to legal academics specializing in the field. The Thatcher administration's confrontation with local governments and its attempt to control their spending provided grist for lawsuits in the 1980s. In turn, the meaning in the legal profession of law as providing an alternative to partisan governance and a curb on it has been resurrected. That ideology as much as anything else has provoked some reorganization in the legal field in response to both the increasing visibility of court decisions and thereby the increasing attractiveness of law as an important governing institution. The focus of this study shifts in the next two chapters, which turn to the broadening and continuing dispute about the point of courts and legality in the British state.

The participatory democratic concerns of social movements in the 1960s was translated into the discourse of legal academics by the 1980s. Rather than emphasizing the importance of the generous policy choice by judges, legal advocates in both the United States and Britain had shifted to a concern with a participatory ethic. American administrative law among both judges and Congress had made that shift by the mid-1970s by widening the law of standing and by lowering other barriers to getting into court and participating in administration (Stewart 1975). That concern had crossed the Atlantic by the early 1980s, with British legal academics urging on British courts equivalents of the American "hard look" doctrine whereby courts should closely scrutinize administrative decision making for its fairness (Craig, 1990a, 1994; Harden and Lewis 1986; Jowell and Oliver 1985). This effort professionalized the popular critiques of government responsiveness. They also urged a reading of case law that would support the ideology of participation as part of British governance, certainly something that would have been a surprise to the parties and intellectuals who had articulated collectivist theory in the early twentieth century.

The task for the next chapter is to trace the reorganization that has occurred and examine what it has meant to participants. All of what I have done so far has addressed the point of view of those advocating or opposing change and their assumptions about what the purpose of court decisions is. However, neither the courts nor those debating them control the meaning of court decisions. The next two chapters will broaden the participants considered to include litigants in cases.

CHAPTER 5

Making Administrative Law

Even without a written constitution the courts in Britain have become significant in the way that those who study constitutional rulings expect: they have, on occasion, overturned policies of the central government. These decisions are part of what many in the profession have seen as a new administrative law, dating from about 1964 (Wade 1994; Drewry 1992). This general administrative law has framed political criticism of British governance and as a result has made lawyers' perspectives on major policy initiatives more relevant.

The post-1964 decisions the profession noticed were useful for addressing elite concerns about Britain's political failure even though they did not capture all judicial decision making. The literature of decline that emerged from Britain in the 1960s ascribed failures in British economic performance in part to its governing system, in which a party is elected to power, then insulated from challenge for up to five years. A Conservative Lord Chancellor participated in this critique, calling Britain an "elective dictatorship" (Hailsham 1976). Leading neo-Marxists have more recently adopted similar language (Hall and Held 1990, 181; for a critique, see Sivanandan 1990). Advocates have included a critique of the failure of law (in the courts) to structure administration while at the same time holding out the hope that law could, if renewed, do just that.

The place of law and court decisions became even more a matter of debate with Britain's partial integration into Europe. Britain became part of the European Community in 1972. What that meant for British sovereignty became a matter for legal, theoretical, and political debate, a part of the reluctance the British have continued to exhibit about being part of Europe. The European Court of Justice could decide cases in which British policy might conflict with European Community law. Britain is also a signatory to part of the European Convention on Human Rights. The Convention requires an adequate internal remedy for complaints as well as containing substantive limits on a member state's policies regarding such issues as immigration and sex discrimination (Kenney 1992; MacDonald and Blake 1991). As cases were brought, Britain's Order 53 became what the government claimed to be the internal remedy. Its political importance has been shaped by Britain's membership in Europe.

The European Convention on Human Rights also provided a referent and context for discontent with British governance by the 1970s. The question of whether Britain could use a bill of rights could refer to the European Convention as an example of the rights people in Britain might want to entrench (Zander 1975; Scarman 1974; Ward 1994; Laws 1995). The intensity of the discussion of a bill of rights increased as a critique of the Thatcher government in the 1980s (e.g., Barnett 1990; Dworkin 1990). The 1970s conservative diatribe against an "elective dictatorship" now has more cautious forms that point out the limits of Dicey's assumption that the common law could protect individual rights when those rights were not entrenched in any way (Carty 1991; Craig 1989, 1990a).

Cases that seemed to create a "new" administrative law therefore found a ready audience. Legal commentators have been eager to find ways in Britain of instituting principles in governing separate from electoral politics. The cases have seemed to offer standards for all of governance. The cases have also seemed important when they address the heart of British justification for governance: parliamentary sovereignty and ministerial discretion. Perhaps surprisingly, given the intellectual disputes described in previous chapters, this means that the individual against the state is not the core issue. Rather, the reasons ministers may use to justify their decisions and the procedures they may use in policy making, often between levels of government, have become key.

As these cases have been repeated and elaborated, lawyers and commentators have taken them to be exactly what the new public law should be about. It should concern questions of broad policy significance. These are not the most numerous cases the courts address in Order 53 judicial review. The most frequently heard cases involve repetitive case-level claims with regard to immigration and homelessness. Challenges to the central ministries are more rare (Sunkin, Bridges, and Meszaros 1993). The common case-level claims against the government are precisely those that some judges, in both judicial opinions and in statements off the bench, have said do not belong in the High Court. The emphasis on the few cases addressing central government's policy-making discretion and the concern to eliminate the case-level appeals has meant that judges and participants see the new judicial review as something that critiques the state. At the same time the cases mean that lawyers are part of negotiations over state policy making. When the government consults with lawyers to design programs that will fit with judicial requirements, the lawyers are incorporated into the practices of secrecy required of the British civil service by the Official Secrets Act.

This chapter will first outline some of the major cases discussed as evidence for a new and revived judicial review. The point is to outline how courts have addressed major issues, not to survey all the cases legal commentators have since considered an important part of judicial review. Judicial review was especially important in local government finance in contributing to public debate in the 1980s; I will discuss that next. This new and intriguing judicial review has led to some efforts to anticipate review on the part of the government; I will outline the reorganization of practice around this field. Finally, I will address how it has colored debate over the need for a new constitution.

"The Greatest Achievement of the English Courts"

The story told of postwar judicial review is that the courts refused to judge the government, certain that new forms of governance meant that law was irrelevant. Suddenly, in 1964, the courts rediscovered their role. That story begins with a chief constable who lost his job. In *Ridge v. Baldwin* ([1964] A.C. 40) the House of Lords held that a police officer was entitled to a hearing before being dismissed, almost a direct refutation of *Nakkuda Ali v. Jarayatne* ([1951] A.C. 56). *Ridge* directly addressed the core concern of the individual against the state. However, it did so in a "new property" context: that is, the chief constable was not a landholder like Lieutenant Commander Marten of Crichel Down. Instead, his "property interest" was in his job. In elaborating procedural requirements the courts were addressing 1950s concerns, but they were not yet addressing the concerns emerging in the 1960s that British governance simply could not handle modern problems of complex policy.

The next major case directly addressed ministerial discretion in an area of corporatist policy making. Courts have held that government ministers have duties under law and that those duties are detachable from the partisanship inherent in British governance.[1] In 1968 the Law Lords held that a minister could not refuse to hold an inquiry into milk pricing simply because the result might be politically embarrassing, though the statute did not require a minister to hold an inquiry (*Padfield v. Minister of Agriculture*, [1968] 2 W.L.R. 24). In 1969 the Law Lords interpreted a statute that excluded review of the Foreign Compensation Commission to mean that review was excluded only if the Commission made decisions it had the authority to make. It exceeded its jurisdiction if it made very wrong decisions (*Anisminic Ltd. v. Foreign Compensation Commission* [1969] 2 A.C. 147), and the court could review a decision for excess of jurisdiction. Legal commentary took *Anisminic* as an announcement that the courts would not attend to statutory clauses excluding review.

In *British Oxygen Co. Ltd. v. Board of Trade* ([1971] A.C. 75), a case decided in 1971, the Law Lords held that a minister must always retain his or her policy discretion: the minister must not promise to bind himself absolutely by rules but must always be willing to take new considerations into account. *British Oxygen* in particular illustrates how much holding a government to law is holding a government to law in a particular cultural context. For *British Oxygen* requires that governing without rules, and thereby to some extent without legal rights, is exactly what is legally required. The discretion that has usually been seen as the hallmark of British administration—the practice of "muddling through"—was not criticized but instead made judicially enforceable.

The British Oxygen Corporation was asking for special consideration for a government subsidy outside any rules. In another case in which adhering to the rules was to the benefit of the claimants the Court of Appeal insisted on the importance of adhering to announced rules upon which people had relied. In Britain people pay annual license fees for the televisions they own; the Home Office had announced a coming increase in the fee. Many people renewed their licenses early to take advantage of the existing fee. The Home Office tried to revoke these new licenses to apply the higher fee. The Court of Appeal held that the Home Office could not revoke people's television licenses simply to collect the new and higher fee (*Congreve v. Home Office* [1976] Q.B. 629).

In the courts, rules began to matter more as a justification for action while elections began to matter less. A central government could not just appeal to its election manifesto to justify requiring a local government to change from a Conservative form of school organization to a Labour-favored one (*Secretary of State for Education and Science v. Tameside Metropolitan Borough Council* [1977]).[2] An elected local government could not just appeal to its election manifesto to justify its increased subsidy to local transit when the first section of the transport statute required the local governments to take into account everyone's interests when making their spending decisions (*Bromley London Borough Council v. Greater London Council* [1982] 2 W.L.R. 62). Parliamentary sovereignty, as well as a concern for the property of rate payers, won over commitments to local election. The case therefore had two important meanings: it emphasized centralization of government control and it did not give overwhelming weight to elections. In refusing to defer to elections (particularly, law skeptics would note, elections of Labour local and central governments (Griffith 1991; Sedley 1987), the case represented commitments similar to those in *Tameside*. Electoral reasons were not adequate reasons for administrative decision.

In 1982 these decisions alongside a few more seemed to reach far enough that in a case on standing Lord Diplock in the House of Lords said that "progress towards a comprehensive system of administrative law [is the] greatest achievement of the English courts in my judicial lifetime." The particular case embodied the odd tensions in judicial review of central government administrators. In the case the House of Lords held that taxpayers' associations could have standing to sue when they had a real possibility of success, but in this particular case they did not. The homage to judicially created administrative law was paid in a case wherein the courts would not allow the claim (*R. v. Inland Revenue Commissioners ex p. National Federation of Self-Employed and Small Businesses Ltd.* [1982] A.C. 617).[3]

Some of the cases, in particular *Congreve,* are somewhat quirky. They can be dependent on the facts and in *Congreve* in part on the particular Court of Appeal judge who heard the case, Lord Denning. Indeed, at least one of the lawyers in *Congreve* saw it that way: he said they took the case "on a lark" and could not believe their good fortune in getting Lord Denning as a judge. However, the case contributes to a narrative legal scholars can tell of courts becoming consistently more willing to criticize central government action, a perception that can in turn make it easier to perceive new cases as also representing change. The courts took the separation of administration from reliance on electoral accountability even further in cases addressing legal duty and election manifestoes.

In addition, statutes enacted in Parliament have more recently relied on rights-based strategies than social programs in the postwar period did. The Homeless Persons Act (1977) tried to address homelessness by requiring local governments to give the unintentionally homeless right of priority for public housing, with rather limited success in the face of the financial constraints local governments have faced (Loveland 1991). Homelessness cases have provided a substantial portion of the judicial review caseload; they have constituted the primary challenge to local governments (Sunkin, Bridges, and Meszaros 1993). Parents have also been given rights to school choice, which courts have sometimes used to shape school priorities (Tweedie 1989). Taxation and land use planning had always had extensive rights of appeal and judge-made standards for decisions. Finally, a few lawyers from the 1960s onward tried to have the courts address how the state was treating low-status people such as gypsies (e.g., *Mixnam's Properties Ltd. v. Chertsey Urban District Council* [1965] A.C. 735), and prisoners (e.g., *R. v. Hull Prison Visitors ex p. St. Germain* [1979] Q.B. 425; see Loughlin and Quinn 1993). The possibility of bringing a suit before the ECHR made for changes as well (Loughlin and Quinn 1993, 502–6). These were individuals against the state, and their cases are mentioned in administrative law textbooks. However, neither these clients nor these cases have provided occasion for celebration of the importance of judicial review. Instead, the cases that provide the discussion of a "new" administrative law, the cases of Lord Diplock's judicial lifetime, are those that address the policy-making powers of central and local governments.

The significance lent to cases such as *Padfield* contributed to a sense on the part of judges that there was a general administrative law in Britain. Judges had made it without the assistance of Parliament but at the same time as judges represented it without encroaching on political preferences. In 1985 the courts reviewed the decision of Prime Minister Margaret Thatcher not to allow unions at the Government Communications Headquarters at Cheltenham. She had not consulted with the existing unions about the decision. The courts held that the union had had a "legitimate expectation" of consultation, based on past practices. However, national security concerns provided an exception in this case, so the government did not have to consult. This case was politically important for its legal evaluation of Thatcher's insistence on limiting corporatist consultation (Young 1989). In his judgment Lord Diplock provided a synthesis of the grounds for judicial review—stating and in part creating judge-made principles applicable to *any* statute or decision by the government (*Council of Civil Service Unions v. Minister for the Civil Service* [hereafter *GCHQ*] 1985):

> The first ground I would call "illegality," the second "irrationality" and the third "procedural impropriety." That is not to say that further development on a case by case basis may not in course of time add further grounds. I have in mind particularly the possible adoption in the future of the principle of "proportionality" which is recognised in the administrative law of several of our fellow members of the European Economic Community. . . . By "illegality" . . . I mean that the decision-maker must understand correctly the law that regulates his decision-making power and must give effect to it. . . . By "irrationality" I mean . . . a decision which is so outrageous in its defiance of logic or of accepted moral standards that no sensible person who had applied his mind to the question to be decided could have arrived at it. (950–51)

"Procedural impropriety" covers both "failure to act with procedural fairness towards the person who will be affected by the decision" and "failure by an administrative tribunal to observe procedural rules that are expressly laid down in the legislative instrument" (951). Two leading practitioners and legal scholars have since elaborated proportionality as a separate ground for review, building both on European principles and *GCHQ* (Jowell and Lester 1989). When the ground for review has been offered to them, judges have proven skeptical (e.g., *R. v. Secretary of State for the Home Department, ex p. Brind* [1991] A.C. 696; however, see Laws 1995). Such suggestions provoke discussion and a sense of activity, however (Boyron 1992). Those disputes shape perceptions about what the courts are doing, no matter how much the grounds for review are simply a hope, which in turn shapes expectations about what constitutionalism ought to mean in England and Wales.

The reasoning proved to be at least as important in *GCHQ* as the result in the particular case was. "Legitimate expectation" as a ground for review has been important in the supervision of local government. Local governments found themselves with new challenges in managing the schools, including a responsibility to allow parents to choose schools. In addition, local governments had to close schools when enrollments declined; in lawsuits the courts have insisted that schools must consult with parents before they close the schools (*R. v. Brent London Borough Council ex p. Gunning* [1986] 84 L.G.R. 168; Meredith 1988). The courts have also held in favor of consultation based on legitimate expectation against the central government, while quite explicitly holding that ministers may change their policies or declare any policy they might choose (Baldwin and Horne 1986; Schwehr and Brown 1991). In doing so the courts have paralleled American developments in administrative law emphasizing participation (Stewart 1975; Sunstein 1983). The emphasis on participation as legitimating government policy, not just elections, has also been adopted in British legal argument critical of the authoritarian strains in British party politics (Craig 1994; Craig 1990b, chap. 11; Harden and Lewis 1986; Loughlin 1992).

However, while the courts were insisting in *Gunning* on consultation as a participatory right, they also insisted that local governments must attend to the reports of their local education committees as a way of incorporating expertise into the decision. The tension between making the "expert" authorized decision and the one arrived at through participation is not easily reconciled. Both the principle of expertise and the principle of participation are, however, critical of justifications of governance dependent only on elections. An emphasis on hearings is part of a concern with legality; the approach also attempts to walk a middle ground concerning the place of courts in democratic governance by addressing only procedure and adhering to the principle that governments may choose any policy as long as they choose it by means of the right procedure. It is exactly this proceduralism that has also been key in American administrative law.

After *GCHQ*, the courts took on yet another controversial issue: birth control for minors. The courts avoided direct engagement with goverment policy by framing the problem as one of legality and the relationship of local government to central government. In *Gillick v. West Norfolk and Wisbech Area Health Authority* ([1986] 1 A.C. 112), the plaintiff challenged the local government's authority to implement a policy of giving birth control to minors without their parents' consent. The legal question was whether the central government had authorized the policy. The public and political issue that the court challenge occasioned concerned families and control of minors' sexuality (Cannell 1990). For legal scholars and judges *Gillick* was one more example of the exciting and important role courts could play in governance (Woolf 1990).

However, the courts also continued their caution in confronting the central government. In 1989 the House of Lords decided in *Factortame Ltd. v. Secretary of State for Transport* ([1990] 2 A.C. 85) that the courts could not subject the Crown—and therefore the ministries—to an interim injunction. According to the House of Lords, the complainants could only get an interim injunction if the legislation under consideration was invalid under European Community law, a question then pending before the European Court of Justice on a referral from the Divisional Court of the Queen's Bench. Courts in Britain could not hold legislation invalid, so there could be no interim relief. *Factortame* stated most starkly the doctrine of parliamentary sovereignty and seemed to raise the question of whether there was a rule of law in Britain. It also exemplified the ongoing reluctance in Britain to incorporate European law. In 1990 the European Court of Justice held, with regard to the question of interim relief, that national courts must decide whether or not to grant interim relief based upon their own assessment of the substance of the legal claims. The Law Lords then held that the High Court could grant such relief in cases raising points of European Union law (*R. v. Secretary of State for Transport, ex p. Factortame Ltd.* (No. 2) [1991] 1 A.C. 603). The question of the government's obligation to obey courts would come back to haunt the government in a refugee case to be discussed in the next chapter.

These cases have conflicting meanings as critiques of British governance. On the one hand, detaching ministerial decisions from partisanship represents something of a startling shift. However, cases such as *Padfield* and *Tameside* do not straightforwardly create legal standards to which ministers must adhere. Instead, they draw on longstanding practices in governance by requiring ministers to do what is best under the circumstances. *GCHQ* both criticizes government and draws on common understandings of corporatist practices to justify their decisions. The notion of legitimate expectations raises questions similar to the due process and statutory provisions cases in the United States: how can a state-created practice give rise to judicially enforceable procedures?

In sum, the most noticeable cases used to note a re-creation of judicial review clearly draw on strands of British ruling practice in order to criticize administrative decisions. They are an innovation in excluding partisanship and political embarrassment as reasons for action by administrators. But in doing so they address the heart of British national-level governing practices. These cases were a doctrine waiting to happen. They do not constitute any one particular standard for administration. They were not predictable and it was hard for administrators to know what to do with them; knowing how to act in the future surely is a requirement of the rule of law. While *Ridge* certainly countered *Nakkuda Ali,* both were one-off decisions in comparison with the frequent decisions courts had been making against planning orders and tax administrators. What made these cases a doctrine, and one that meant courts were active against administration, is the context into which they fell. That context was one of acute elite anxiety about the capability of British governance to reform itself and to attend to legality in administration. Efforts for an administrative court had failed before 1981. So had the effort to impose a statute that would allow for judicial review on the merits of decisions. What was left was to encourage judges to change how they decided and in turn to amplify whatever decisions they did make. (For an example of the later celebratory reception of these decisions from an American who had long attended to British administrative law, see Schwartz 1987.)

Such high-profile decisions along with some others have given the courts the reputation of at least *possibly* overturning the central government. They do not readily constitute a coherent doctrine. While the cases receive substantial attention in the press and in the profession, they have not been increasing rapidly in number. In 1985 the High Court heard 113 cases, 47 of them immigration cases (Sunkin 1987a, 458–60). Between 1987 and 1991 applications for leave for judicial review against the central government in areas other than immigration comprised between 8 and 12 percent of the judicial review caseload, though the numbers were dropping in the first part of 1991. The numbers of applications did not seem to go up consistently either, ranging between 129 and 189 per year. The number of cases going on to a full hearing is much smaller. The application rate against local governments increased in that period, largely in education (Sunkin, Bridges, and Meszaros 1993, 23–27). Furthermore, outside of immigration the central government seldom loses. While complainants do bring cases, the numbers are neither as large nor as rapidly increasing as the extensive attention paid to administrative law in the profession would suggest.

Will You Obey the Law? Meanings of Legality from the 1980s

The cases and the potential they hold for political argument are important well beyond their numbers, however. The use of the courts became part of the bitter political fights of the 1980s and aided in organizing the political world into law abiders and lawbreakers. That organization included the government; one telling criticism of both the Conservative and Labour parties that has gained attention in debate is that they cannot abide by the law. Therefore, while the number of cases could matter if the focus were on court decisions, it is not the key component of understanding what legal decisions have meant in the culture.

The Conservative party has long relied on rule-of-law claims and imagery. By this the party quite specifically has meant punishing crime. On the other hand, the rule of law has very quickly become linked to a meaning of law critical of government authority—an entrenched bill of rights. A bill of rights and a written constitution are about having a lawful government. Therefore, with increased attention to the courts, the law-and-order framework could on occasion be turned against the Conservative government to criticize it when the courts offered any criticism whatsoever. When the courts refused to offer such a critique but might have, the ideals of legality could provide grounds for critique.[4] The courts have long had critics, dating back to the early-twentieth-century *Taff Vale* decision, who have argued that the courts are nothing but a Tory institution. More recently, Professor J. A. G. Griffith of the London School of Economics wrote a book, popular enough to have been published in several paperback editions, explaining the court system and criticizing it as Tory while holding an implicit ideal that the law actually can be neutral or fair. There are two directions for criticizing the government when the courts have judged: the central government can be criticized as not living up to its own standards as interpreted by Conservative judges if it loses in court. If the government does not lose, critics can dismiss the judges as simply Tory and unwilling to adhere to the true ideals of law. Either way, the Conservative emphasis on law and order as a means of crime control has an answer in law as an aspiration to fairness once the courts become involved in any politically charged issue.

This tension between law and order and an ideal of legality appeared particularly starkly in the mid-1980s when the miners struck. The strike was long and bitter, lasting from 1984 through 1985. The specific issue was whether the government could close pits that it saw as not feasible to run. However, in the context of the Thatcher government's priorities the strike was a test of the power of the government to control the unions. As an old industry that the government had nationalized in 1947, mining represented the collectivist approach to policy making that the Thatcher government claimed to be determined to break. The miners faced repeated court injunctions against some picketing practices; many were also arrested for a variety of offenses, from participating in riots to picking coal. Critics of the arrests could portray the courts as nothing but Conservative party tools (see, e.g., Samuel, Bloomfield, and Boanas 1986). The National Union of Mineworkers focused on and condemned police violence (Jones 1986). However, Conservative government officials and members of Parliament were much more publicly successful at framing the issue as one of law and order with the miners on the wrong side. The Conservatives made sure to emphasize a close connection between the Labour party and the National Union of Mineworkers. Conservatives asked over and over in Parliament whether the Labour party endorsed the miners' breaking the law (Krieger 1986). In asking that question the Conservatives were replaying the Fare's Fair dispute of 1981. During that debate as well the Conservatives had asked if the Labour Party would tell the Greater London Council to obey the law.

Legal ideals and criticisms provided powerful symbolism in other legal-political issues as well, readily raising questions of administrative power, accountability, and law. The government prosecuted people for violation of the Official Secrets Act, the extremely restrictive act that makes it illegal for state employees to release information. Clive Ponting, a high-level civil servant, was prosecuted for leaking information about the way the government had misled the public concerning the conduct of the Falklands War. The jury refused to penalize him. Ponting wrote an indictment of secrecy in British administration framed in rights-based and constitutionalist terms, entitled *The Right to Know* (1985). Finally, the serious problems of violence during football games during the mid-1980s also provided a place to debate the importance of the rule of law, by which the Conservative government meant severe penalties for those involved in riots. In August of 1984 the government issued a report on violence among fans at football games; Parliament debated it, with the rule of law as part of the framing of the debate. After the Heysel Stadium disaster in May of 1985,

Fig. 5.1. "Excepting you, my lady." (From *Manchester Guardian,* 23 November 1984. Les Gibbard: *The Guardian.*)

at which forty-one people were crushed to death, the government issued a new bill expanding the enforcement powers of government officials. Parliament discussed the bill, once again raising the question of whether the Labour party agreed that people should follow the law (*The Times*, 15 March 1985; 6 April 1985; 3 May 1985; 4 July 1985; 12 July 1985; 25 October 1985). Yet an entirely different interpretation of the disaster would have avoided the rule-of-law question. The football stands had no seats—they really were stands. There was no clear limit on the number of people who could be admitted to the stands, and controls on entry were lax.

The miners' strike, the official secrets prosecutions and the framing of fights at football games highlighted the rule-of-law arguments as well as their accessibility as a critique of a Conservative government. If a Conservative government would rely so heavily on the rule of law as a criticism of both mass behavior and political dissent (Jessop et al. 1984, 45, 57), the deeper appeal to fundamental principles would provide an ironic critique of a government claiming to emphasize the rule of law. This context faciliated organization around constitutional concerns, many of which centered on the conduct of the administration.

GCHQ provided just that commentary. The House of Lords decided the case during the miners' strike. Parliamentary debate and the newspapers took the opportunity to say that the Conservative government was exempting itself from the obligation to obey the law.[5] *The Guardian,* the left-leaning national newspaper, contrasted Mrs. Thatcher's insistence that the miners follow the law with the decision, explaining that she was exempt from that requirement (fig. 5.1).

The central government's effort to control local government finance in the 1980s illustrates the significance of court decisions as part of partisan debate. It also illustrates the importance of the dichotomy between those who abided by the law and those who did not—and how the Conservative argument, that one must abide by the law, could be turned against the government. Local government finance also illustrates the importance of judicial review in public debate within the new context of judicial review; that is, these cases do not concern the individual against the state but state management and struggles for control between levels of authority.

The Courts, Administrative Law, and Partisan Debate

Ken Livingstone, the flamboyant Labour party leader of the Greater London Council (GLC) in the early 1980s, took on the central government's concern with controlling spending in the 1981 local election. In London the Labour Party ran on a policy of increased transportation subsidies with the catchy title "Fare's Fair." Once the Greater London Council implemented the policy, a local council within greater London challenged it in court. A local authority claimed that the GLC had a fiduciary duty in spending tax dollars, or rates, from the borough councils and that the GLC was not living up to that responsibility. Furthermore, the governing Transport Statute, enacted by Parliament, required the GLC to take all interests into account. The GLC lost in court, not entirely to Ken Livingstone's surprise. However, the case led to what most of the cases between central and local government concerning local government finance led to: a debate in Parliament and publicity.[6] Court cases allow one to get time in Parliament, which does not have the reputaion of being easy to do. Cases are a way to get on the national agenda. While the Conservative government could insist that the GLC had an obligation to obey the law, the Labour party could talk about the bias of Tory judges. This dispute would play itself out over and over again in the courts throughout the 1980s. The courts were involved in a key political issue that eventually was part of the reason for Mrs. Thatcher's resignation, the reorganization of local government finance (Travers 1986). Control of space in the 1980s was in part a control of socialism (Harvey 1989, 236–37); courts played a part in the dispute over controlling space. Local governments used the courts to resist the control of central government and to publicize that resistance. Along with the cases already mentioned, the local government finance cases both participated in arguments about courts and law and brought lawyers and lawyering into state management. The local governments played this struggle out in part in court. The local governments would often lose, but court cases would keep local government finance in the newspapers.

An early local government finance case raised expectations that perhaps local governments could win (*R. v. Secretary of State for the Environment ex p. Brent L.B.C.* [1982] 1 Q.B. 593). In 1981, in controlling the level of grants a local government would receive from the central government, the central government refused to listen to further representations about local government needs. As one lawyer remembered, that "leapt out" at him as an issue; since the *British Oxygen* case in 1971 the government had always had a responsibility to consider individual circumstances. Local governments carefully set up the case, requesting further attention from the minister to make sure that he refused. He did, and a court case was brought on the grounds that the minister had the responsibility of deciding while keeping an open mind. The local governments raised other issues, including the claim that the government had made decisions that violated the requirements of *Wednesbury* concerning reasonableness. The local governments won, but only on the question of consultation. They did not win on the substantive issue of preventing the central government from controlling their spending; they did win the ability to criticize the government for not obeying the law.

Parliament immediately discussed the case, though briefly. One Labour M.P. illustrated the usefulness of a judicial decision against the government in Parliamentary debate:

> Does he feel no shame that while he continuously warns others not to break his laws he has now been discovered to be the one who has broken his own laws? Hon. Members have accused him of being a self-appointed commissar. He has now been found guilty of acting like a commissar by, in the words quoted by Mr. Justice Ackner, highhandedly placing convenience before justice. (*Parl. Deb.*, Commons, 6th ser., vol. 13 [1981]: 427)

After the decision the minister, in discussing financial controls on local governments, hastened to assure Parliament that he would continue to listen to representations by local governments (*Parl. Deb.,* Commons, 6th ser. [1981]: vol. 14, 225, vol. 15, 310, vol. 15, 322; [1982]: vol. 18, 155, vol. 34, 164–65). M.P.'s would complain that the minister had not listened to representations from their area (*Parl. Deb.,* Commons, 6th ser., [1982]: vol. 18, 165). On the one hand, it illustrates how little bite court decisions might have: consultation, even if limited and not shaping decisions, had been an ordinary practice. References to consultation might not be the result of the court decision. On the other hand, the Thatcher administration had insisted it was changing those practices. But the court decision gave some reason to the minister to continue to refer to consultations. That court case and legal images continued to color the debates. When in February of 1982 Parliament considered changes the government was making, one Labour M.P. said:

> The Secretary of State, who lectures local authorities about the need to conduct themselves lawfully, has been conducting himself unlawfully ever since last June. If he were not a Minister of the Crown with an obedient

majority ready to bail him out, he would by now be helping the police with their inquiries. (*Parl. Deb.*, Commons, 5th ser., [1982]: vol. 18, 168)

In England and Wales, people accused of crimes "help the police with their inquiries." In Parliamentary debate policy disagreements were made analogous to the commission of ordinary crimes, thanks to court decisions.

Local governments continued to use court cases as a way of gaining the attention of the central government. One local government solicitor maintained that further consultation sometimes did lead to an increase in the initial grant decision. After *Brent* the minister still cut the grants of the local authorities that had sued. He said in Parliament that in response to further representations he had changed some of the ways of calculating grants after further consultation (*Parl. Deb.*, 6th ser., Commons, [1982]: vol. 18, 155). Much of what the local governments compiled, however, was a record of losses in the courts through the middle 1980s.[7] But they still brought cases in part to gain publicity, and court cases shaped that publicity (*The Times,* 2 March 1985, 2; *The Guardian,* 29 March 1985, 15). An expectation that the law should be fair and neutral colored that effort.

The early controls the central government imposed involved setting the levels at which local governments could set their rates (local property taxes). The government would control rate levels for local governments it believed were overspending based on calculations of local need. The central government finally changed the basis of local taxation from property to a per-head tax in 1990. The government called it a community charge; the many people opposed to it called it a poll tax. One purpose the Thatcher government had was to shift the responsibility for what it saw as the profligate policies of local governments onto the individual voters (rather than businesses) and therefore the local governments themselves. Local governments also challenged the government's poll tax efforts in court. These cases, too, were important in setting elite debate; the government also saw the cases that way.

For example, the government distributed what it called an informational leaflet on the poll tax, or community charge, in 1989. It was challenged in court, and the courts issued a temporary injunction. Waiting on the judicial decision was accompanied by "considerable hand wringing" in the government and civil service (interview, 1990). The courts' involvement in the issue created an opportunity for discussing the rule of law and the proper role of the courts in the newspapers. Indeed, the conservative jurist Sir William Wade thought they were overstepping their proper boundaries by judging in an area where there could be no law to apply. The government, he argued, had the power to distribute the information it wanted to distribute (Wade 1989; Sedley 1989). As it turned out, the temporary injunction the courts issued against the informational pamphlet was not sustained in the final High Court judgment. The judgment was actually critical of the leaflet as misleading (*The Guardian,* 18 May 1989, 5). That point

"No thanks — not in my back yard!"

Fig. 5.2. "No thanks." The poll tax injunction. (From *Manchester Guardian,* 11 May 1989, p. 6. © Les Gibbard: *The Guardian.*)

became part of parliamentary debate criticizing the leaflet as "party political," and illegitimately so, rather than informative (*Parl. Deb.,* Commons, vol. 153, 899–900, 903–4 (23 May 1989). That the courts had said so contributed to debate. "Considerable hand wringing" did not occur because anyone thought that courts would make it legally impossible to implement the poll tax. Instead, the courts became a source of embarrassment because such political hay could be made of their decisions (see fig. 5.2).

In April of 1990 local governments applied for judicial review of an issue about the poll tax. During the hearing for the application the courtroom was filled, with many observers standing on the steps and in the back of the room. The poll tax case was politically compelling. From the beginning it was unlikely the local governments would win. Yet it would provide one point of resistance to the government and one focus for public debate.

While the local councils could set the level of the community charge, or poll tax, the central government could cap the charges, ordering the councils not to spend beyond a certain amount. The local authorities claimed that the application of charge capping to particular councils followed no set principles, as the statute required, and was therefore unfair. The grounds on which the secretary of state could cap the charge were that the decision "shall be made in accordance with principles determined by the secretary of state . . . and those principles shall be the same [for all authorities within the same class]" (Local Government Finance Act 1988, Part 7 § 100 [4]). If the judge granted the application, as was generally expected, the challenge would be heard in court. If the challenge were then successful, better and fairer principles would have to be devised. If the poll tax were to be dismantled, which was a topic of discussion by everyone from cabinet ministers to civil servants to constituents, it would not be by the court. Yet debate over law and courts in the 1980s and the long series of cases regarding local government finance leading up to this case meant that the courts were part of the highly politicized struggle over the poll tax. Courts could not transform the partisanship of British governance; the practice of framing issues solely in partisan terms is too well entrenched. Rather, the aspired-to neutrality of the court became one more source of partisan dispute.

The poll tax case addressed part of the public poll tax debate: whether there were any defensible principles used in setting the levels of central government support or whether instead the central government had largely calculated financial support based on the partisan composition of each local government and its significance to the central government. That had been an issue from the early 1980s onward (see *Parl. Deb.*, 6th ser., [1982]: vol. 34, 168–72). While the minister was supposed to have used some general principles, they were not immediately discernible, and the newspapers discussed disparities between councils that seemed suspiciously targeted, differentiating between Labour and Conservative councils (see, e.g., Cohen 1990).

This case had the potential of ruling against a high-profile policy of the central government. Even the application for review received considerable coverage, highlighting the role that law in courts can play as political critique in Britain. An editorial in *The Independent*, a national newspaper, stated the issue well:

> The Secretary of State for the Environment should certainly be obliged to demonstrate that the way in which he drew up his list of 21 councils, not

> one of which happens to be Conservative-controlled, was legal and procedurally proper, and was not, to cite Lord Diplock's definition of irrationality, "so outrageous in its defiance of logic or of accepted moral standards that no sensible . . . person could have arrived at it." Such a huge volume of legislation giving so wide a discretion to ministers has been passed by this Government that judicial review is at present a particularly important safeguard against the abuse of executive power. (Cohen 1990)

Court cases have made it possible to invoke the law as a critique in political argument and not just for those aligned with either major party. As it turned out, the courts, through and including the House of Lords, held for the central government (*R. v. Secretary of State for the Environment, ex p. Hammersmith and Fulham London Borough Council* [1990], *The Times,* 5 October 1990, 36). The local authorities see these in part as media efforts to criticize the government; the Association for Metropolitan Authorities worked with the media regarding the poll tax case. The policies of the Thatcher government aimed at dismantling local councils alongside the longstanding and conflicted image of law and courts as either neutral and outside politics or as Conservative made local government finance cases common and noticeable in the 1980s. Each argument or loss in the courts provided further discussion in the newspapers about rate or charge capping, allegations of unfairness, and the role of the courts (*The Guardian*, 6 June 1990, 2; 16 June 1990, 2; 28 June 1990, 2, 4). That these cases existed at all depended less on judicial attitudes regarding accountability than on images of law in British culture and how those meanings could be mobilized.

Once the poll tax was enacted, one form of political resistance was a refusal to pay (Lee 1990). The importance of the courts in the day-to-day politics of this issue was not derived from any broad statement of principle by the higher courts. Rather, the low-level magistrate courts responsible for enforcing the poll tax were important. Organized protests raised broad objections to the poll tax in magistrate courts; the government responded by requiring people to tick off standard defenses on forms in an effort to close off political debate in the magistrate courts. It was also an effort to speed up the handling of cases. The process costs made these lower-level courts in ordinary enforcement proceedings, not the High Court operating by way of judicial review, the final important actors in the poll tax dispute (Thomas 1992).

The existing political cleavages in Britain are partisan (Ashford 1981). Party debates and the problems of elected officials provide the material for what is considered political. That which is not partisan is not political. Parliament largely debates rather than works out the details of legislation; the courts cannot change that. The executive controls lawmaking; the courts cannot change that. Because those are the existing debates, court decisions have the capacity to be treated as important to the extent they can be fit into partisan debate. The issues fit together: court decisions are useful in political debate because the courts can be portrayed not as partisan but as legal.

That importance in public debate contrasts with why judicial review of case-level homelessness decisions have been important to local governments. For local governments review can pinch their policy-making discretion much more tightly. Cases have limited discretion in distributing housing and allocating children to schools. Where local governments have been able to avoid those decisions, they have (Loveland 1991; Tweedie 1989). Similarly, the repetitive cases in immigration pinch the government's discretion; it is sometimes ordered to admit particular applicants.

Homelessness claims continue to be a dominant part of the caseload; they have also been a site of struggle for those concerned with the administration of government services. For example, in one borough in London feminist organizing has focused on the ground level, as it did in the early twentieth century when male legal scholars were arguing about the abstract powers of the state. In this borough, the women's associations pressed the local council not to define women who left abusive partners as "intentionally homeless." If they had defined them as intentionally homeless, the authority would not have had responsibility for housing them. While the authority was concerned, it eventually defined victims of domestic violence who left their homes as intentionally homeless and therefore outside the bounds of the act because they did not have the resources to give priority to the women (interview 1990; Loveland 1995). The making of administrative law as a principled discourse often remains apart from the concerns of people who consume public services. Yet those lower-status issues provide much of the judicial review caseload (Sunkin, Bridges, and Meszaros 1993).

Judicial Review as Legal Control of Government

The British central government is notoriously closed to detailed analysis and critique (Gelb 1989; Heclo and Wildavsky 1981). Administrative law has sometimes been portrayed as having the potential for opening the government to critique through the courts (Ashford 1981, 17). That is why the cases that limit ministers' discretion in choosing to order inquiries or that limit the reasons for which a minister can act are so interesting to participants. One barrister argued that the significant part of judicial review was about "managing governance," not about case level decisions (interview, 1990). Another called administrative law "terribly exciting" for that reason, adding that it must be even more so in the United States since American judicial principles are so much more developed and important (interview, 1990). This barrister was addressing local government finance cases, not case-level decisions regarding housing or immigration. But what critique or control can judicial review provide?

What judicial review can do is dependent on the conditions under which it works—which is still a parliamentary system with a government that has few incentives to give judges very much to review. Like all political change, judicial review is not some change wholly external to the existing system and somehow intervening in it; it emerges out of a particular path and in a particular context. Both shape what it means (Krasner 1989; March and Olsen 1989; Skocpol 1985). Whether judicial review can control administrators is a question dependent on the institutional field in which judicial review works. The very forces that limit the availability of judicial review in the first place imply that the judicial review that is available will fit into existing channels.

Major advantages of Order 53 cases are that they can be scheduled and decided quickly. There is a three month time limit on filing an application. Judges also have discretion to limit it further, dismissing cases not brought in a timely fashion. The poll tax case was scheduled for three weeks after the hearing for leave. Speed makes for limited time in which to establish the extensive record common in American administrative law cases. In addition, judges seldom order discovery, which means that neither plaintiffs nor judges have access to much of the information that contributed to a decision (e.g., Sedley 1990: 351). In the poll tax case, the petitioners' request for a discovery order against the minister was turned down with the comment that the judge was sure the minister would freely share all the documents and evidence. The comment provoked laughter throughout the courtroom. A petitioners' barrister respectfully disagreed with the judge, basing his statement on past experience with the ministries. But that approach, embodied in the rules and not just in the particular judge's attitude, is consistent with the existing practice in British government. A centralized administration, with little incentive to share information, can decide what is important to know. Administrative law offers limited opportunity to break open the closed practices of the administration no matter what the substantive principles. The practice of secrecy is unlikely to change; once again, ministers and the executive control the law reform agenda and the parliamentary agenda. The Law Commission in its 1993 consultation paper on administrative law recommended against changing the rules making discovery so discretionary, much to the disgust of commentators eager to see the expansion of the role of courts in evaluating policy (Cane 1993, 893).

The statutory bases for extending administrative procedures or developing standards for their evaluation are limited (Harlow 1987). Standards such as the one governing the poll tax, that decisions "shall be made in accordance with principles determined by the secretary of state," are common.

The courts themselves have limited the availability of judicial review by making a distinction between public and private law that the enacting Law Commission did not seem to intend. Private law rights are analogous in some way with problems that one might have with someone other than a government authority. A suit claiming that someone had committed a tort, or private legal wrong, could occur against a public authority or a private person. That would be a private law right. Some actions are in their nature more governmental, at least as lawyers might see it, and have implications beyond the case at hand. Those are public law questions. This distinction, while very difficult to make, was enshrined in law in 1983 when the House of Lords held in *O'Reilly v. Mackman* [1983] 2 A.C. 237 and *Cocks v. Thanet District Council* [1983] A.C. 286 that public law was an exclusive remedy. In *Cocks,* for example, the High Court decided that the duty under the 1977 Housing (Homeless Persons) Act to investigate whether a family was homeless was a public law function. If one went by private law when the appropriate procedure was an application for judicial review, one's claim would be dismissed. The plaintiffs in *O'Reilly* sued the Board of Prison Visitors, claiming a breach of natural justice in their disciplinary proceedings. They proceeded by a writ rather than application for review because the time limit allowed for an application had already expired. Both the Court of Appeal and the House of Lords held that the application for review was the only system available for suit against public authorities. In the Court of Appeal, Lord Denning supported his decision by saying that if the plaintiffs could proceed by ordinary action, public authorities "would be harassed by all sorts of claims." Lord Diplock in the House of Lords agreed:

> The public interest in good administration requires that public authorities and third parties should not be kept in suspense as to the legal validity of a decision . . . for any longer period than is absolutely necessary in fairness to the person affected by the decision. (*Cocks,* 284)

Changes in Order 53 had consolidated the discretionary control of the courts concerning what complaints to hear. Ironically, given the interest in and concerns about expanding judicial review, the courts have a deep sympathy for the "needs of good administration"—in other words for flexibility, speed, and lack of legal accountability. Quite apart from what the lawyers have seen as contributing to technical legal rationality, the courts have sometimes been concerned with administrative flexibility (Offe 1985, 301–2).

The division between public and private law makes public law remedies less available.[8] The justification is that public law is an important remedy useful for claims regarding roughly what we might call public goods—issues in which the benefits of making the claim do not accrue primarily to the individual claimant but to a wider public.[9] Even practicing lawyers in the field find the distinction between public and private law questions difficult to use, yet it has support from leading judges (e.g., Woolf 1986b). Given that the politics of legal change is one of expertise, relying on the Law Commission and the decision making of judges, the perspectives of leading judges matter. The private law–public law distinction will continue to make for a separable, public law, which Dicey had seen as emblematic of the problems in continental law. While it might create an unworkable distinction, it contributes to the elevation of public law as a constitutionalist discourse reserved for important public policy questions.

The creation of a separate public law in the 1980s is filled with irony: it creates what conservative scholars from Dicey through writers in the 1960s had feared from public law, a realm of executive privilege. Yet it did not do what pro-state scholars had wanted to do; public law had a different meaning when the welfare state was expanding. It did not create a public law entirely sympathetic to administrative priorities, which welfare state scholars once took to be the distribution of benefits.[10] *O'Reilly* did not fit any scholar's sense of what was important in public law in 1950s and 1960s scholarship—protecting some group of individuals—and it has been widely criticized.[11] Yet, even while the new judicial review has been continually circumscribed in comparison to the original ideals, it has looked like the one institutional opportunity for challenging the central administration.[12] The reputation for overturning government action in important public policy issues is more important than actually doing so; central government is still more likely to win in claims against it (Sunkin, Bridges, and Meszaros 1993).

Despite the limits on what judicial review can accomplish, administrative law has seen reorganization in the practice of law inside and outside the administration. That reorganization is in part an effort to anticipate litigation so as to avoid embarrassment. But some reorganization is less dependent on the existence of cases than on the meaning and significance of administrative law principles as ways of criticizing the government in ways that invoke constitutionalist discourse.

Case Law and Adaptation of an Organizational Field

Administrative law decisions are seen by academic lawyers as necessary for making the administration abide by the law (Craig 1994; Wade 1989). That approach also accords with the views of scholars who study administrative procedures from a principal-agent point of view: statutes are written in part to give courts, as agents of the legislature, a way of controlling the bureaucracy (McCubbins, Noll, and Weingast 1987). Courts simply neutrally interpret those rules. In Britain, where the legislature and upper level of the executive are united, the rather limited directions given in statutes are not necessarily designed to control the policy-making decisions of the upper level of the government. Indeed, what administrators want is an ability to flexibly pursue the goals set in legislation or by ministers; Claus Offe has called this functional rationality (1985). The parliamentary system in Britain makes that possible.

Legal rationality, or following rules, does not allow that flexibility. To the extent that the courts read statutes as though they are intended to control upper-level policy making, they take on a role not predicted from a control point of view. Instead, they take on the constitutionalist perspective of finding principles of governing not dictated by elections or legislation. Those principles are what make administrative law appealing to participants. The control perspective that academic lawyers emphasize only makes sense if the unity of the legislature and executive are ignored.[13]

Reformation around administrative law includes bar associations and lawyers within central administration who are increasingly responsible for watching for and educating administrators about administrative law. The courts do not decide a large number of cases each year, so that administrative law does not provide a specialization for many lawyers. The vast majority of solicitors who have taken applications for judicial review have taken only one case in a year (Sunkin, Bridges, and Meszaros 1993, 32–35); the exception is in immigration, the subject of the next chapter. The level of specialization among barristers is not available. The point for solicitors would, however, also hold for barristers: there are not enough cases for judicial review to provide a complete practice for many. One barrister working on local government issues said that at the height of litigation in the mid-1980s she and two others were "popping up like Topsy" in the courts. That experience led to a reputation for doing policy-level administrative law work, drawing her into environmental litigation based on European Union (EEC) standards.

In Britain, lawyers as a profession in the past have not been very tightly integrated into the party or administrative governing elite (Abel 1988b). However, in holding themselves as somewhat independent of partisan governance, lawyers in Britain throughout the twentieth century have had the ability to do what many claim is the particular virtue of the legal profession in the United States—articulate public values through a detached normative consideration of the meaning of a statute.[14] They have claimed a much more circumscribed role than legal academics in the United States do, but administrative law cases and changes in governance the Thatcher administration brought allowed a widening claim despite the lack of a written constitution.[15] Without a written constitution, administrative law (and now particularly administrative law that addresses partisan issues) plays into concerns increasingly raised in the culture of the "chattering classes"—in *The Times*, *The Guardian*, *The Independent*, and the *New Statesman*—about the need for a constitution (Dworkin 1990; Crick 1990; Ellis 1990; Lester 1990a; Noble 1990; Siedentop 1990). That has meant the development of lawyers' organizations that urge the relevance of lawyering to political accountability. The courts do not have to do very much to encourage such hopes that legally enforceable accountability could be part of British practice.

In 1990 Stephen Sedley, then a Queen's Counsel, worked with others to form the Public Law Project,[16] which has drawn on an elite concern about the lack of a constitution. The project connected that concern, though, with concern about disadvantaged groups more than "managing governance." The lack of a written constitution in Britain allows people to claim that very wide and broad concerns are fundamental to governance. The Public Law Project urged "it is widely accepted in Britain that there exist uncontroversial and fundamental rights, among them rights to fair and open government and of ready access to justice" (Public Law Project 1990). The project has since funded research on judicial review litigation as well as provided representation in test case litigation (Sedley 1990; also see, e.g., *R. v. Council of Legal Education ex p. Eddis* [1994] CO/1223/94).

The Administrative Law Bar Association (ALBA), with about four hundred members in 1990 and growing, participates in discussions about constitutional change and administrative law in Britain. It was formed in 1986 by barristers who thought it would be useful to have a place to discuss important new developments in administrative law. One barrister involved in founding it said that not many barristers were practicing administrative law; ALBA grew out of an academic interest (interview, 1991). Most bar associations in Britain are limited to barristers. ALBA incorporates barristers, solicitors, judges, legally trained civil servants, and academics. It also provides a context for what one member called "cocktail party discussions" of administrative law (interview 1990). ALBA has also supported the organization of a Crown Office users' committee. The aim was to improve operation of the Crown Office, the office in charge of administrative law practice in the courts.

ALBA became in the perception of some members the "most fashionable organization" to join, the "in thing" (interview, 1990). Much of what ALBA has done is meet, and at their evening meetings the members have heard papers on French administrative law, civil liberties, human rights, and racial discrimination law. The mention of the protection of individuals against the state is routine and essential for the position of the association—what else does the common law have to offer? Indeed, ALBA has supported the Public Law Project (Public Law Project 1990). The topics and the way they are discussed suggest the interest in European issues and approaches that has been developing in the profession, including a concern for participating in the management of issues between state organizations. The European Court of Justice and Britain's acceptance of its particular orders, along with an intellectual interest in the French system of administrative law as a way of efficiently attending to state and individual interests, represents a European affinity common to discussions of law and rights in Britain.

Where individuals' claims or rights might be at stake, speeches before ALBA have often taken them to be about the competing powers of state institutions, a framework that generally mirrors the focus of judicial decision making. For example, the Equal Opportunity Commission's power was the focus of a judicial review case regarding the Commission's decision to investigate the allocation of school places to boys and girls (Lakin and Whitmore 1989). In recognizing the mediation and creation of interests by institutions, ALBA's view of judicial review is less romantic than that of activist lawyers in the postwar period who were concerned with the individual against the state. In the 1950s property holders subject to planning decisions provided the clientele worthy of concern. Planning law has provided principles of administrative law, but it has its own statutory appeals. Therefore, administrative law was separated from any high-status individual client base. The interest in state management elevates the status of the area away from the clientele of state services. Cases such as *Padfield* and *Bromley* give a legal basis for lawyers' involvement with state management.

With regard to individual rights, members of ALBA have listened to talks on the European Convention on Human Rights. Speeches on French administrative law and the Conseil d'Etat demonstrate an interest in the latter's significance in administration, though again with regard to managing government procedures and decisions:

> If for example, the third London airport question, or the Sizewell Be [*sic*] question or the Hinckley Point question had arisen in France rather than here, instead of having a public enquiry and then a ministerial decision, you would have a ministerial decision which would then be challenged before the Conseil d'État and before the Conseil d'État they would not only hear everything the minister had to say and everything all the pressure groups in the world had to say, all on paper of course, but they would apply their own balancing of the merits and demerits of the decision afresh, they would apply what they call a balance sheet decision. (Bridge 1988, 10)

The emphasis on addressing "merits and demerits" and thereby becoming part of central government policy making fits as well with the centralization of judicial review practice in London. Most cases that are brought in London rely on London practitioners (Sunkin, Bridges, and Meszaros 1993). A possible challenge to that London base came in the Courts and Legal Services Bill of 1990. The public focus was on the abolition of the distinction between barristers and solicitors and on the abolition of the solicitors' monopoly on conveyancing. In addition the Lord Chancellor's Department considered moving Order 53 out of the High Court, allowing the county courts throughout the country to hear judicial review cases. This would have moved cases out of London. Officials within the Lord Chancellor's Department had justified putting the cases in county courts by arguing that this would make the process less expensive and more accessible.[17] ALBA worked against that; one leading member called it "quite inappropriate" (interview 1990). It would have decentralized the new and engaging practice, though one lawyer speculated that specialists practicing in London might have just traveled throughout the country, as they do for planning law. An official within the Lord Chancellor's Department gave that department's version of the justification for conceding and allowing practice to stay in the High Court in London: practice is new, technical, and full of high principle. It is unsettled. To have the county courts making politically contestable orders against the central government would at least be (a milder) "unsuitable at this time" (interview 1990). While administrative law creates an ability to challenge the government, the centralization of the state in London is reinforced by keeping the practice in the High Court. In bringing courts and lawyers into the network of governance, the new administrative law follows channels already made.

The changes in administrative law have found organizational adaptation in administration. Treasury Solicitors, the government's chief legal officer, during the late 1970s and 1980s believed that some cases that were being lost did not have to be lost. They also believed that not all cases were avoidable; in litigation against the central government the courts did not seem to be developing clear standards, and it was therefore difficult to see how to incorporate them into administration (Kerry 1986). A group of senior officials and lawyers formed a working group on administrative law to discuss how to better address judicial review. They supported improving the education of civil servants in administrative law (Sunkin and LeSueur 1991). That is not the same as saying that particular decisions from the courts became predictable or avoidable. What is most predictable for high-ranking civil servants is that policy innovations will probably land in court; what the outcome will be is less clear. However, the effort within the Treasury Solicitor's Office continues, and the hope has been that routine cases can be avoided, ones regarding, for example, the giving of reasons in individual cases or the requirement to keep one's mind open to new considerations. In part as a result of the working group on administrative law, the Treasury Solicitor's Office now has an official whose responsibility is to organize and explain issues of judicial review to the departments generally. The idea that administrative law is something general, not just a collection of cases from and specific to land use planning, tax, or immigration law, gained administrative backing when someone was put in charge of the issue within the Treasury Solicitor's Office, separate from the specific departments.

That job was created when a civil servant in the Treasury Solicitor's Office wrote a pamphlet for distribution within the administration entitled *The Judge over Your Shoulder* in 1987. The pamphlet provided a primer on administrative law for administrative officials who were not legally trained. The core of the booklet states the requirements that the judges stated in *GCHQ*. The advice is so general that it may be most useful as a way of telling civil servants that they might have a reason to consult departmental lawyers. Most of the advice is about *forms* of making decisions. Or, as *The Judge over Your Shoulder* reassures decision makers: "The powers which the judges have built up over the years are not limitless. . . . It can happen that the same decision is reached second time round without taint of illegality" (15).

The Judge over Your Shoulder evoked criticism for not treating the rule of law (housed in judges) as intrinsically valuable. It treats judicial review as something one plans for and does not anticipate with particular relish. The rule of law, meaning what judges do, should be treated instead as a matter of what is correct; that the government finds itself in court frequently should be seen as a sign that there is something wrong with its policies (Bradley 1988, 4). The availability of judicial review has made legal critique seem more relevant to politics.

Organization of administrative law has also been reinforced by the selective and scattered case reporting system. The law reporting system in Britain is highly selective. Only a small portion of cases appears in any of the official reporters—one estimate is roughly 30 percent of the Court of Appeal cases are reported (Atkins 1991). These are selected by barristers who have the responsibility of choosing the cases that are important. Three national newspapers, *The Guardian*, *The Times*, and *The Independent*, also have reporters. They also select cases, but their reports add substantially to the number of cases reported. Finally, some cases remain unreported. The difficulty of knowing case law reinforces the importance of networks of people who do know the decisions.[18] Some of the organization in the administration has been exactly around that issue—improving access to relevant legal knowledge.

The Treasury Solicitor's Office began to issue occasional digests of administrative law cases the office saw as relevant across the departments. The Crown Office has employed barristers to manage cases, which includes scheduling and compiling relevant cases for the judges. These lawyers specialize in areas within judicial review, creating the beginning of a law clerk system for the Crown Office. Finally, the Crown Office in conjunction with Richard Gordon, a barrister, started an administrative law digest. It specializes in administrative law and reports many more cases than the general law reports do (Bradley 1989).

Finally, more barristers participate in litigation for the government. The government has long maintained a "Treasury junior," a barrister whose responsibility is to litigate for the government. His status has exemplified the blurred state-constitutive status of the legal profession, particularly as it exists in Britain. Barristers are formally forbidden from having one continuing employer. Rather, they are briefed by solicitors for a series of clients (Abel 1988b). The number of barristers in addition to the Treasury Junior who take cases for the government has increased with the expansion of judicial review, particularly involving local government. The central government has also consulted with lawyers outside the government on the design of programs.

Attention to administrative law would suggest that the government, if prudent, would try to incorporate the standards of judicial review before cases happen. It would suggest that they should incorporate legal advice, as the Treasury Solicitor's Office tries to encourage with its law digests. That could well include consulting about how best to design programs, which federal, state, and local governments do all the time in the United States. They do, but the way it is discussed evokes the controversy of *The Judge over Your Shoulder*. To plan, worry, and strategize is to treat law as something unpredictable and ordinary rather than an expression of the right way of governing that everyone ought to know. Rulings by courts could more readily be seen as the embodiment of the law and its rightness when the decisions were less relevant; the price of relevance has been a certain amount of demystification. Furthermore, once lawyers consult with the government on a policy they are bound by the Official Secrets Act, an act the Thatcher administration chose to enforce in some cases that received wide publicity. The emphasis on secrecy important to some in or working with the administration points out the incorporation of lawyering into secrecy rather than lawyering as a disruption of secrecy in the administration.

The routine practice of secrecy and consultation lends an air of the government doing something wrong (Bradley 1989). Criticism of *The Judge over Your Shoulder* addressed secrecy. Professor Bradley complained (1987, 2) that it had not been ordinarily published (though the office distributes it to thousands of civil servants and said that it regularly sends them to students who request a copy for study). Furthermore, the pamphlet had been accompanied by a confidential memo outlining steps departments could take to protect themselves against judicial review, including hiring outside counsel (Bradley 1987, 3). The composition and commission of the group that met in the mid-1980s to decide what to do about judicial review has remained confidential (Sunkin and LeSueur 1991, 165–66).

Checking with the lawyers came up in the administration after *Tameside*, the 1976 decision that held that the government had to attend to all relevant considerations in administrative decisions. The Treasury Solicitor's Office sponsored a "massive post-mortem" to avoid similar cases in the future, though it found itself making the frustrating instruction to pay attention to all relevant factors when making a decision, a standard a solicitor in the administration said was quite close to useless.[19] After the 1981 *Fare's Fair* controversy regarding transport subsidies by local governments, local authorities consulted over many decisions to spend money—including whether they "could repair the tube station lift."[20] However, when court decisions have addressed core concerns local governments face, local governments have tried to avoid the decision. For example, a 1984 decision would have made it extremely difficult for schools to ever deny a child in England or Wales her parents' choice of school. The response of local education authorities was to ignore the decision. In Scotland, where it was more difficult to ignore court decisions, educational authorities settled cases when parents chose to appeal (Tweedie 1989, 196).

By the late 1980s consultation in the central government did not await a court suit. *Tameside* in 1976 had been a surprise. It no longer would be a surprise to have central policy decisions addressed in court. For example, the government instituted a Social Fund, a new way of allocating some welfare benefits (Drabble and Lynes 1989). It consulted with barristers on how to design the program. Questions addressed how much discretion the government would have with different strategies of distributing funds and different ways of drafting the legislation. Everyone involved expected the program to be challenged in court, and it was, in *R. v. Secretary of State for Social Services ex p. Stitt* ([1990] CO/1026/89) precisely on the broad discretion the statute granted the ministry. But a court challenge is a challenge on procedures and therefore not a reason to abandon the program.[21] Indeed, the Court of Appeal in *Stitt* deplored the extensive grant of discretion but held there was nothing the Court of Appeal could do about it. The task for lawyers advising government has not been to limit the government's discretion to choose a policy. Indeed, the government consulted extensively with lawyers when drafting the Social Fund program (interviews, 1990) resulting in a program with what judges claimed was more unfettered power than that in any other Act. The government's barrister responded that there was a first time for everything (*R. v. Social Fund Inspector and the Secretary of State for Social Security ex p. Healey, The Times,* 5 July 1990). With a majority in Parliament the government can get its policies adopted. Instead, the objective has been "to 'protect Ministers' from embarrassment in the courts" (Sunkin and LeSueur 1991, 172).

In accord with emphasizing major policy issues as what is important in administrative law, a leading judge has argued that the government should create a Director of Civil Proceedings. Lord Justice Harry Woolf has long been involved in administrative law. He was the Treasury junior, then one of the first judges on the Crown Office list, the list of judges focusing on administrative law. He has had an ongoing interest in administrative law, and he commands respect across the political spectrum within administrative law practice. In 1990 the government chose him to conduct the inquiry into prison riots (leading judges are often chosen for major government investigations [Stevens 1993]). Lord Justice Woolf's proposal for a Director of Civil Proceedings requires consideration as a statement of an important legal official whose ideas gain attention from the profession and from those most responsible for changing practices, the civil service.

The director, as Lord Justice Woolf envisioned it, would be an employee of the central administration and would choose the cases that are worth public backing—ones that raise important public policy and law questions (Woolf, 1986a, 1990, 108–13). Like officials within the Lord Chancellor's Department, Lord Justice Woolf would like to see housing and immigration cases handled by administrative tribunals; the proceedings are too fact based to require the attention of the High Court (77–81). A director would handle cases that challenge principles of governing of the central administration; examples include the challenge brought to the Department of Health and Social Services' distribution of a pamphlet to minors on birth control. It is this type of case that seems to have a wider public benefit rather than simply being of interest to the complainant involved (see *Gillick v. West Norfolk and Wisbech Area Health Authority* [1986] 1 A.C. 112). Indeed, as legally framed it had little to do with individual rights.

Such a director would be institutionalizing an effort at public criticism but through the existing extremely centralized administrative system. Institutionalizing an official who would screen complaints for their importance would contribute to that centralization while at the same time intending to critique it. Such a critique and the actual consolidation it represents fits with the elite profession's efforts to keep Order 53 proceedings in the High Court. It both criticizes centralization of government authority and participates in that centralization. The director would also further analogize Britain's administrative judicial review with constitutional review in some European states where only specified agents have standing to challenge the constitutionality of legislation (Stone 1992).

Lawyers through ALBA and public discussion have claimed a place in politically contentious areas of governing under claims to expertise in legality in the administrative state. What is more, many already involved are interested in claiming a more extensive role. The legal profession in England has often had a somewhat constricted approach to what their expertise entitles them to say whether as judges or political advisers. New court decisions give lawyers the cultural authority to claim more (see, e.g., Beloff 1995; Laws 1995). By 1995 some judges' sense of authority had reached far enough that Lord Irvine, the Shadow Lord Chancellor, reminded judges in a talk before ALBA that they could not overturn legislation (Irvine 1995).

Terence Halliday has argued that the profession's epistemological base makes up the profession's claims to expertise in public affairs. Its broad reach, and the effectiveness of it, are in part dependent on the broad normative scope of being expert in "the law" (1987). Halliday has also attended to the social context supporting claims to expertise—the organization of the profession, its inclusiveness, and the politicization of the context. The experience and organization of administrative law points to another factor left implicit in the American context. The increased ideological power of the profession stems in part from judicial decisions increasing the relevance of the profession to political debate—a version of what Tocqueville noted in the United States. Court judgments provide a resource for the already organized profession to claim expertise in public affairs. The expanding territory claimed by English administrative lawyers in constitutionalism highlights the ability of the profession to mobilize and reframe existing knowledge to expand cultural authority when court decisions have made it plausible (see, e.g., Graham and Prosser 1990; Lester 1988). For example, Professor J. A. G. Griffith claimed a scandal regarding a cabinet controversy over government support of a helicopter business in 1985–86 as a constitutional problem, one that could be addressed in part with a rule-of-law government and courts that insist on proper principles in public law (1988). Even the British consideration of the Maastricht Treaty of the European Union was heard as an application for judicial review (*The Guardian Weekly,* 25 July 1993, 1; Rawlings 1995). So was the government's rail privatization (*The Times,* 25 November 1995, 2). Neither challenge prevailed. Constitutionalism has become a routine category lawyers use to criticize almost any part of British government. In turn, it takes on a wider reality through the discussion of the possibility of a written constitution and bill of rights, documents that would address administrative state power.

Lawyers have been brought into governing in ways that highlight some of the ironies of administrative law as critique. By participating in the secrecy surrounding consultation, which is required by the Official Secrets Act, outside lawyers have been drawn into the governing elites' administrative practices rather than being able to find a way to disrupt them. The creation of administrative law through judicial review has not done all that commentators might have expected.

Including the conflict between central and local government and dismissing case-level claims as uninteresting excludes immigration law and homelessness claims. Excluding both fits with the perception of what judicial review is for. Immigration cases, many officials and lawyers outside the Home Office believe, ought to have a separate and more accessible statutory appeal system; there is no reason for them to go by way of judicial review (Woolf 1992). (Before 1993, applicants could only take some issues on appeal from outside the country. That makes judicial review before leaving more attractive.) While lawyers support judges' role in governing, that support connects with an interest in a constitution rather than a concern for particular individuals and their complaints. That is what tribunals are for and after that perhaps county courts. Judicial review should instead address broad issues of policymaking, exactly what even conservative legalists in the 1950s had argued should not be in court. By the 1980s, the issues in judicial review that fit the old paradigm of the individual against the state were immigration and homelessness, which did not raise issues compelling to elite lawyers.

The newer meaning of judicial review and administrative law recognizes lawyers as part of a governing elite, one that is separate from partisanship yet involved in important policy decisions (see e.g. Beloff 1995; Laws 1995). That echoes the role academic lawyers argue for in the United States, where lawyers in administrative and constitutional law are to call the country back to its governing principles and virtues, apart from self-interest or partisan division. The elite part of the profession is as eager to have a nonpartisan republican role in governing as it has been in the United States.

Considering the mass claims cases to be less important, more about individual claims than about principles of governance, would contribute to an existing division within the profession and legal practice. Issues of principle are the ones that legal elites take to be universal, general, and important. They are nonrepetitive. And they have high-status clients who are not claiming benefits from the state. (For an example, see Beloff 1995, 145–46.) The courts themselves have supported this understanding of what is important; in 1986, courts told applicants that immigration and homelessness cases were wasting the courts' time (see also *R. v. Secretary of State for the Home Department, ex p. Swati* [1986] all E.R. 717).

The Rule of Law and Partisan Debate

The attention that administrative law has received would suggest that there has suddenly been a significant increase in the number of cases in court. Indeed, the number of applications for leave went up significantly in the 1980s. However, when cases are analyzed by category there has been a substantial increase primarily in the number of immigration and homelessness cases filed (Sunkin 1987b; Sunkin, Bridges, and Meszaros, 1993). Since 1987 local governments have also been subject to an increasing number of claims in education. Despite the attention the policy-making cases against central government get, since the early 1980s there has not been a substantial increase in the numbers of those cases (Sunkin, Bridges, and Meszaros 1993). One response to that information would be to say that those who think the area of law is growing or important are mistaken (Sunkin 1987a). Indeed, one lawyer enthusiastic about the enterprise still noted that administrative law could hardly constitute a full-time practice for many lawyers unless they were in immigration; there weren't enough cases (see also Ames 1993). But administrative law cases challenging central government gain attention because these cases fit into the existing debate about political accountability and a new written constitution for Britain. Commentary outside of lawyers' groups makes the constitutionalist significance of judicial review evident.

In particular, Charter 88 was formed in 1988 to muster popular support for a bill of rights and a written constitution explicitly outside the party system. Charter 88 is modeled on Charter 77, the human rights movement in Czechoslovakia formed in 1977. Playing on the image of Charter 77 has provided a critique of British government. Charter 77 asked the government to follow its own law, and it protested secret arrests, brutal police practices, and the lack of freedom of speech (Adams 1992; Samal 1988). To name an organization Charter 88 is both to link the movement with the democracy and human rights movements of the 1970s and to find a footing for human rights without an existing written constitution, a footing appropriate for critiques raised in Britain. Europe was the important reference point. Charter 88 opened its "Prospects and Plans" with the following words:

> CHARTER 88, as an idea and as an organisation, was born not of a carefully planned strategy with fully fledged tactics, but on the beginning of a wave. Popular democracy is its name; Europe its present continent; CHARTER 88 embodies its hopes in the United Kingdom. Through popular, peaceful change the Charter aims to bring about as soon as possible a modern written constitution in Britain, with human and political rights entrenched in law. (Charter 88, n.d.)

An emphasis on legality has appeared throughout the Charter 88 material. Its pamphlets have addressed the new administrative law in a critical fashion. The pamphlet entitled "Redress for All State Abuse" noted:

> * There is no right of access to courts—you can't challenge an abuse of power without a judge's permission. Between 30 to 40% of applications for judicial review are simply turned down without a full hearing . . .
> * There is no statutory obligation on government authorities to comply with a code of good administrative conduct.
> * Judges have discretionary powers to strike down decisions made by ministers or civil servants on three counts: that they are unlawful, perverse or procedurally unfair. But there is no domestic Bill of Rights to provide speedy and effective remedies for state abuse of our fundamental liberties.
>
> It seems to suit our rulers very well to keep us subjects, without rights or redress. For example, Samuel Stitt recently applied for judicial review of a social security ruling. He was turned down by the Court of Appeal. The Court clearly felt that Stitt had a case and found it remarkable that Parliament should have given the Secretary of State such unrestricted power. But as it had, there was nothing to be done about it. (Charter 88 1990)

These critiques focus on legality: people should get hearings before courts turn down their applications for review, and government should operate by rules. The extremely limited role of the courts also, ironically, plays into the debate over a constitution. An appeal to fundamental principles reaches beyond what the courts have done and provides a critique of the courts, as Charter 88 used *Stitt*. Charter 88 advertised for support using issues that have been both partisan politically compelling and within administrative law—including the poll tax and GCHQ. The limited criticism by the courts of governing practices is used as evidence of the need for a new and written constitution (Graham and Prosser 1991). What the courts would do with a potential bill of rights in Britain is a topic of much discussion; those few cases in which they have addressed central government power explicitly can provide a signal. Those cases are in administrative law (Lester 1990b).[22]

While in power the Conservative party was not about to endorse a claim for a constitution, particularly when many concerns focus on administrative accountability. Those advocating a new written constitution have recognized that no party had much of a reason to endorse one unless it seemed to offer a significant electoral advantage. Yet the constitutionalist claims echo throughout political argument. In 1991 Roy Hattersley, the deputy leader of the Labour party, revealed a plan for a "Charter of Rights" (*The Times,* 9 January 1991, 3). In July of 1991 the Prime Minister, John Major, issued a "Citizen's Charter." It argued for more efficient service for consumers of public goods, including national health insurance and public housing. As several critics have argued, the Citizen's Charter moved from the concern of citizens as participants in policy choices represented in Charter 88 toward citizens solely as consumers of public services with little interest in what those policies are (Barron and Scott 1992; Drewry 1993, 251–52). But it was just that constitutionalist framework that made sense to some critics of the Conservative government.

Organization around law and the rule of law relies on the idea that there is certainty in an abstraction called law rather than a set of practices and particular laws or particular judicial decisions. Debate in Parliament criticizing the government, Charter 88, and other public commentary have all relied on law as having certain fundamental principles available to criticize the government. Christopher Hitchens in *The Nation* pointed out surprising effects of the Thatcher administration; one was that " 'Thatcherism' has made possible a movement for a serious, law-based constitutional republic in Britain and has hacked away at the encrusted institutions and attitudes that stood in its path."[23] By 1995 *The Economist* could run a series on constitutional reform that drew on judicial review (14 October 1995). Charter 88 has emphasized political participation and discussion about what a constitution *should* require; it has been very open-ended. Charter 88's main statement includes a call to "[s]ubject executive powers and prerogatives, by whomsoever exercised, to the rule of law" and "[p]lace the executive under the power of a democratically renewed parliament and all agencies of the state under the rule of law" (Charter 88, n.d.). These images provide a reason to bring cases, and to discuss them, whether or not the challengers prevail. Even *Time Out*, a popular London weekly that publishes information on entertainment as well as articles on popular culture, now notes judicial review cases that raise political issues (e.g., "Green Legal Challenge" 1990). Important political issues are brought to court despite the unlikelihood of success.

A rule-of-law image is particularly ironic in light of the legally enforceable duty to retain discretion in Britain. The popular attitude toward law implies a kind of certainty and rule boundedness that, perhaps predictably, does not appear regularly in judicial decisions or administrative practice. The cultural importance of that imagery explains the importance of administrative law despite the limits to the critical principles the courts have found and despite the government's ability to revise any decision with which it is unhappy. Public meanings play into parliamentary debate. Time in Parliament to debate issues is a scarce resource, one for which departments maneuver and that civil servants often want to avoid. Court cases can provide that time. Next, the opposition uses time in Parliament to embarrass and criticize the government about its policies since they can seldom be changed or defeated. While the government may not have to worry about losing, it does worry about embarrassment. Oppositional party politics also makes its way into the newspapers and popular commentary. A judicial decision is a resource for criticism. Departments know that. For example, local government finance cases throughout the 1980s, as well as the *GCHQ* case, provided rich material for editorials and cartoons. The new cases have met with public discussion and an adoption of judges' language and standards within administration and in public debate. The *Gillick* case regarding the responsibility of the minister in distributing information about birth control to minors provided an occasion for parliamentary and newspaper debate about sexuality and the family in England (Cannell 1990). While the new decisions or concerns about them do not seem to have led to a prohibition of any particular decisions within government—the government did not abandon the Social Fund scheme or the poll tax in response to judicial review but consulted on how to design them—they have played into a heightened awareness of the possibilities legal critiques seem to offer in a time of discontent with partisanship.[24]

The Courts and Political Choice

The courts' engagement in central policy disputes has resurrected old concerns about the democratic accountability of the courts even though they have not generally overturned policies of the government (Bell 1984; Charter 88 1990). A radio discussion of administrative law stated that well: "Q.C. v. M.P." (BBC 1990), broadcast in April of 1990. By 1995 news programs on television and long newspaper articles discussed judges as against ministers, largely as a result of judicial review (Cohen 1995; Ward 1995). To frame the issue that way is to highlight what is most politically compelling about judicial review, particularly to elite lawyers. First, that debate places elite barristers, called Queen's Counsel, on a par with members of Parliament. That is a shift in a system in which lawyers and legal knowledge have not been important in governing. Second, it frames the debate as one of political choice represented by M.P.'s against law. But that does not entirely capture the place of judicial review.

Changes in response to judicial review are in administrative procedure—one consults where one hadn't and should have, or insists that one's mind is still open to new considerations. Administrators reconsider decisions. Curiously, the rule of law in practice has quite a different meaning from what it has in governing theory. The rule of law is supposed to require courts to hold administrators to standards in statutes. One would think that could well mean substantive standards—that is, if a statute directs an administrator to make a judgment about the need for revision in milk pricing policy, that administrator could be held to have made the wrong decision if he or she decided on the wrong basis. However, in practice cases are virtually always about procedures rather than fundamental principles of what policies may be.[25] The substantial litigation around changes in financing programs from local governments did not finally stop the centrally initiated changes. Instead, it primarily colored public debate and slightly enhanced the bargaining position of the local governments. The image that the courts are squaring off against the central government seems much more pervasive than any decisions actually overturning central government decisions are. Finally, if judgment from courts is less democratic than policy initiated by the central government, that problem is rather easily remedied through government revision, whether of the statutes held not to authorize action or of the actions themselves.[26] That is less true in case-level decisions interpreting statutes or rules regarding homelessness, allocation of children to schools, and immigration. Local governments in particular have sometimes found that court decisions interpreting central government statutes limit their discretion and local governments cannot change the statute. The most they can do is to sometimes ignore court decisions (Tweedie 1989; Loveland 1995). Yet it is not case-level decisions, with their close reading of statutes rather than assertions about ministerial power, that occasion the discussions of democracy and the rule of law.

The image of courts against democratically elected legislatures, with the implication that one side or the other wholly wins or loses, seldom captures the place of judicial review in governance. Even the postwar-created European constitutional courts, which do have the power to overturn legislation, often have limits to what they can do. Their members are often chosen both for expertise and as members of a party. The French Court Constitutionnel considers legislation before it has been implemented. The national legislature can and does revise legislation in light of decisions. The Court Constitutionnel seldom completely halts central government policy (Shapiro 1990; Stone 1992). Even less in Britain do the courts directly overturn government legislation. They can require reconsideration, which can increase the costs of a policy to the government. But they do not hold that legislation is against some fundamental principles. Instead, they read statutes through judicial interpretive principles, generally concerning procedures, and evaluate an administrative decision against the interpretation. Even central government decisions under statutes are not straightforwardly democratically authorized; they are discrete decisions undertaken by executive ministries under the authority of a statute. They are not the statute itself. Even less are decisions by ministries or local governments in case-level policy making such as housing or immigration or school placement allocation simply an execution of the will of the people.

However, to point out that the courts using judicial review in England and Wales decide under severe constraints is not to say that judicial review is meaningless either. It can increase the costs to government of making decisions by requiring reconsideration, by requiring that policies are defended in court, and sometimes by embarrassing the government in debate. It also constrains case-level decision making.

Even in Britain, with its judiciary conventionally understood to be so conservative, it would be a mistake to conclude that the court decisions mean nothing because the government can revise or avoid them and because courts have no constitution from which to build a critique. Instead, the new judicial decisions have to be understood in the context in which they are made. The attention they get in partisan debate is significant. Decisions provide a way to criticize government that is useful precisely because it looks nonpartisan. That usefulness has been part of the reason for reorganization in the field of administrative law. In Britain the enthusiastic reception of a revived rule of law misses the uncertainty intrinsic to the enterprise of interpreting statutes through broad principles.

The new administrative law has increased the relevance of lawyers and legal expertise to administrative policy making in England and Wales. The simultaneous and related interest in a new constitution has made it possible for legal expertise to seem relevant to governing in a way that both fits into partisanship as the relevant debate in Britain and offers something separate from partisanship. The emergent debate is very statist, largely not oriented toward individual complaints about the delivery of services but about public management issues between organizations. *GCHQ* provided an important example: the judge-stated duty of the government to consult was abrogated in this case due to national security, a state priority separable from partisan purposes. These issues of central government responsibility to operate under rules and of relations between central and local government are what have evoked interest and participation by an elite part of the bar in England. Administrative law is an area of law that is relevant to most people's lives (Smart 1989). Yet at the moment of its institutionalization in Britain as a critique of governance it has become more abstracted from people's lives. Leading lawyers urge the more extended use of tribunals and ombudsmen for the routine complaints people have about government programs. Immigration and homelessness claims are still the main component of the administrative law caseload. The courts have deplored the appearance of those cases in court (e.g., *Pulhofer* and *Swati*). Lawyers have cited these issues as a warning sign of retrenchment: too many applications are made "without a proper basis."[27] In signaling that division of concerns between what is important and what cases are improperly brought, the profession has made its bid to participate in principled governing in Britain. Courts and the law they make are critiqued as embodying abstract universal reason; therefore, they have little to offer people trying to criticize the state (Smart 1989). Paradoxically, the image of abstract reason is what makes courts attractive as critics of a centralized and highly partisan government.

During the 1980s and into the early 1990s no one critical of the Conservative government was winning in any traditional political domain. Internal strife made it difficult for the Labour Party to present itself as a plausible alternative to the Conservatives. Administration was closing out corporatist consultation. The central government was abolishing the local governments that provided a home to municipal socialism. The courts, despite their unwillingness to rule against the central administration very often at all, provided a place for critique that the government could not abolish without seriously encroaching on its own rule of law ideology.

CHAPTER 6

Narrowing It Down: Immigration Practices

> My name is Karim Amir, and I am an Englishman born and bred, almost. I am often considered to be a funny kind of Englishman, a new breed as it were, having emerged from two old histories. But I don't care—Englishman I am (though not proud of it), from the South London suburbs and going somewhere. Perhaps it is the odd mixture of continents and blood, of here and there, of belonging and not, that makes me restless and easily bored.
>
> —Hanif Kureishi

The problem of belonging in Britain is acute for people who have moved there from the Indian subcontinent, Africa, or the West Indies—the New Commonwealth—or for those whose families did. The Commonwealth organization, reformulated over the years and consolidated in the British Nationality Act of 1981, holds that they are British. Once they would not have been considered ethnically English, even if British, but in recent years some scholars have begun to argue explicitly for a construction of black English ethnicity (Gilroy 1994). The treatment of those who live in Britain and whose families were once from the New Commonwealth has held they do not belong in the British Isles. The problem is even more explicit for those born in London of a Commonwealth parent or parents, such as Karim, the character speaking in the epigraph above.[1] Karim's situation is that of most people considered black in Britain. Rather than being immigrants, more than 50 percent now were born in the British Isles (Anwar 1991). Yet a dominant political meaning of blackness in Britain still often assumes that people of Asian, African, and Afro-Caribbean ethnicity are immigrants and do not belong. Therefore immigration is a politically sensitive issue, not simply a question of what to do concerning people arriving in Britain now but implicitly and sometimes explicitly a question about how much people already there belong. Immigration therefore is a politically significant site for examining the racialization of citizenship (Mohanty 1991). It has also been one of the most politically charged and vibrant sites for community organizing against the Conservative government (Sivanandan 1990). The legal discourse of immigration domestically and in the European Court of Human Rights depends on the administrative law categories developed in earlier chapters. Yet those most concerned with administrative law and legal accountability as a general topic seldom deal very extensively with immigration law.

Not surprisingly, the cultural problem of belonging for racialized minorities in Britain has had its counterpart in the legal status of immigrants. That status was left open in the 1950s, when Commonwealth immigrants moved to England to live; as Commonwealth members they were entitled to move freely there and to look for work with British employers. From the early 1960s on the government began to worry about assimilation and in November 1961 began a voucher program to control Commonwealth immigration in part on the basis of race (Layton-Henry 1992). Britain abolished this political understanding with the Commonwealth Immigrants Act of 1968, which refused to allow Asians in East Africa, Commonwealth citizens, to escape to Britain when Africanization threatened them in Africa. The legal position of Commonwealth immigrants was finally consolidated against the interests of those from the "New Commonwealth" in the Immigration Act of 1971 and the Nationality Act of 1981.[2] In discriminating between those from the "New" and "Old" Commonwealths the government distinguished between people from the Indian subcontinent, Africa, and the West Indies on the one hand and those from Australia and New Zealand whose families had moved from the British Isles on the other.

Britain has used exclusion of immigrants as a way to address its race problems. The belief is that immigrants and ethnic minorities need to learn how to become English, and that that acculturation will work best if there are only limited numbers of racial minorities to acculturate and to whom native English, Welsh, and Scots must become accustomed. Immigrants and native-born citizens of Asian, African, and Afro-Caribbean ethnicity have challenged that model and claimed the legitimacy of their cultures within Britain.[3] Conflicts over language in schools and over Salman Rushdie's *The Satanic Verses* have exemplified cultural struggles over belonging.[4] It was made acutely visible when a member of the government, Norman Tebbit, said in the spring of 1990 that a test of belonging is whether people cheered for the English cricket team. England effectively exported cricket, and within Britain there are many supporters for the excellent West Indian team and other Commonwealth teams. Norman Tebbit was roundly criticized for his comment as a race-based statement that insulted citizens. Citizenship, on his model, is not a legal status but a matter of culture. This issue has often emerged historically in societies with waves of immigration.[5] While antiracist activity has had to immediately confront the cultural issues of what it means to be British, political action has also criticized the immigration rules and statutes as racist and sexist. For example, before 1985, women were disadvantaged in their ability to bring their husbands into the country. That has been addressed through litigation and through other forms of political action, including critiques of the way the legal system has treated people (WING 1985).

A related immigration question is the status of refugees. As a signatory of the U.N. Convention on Refugees, Britain must admit people who have a "well founded fear of persecution" on the basis of their membership in a social group in their home states. However, that has also been a politically contentious issue and in 1987 and 1989 a source of waves of cases.

The Immigration Acts, the adjudicators who interpret them, the Home Office, which designs guidelines under them, and the Immigration Appeals Tribunal, which decides appeals from adjudicators, are all concerned with background questions of exclusion from Britain. They work on a policy that is not generally contested within the parties: neither race discrimination nor immigration have been popular electoral issues. One part of the Conservative party has long been actively against immigration and sympathetic to the racism that was part of an English sense of being threatened by outsiders. The Labour party has also been restrictive while sometimes taking the public strategy of avoiding the issue or criticizing the government when the Conservatives are in power. An example of that is the 1988 Act. Labour criticized it continually in Parliament; the government pointed out that Labour had made no commitment to open immigration (Layton-Henry 1992, 206–10). Similarly in 1993 and 1995 debates Labour avoided the vote-losing argument in favor of asylum-seekers and against the government. Local Labour governments have sometimes been more sympathetic in their practices with regard to schooling and rules regarding discrimination. The avoidance of the issue has also extended to a leadership consensus to try to minimize the importance of racial categories in national politics (Messina 1989). When immigration has been politically raised as an issue by the parties, it has usually been in support of a fear of too much immigration into Britain. Getting other perspectives on immigration into parliamentary discussion and its accompanying national attention is difficult, to say the least.

Litigation in Britain addresses immigration. Participants see it as providing an opportunity to break through elite consensus in addition to providing an ability sometimes to win for individuals in court. Litigation offers opportunities for a political critique of racial problems in Britain and the race-based practices of immigration law. Preferences regarding litigation are endogenous to the political system, deeply responsive both to the problems the immigration system has created and to the incentives and format created by the courts themselves. The courts require narrow arguments, and therefore lawyers make them. Stuart Scheingold has said of radical lawyering in Britain that "radical lawyers are both resistant to, and influenced by . . . forces of conventional professionalism" (1994). It is easy to believe from an American perspective that the courts do little that is relevant to public debate or other forms of politics in immigration and that lawyers can do little that is useful for clients. But that is not how some participants see it.

While the last chapter addressed what might roughly be called a public goods type of litigating—litigating between organizations over issues that are most significant for their participation in national politics and revision of policies—this chapter will be addressing litigation that largely benefits particular individuals—litigation to be permitted to live in Britain, brought often by lawyers who work within the profession but try to incorporate political resistance into immigration law. As we will see, this litigation spills over into national politics.

But how do practitioners find opportunities in immigration law? There is no bill of rights in Britain to use to critique statutes. Indeed, litigation is often based on interpretations of Home Office rules as much as on statutes. Worse, the British courts have been generally understood to have an apolitical, unprincipled, and narrow approach to interpreting statutes. Indeed, within legal theory that is often taken to be their only justifiable position (Cross 1977). When the "apolitical" idea is debunked, critics argue that the courts' approach is inherently conservative and provides little ground for criticizing administrative practices (Griffith 1991). If the courts have narrow understandings of statutes, ones that favor government priorities, why take any cases? Once cases have been through legally trained adjudicators and administrative tribunals, any administrative decision wholly outside plausible statutory interpretation will have been excluded. And, the conservative courts argument would go, there is no point in challenging the principles of decisions. Courts in England will not aggressively challenge administrators. (For a consideration of courts' role in immigration, see Legomsky 1987.) The other side of the same approach would argue that the courts have become more active in recent years, which usually implies a change in judicial ideology toward making the "fair" decision (Paterson 1982). Immigration cases, then, must be part of the courts' new activism based on emergent judicial attitudes critical of administration.[6]

A better answer than the one provided by the deferential or activist courts perspective requires two things. First, it requires an appreciation of legal interpretation. Statutes and rules must always be interpreted in a context and through interpretive principles; plain meanings are only plain to some specified group, and they are only plain within a context.[7] That the courts retreat into the language of rules does not answer the question of what those rules mean to them and other participants. Once decisions are made, they are available for others to use for a variety of purposes, not all of which are tied to what the courts might have meant to do.

To address these questions, I interviewed nine lawyers in the spring of 1990 and 1991, both barristers and solicitors, who practiced largely in immigration. I used a network sample approach, in which I asked practicing lawyers for the names of others significant in the practice of immigration law. I talked to many of the lawyers repeatedly said to be very involved in immigration law in private practice. Most of them were ethnically English men; two were men of South Asian ethnicity, and two were white women. The sample means that I did not talk to lawyers those practitioners are concerned about—solicitors and barristers who only occasionally take cases. Nor did I talk to clients to address how they saw their cases or how they saw their lawyers.[8] While the sample is neither representative of all who practice immigration law nor complete with regard to experience in litigation, it is useful in addressing what lawyers see as possible to gain from the legal system.

I also listened to a group discussion of immigration law issues, which incorporated ten more lawyers. It was a regular meeting of an organization that educates and shares information, the Immigration Law Practitioners Association (ILPA). That group was more diverse by race and gender than was my network sample of lawyers. Indeed, only one of the lawyers in my network sample appeared at the ILPA meeting, though lawyers in the network had been active in organizing the group.

Lawyers practice in immigration both for business executives and in cases they see as more politically charged. Because of the link between race and immigration, lawyers can see working on immigration for refugees and families from the Middle East, Africa, and the Indian subcontinent as a kind of political work. As one lawyer told me, her law work was all part of "sixteen-hour days working on antiracism."

This chapter addresses the choices made by litigators within the law of three subfields within immigration—refugee cases, rules governing exceptions from deportation for reasons of "compassionate circumstances," and rules governing settlement of people who marry those who have a right to live in Britain. All these issues raise the question of what one can get out of litigation.

What Decisions Mean

In immigration law the significance of the relationship between the particular and universal aspirations in law becomes clear. Immigration litigation is highly particular, making claims against changing rules, statutes, administrative practices, and judicial interpretations of them. The relationship of immigration law to the politics of race in Britain means that it does not share a political context with most other areas of administrative law. Yet in litigating the claims lawyers hope for favorable decisions, good press, and some public concern based on a dense rule-of-law ideal that they see the government too often ignoring. Using rule-of-law ideals to criticize government action depends not on the specific politics of race and immigration but on the universalized claims to due process and what it means to treat people well in law, even though the rules in immigration are highly particular to that field. Immigration law, including the hopes that practicing attorneys have for it, embodies the tension between the specific and the abstract that is part of the making of legal ideals.

But how does law provide that kind of critique in British politics? Why go to court? If all of politics is channeled through Parliament and administration in Britain, why not work there? The problem is well stated by the British Left, which has long mistrusted courts, and by some American critiques of courts. The critiques make tremendous sense, particularly within the British context. Rights individuate complaints and lead people into complacency about government as being fair.[9] The British Left has long mistrusted courts, based in part on unions' experience in labor law. Carol Smart (1989) has raised problems with the use of law for progressive change for feminists, but these concerns apply even more broadly. She argues that the law is a self-contained discourse, one that closes out other critiques as irrelevant to law; law is the authority on governance. This critique collapses litigation in individual cases under existing rules, litigation under the European Convention on Human Rights, litigation for changes in policy based on critiques of existing rules, and efforts to change legislation that legally governs relationships. The forms of argument can be different in these different areas. For example, efforts to change legislation are often based on wide-ranging arguments regarding social justice. Smart's critique also depends on a belief in the masterfulness of law—that its language is accepted in all forums. Most of the immigration litigation, challenges to applications of the rules in particular cases, would be part of the most narrow use of law and therefore most open to Smart's critique. Such litigation is, similarly, most open to the critique of rights and litigation as individuating complaints. Whether a woman legally residing in Britain is consulting with legal services about her divorce settlement or an immigrant is consulting about the conditions under which she can stay, they are working with interpretations of rules in particular cases rather than collective political challenges to the rules themselves. While not resurrecting the argument that legal interpretation or practice is politically neutral, this approach does hold that it is not a useful or effective form of politics.

Reading from a doctrinal level alone, without asking participants about possible meanings of litigation, stunts understanding of what is possible within legal strategies. Doctrine, or one person's reading of it, does not contain all the cultural and political meanings of litigation. It should be an empirical question whether the use of rights, even mundane and changeable rights such as those in interpretations of immigration rules, is politically enervating and individuating. As Richard Delgado (1987) and Patricia Williams (1987) have argued for the United States, from the point of view of people who have been denied selves by dominant social groups, some formally recognized selfhood or autonomy can be important. It affords some protection against prevalent social abuses. Distance can make room for political activity and assertion, rather than obliterate it. Patricia Williams (1987) also argues for that even within the formalities of a lease; those advantages are not reserved for claims under a bill of rights. Such an argument invites turning to a legal system known for its hostility to claims based on wide principles as a limiting case for evaluating the possibilities of narrow legality. It invites rethinking the problem of individuation. Within immigration in Britain, lawyers argue that individuation could make immigrants more acceptable by making them human.

> There is a difference between immigration as an issue and caring about individual cases. People do care about children and they do care about people being persecuted. They can relate to that. There's been a continuing high level of interest in the press on refugees, on, for example, primary purpose, which has provoked an endless stream of misery. And people care about those issues. You can tap that support. And that eventually gets to judges. As Lord Scarman said in the early proceedings in *Khawaja* [discussed below], it is idle to pretend that judges don't read newspapers. (interview, 1990)

By raising questions through particular stories, litigation can appeal to the very particular human commitments we have, commitments not easily subsumed under general rules. Yet particular human commitments make up many of our judgments (Nussbaum 1991b).

An ordinary victory in court for a claimant could be accorded some respect as important for that person. The critique of rights also treats political organizing and litigating as mutually exclusive rather than reinforcing. At one level, that could be right: in the abstract, resources put into one strategy could have gone into another. However, strategies need not be mutually exclusive, and the skills lawyers have might be best suited to political work through litigation. Finally, the argument for the problems inherent in litigating for claimants avoids the concrete "compared to what" question. While political organizing provides the general frame of an alternative strategy, it only makes sense where one can talk about the expected outcomes of organizing in a particular context. If political effectiveness for immigrants or ethnic minorities looks difficult in Parliament or in other political discussion, then the difficulties of accomplishing anything through litigation could diminish in comparison. Litigation, with all its limits, could offer something.

The significance of litigation rests in part on the British government's ability to exclude groups (other than producer groups) from policy making (Crouch and Dore 1990). Even in domestic race relations representatives of racialized minorities to whom the state listens often come from the state-created community relations councils. These are often criticized as representing more conservative perspectives on the significance of race in British politics (Katznelson 1973; Sahgal and Yuval-Davis 1993). Litigation for individual clients does not depend on the state's consent to consult about policy-making. The closure of the British political system does not mean that it offers no strategic challenge. Indeed, highly repressive political systems offer opportunities to make claims within the existing framework (Scott 1990). Sometimes governing principles offer openings to make claims for people disadvantaged and within the political system. Much substantial change has initially been framed as claims within existing frameworks, exploiting contradictions and tensions within them, and for particular individuals. Within the United States organizations and individuals use legal rights talk as a way of mobilizing and making claims for equality (McCann 1991). At first glance one might simply attribute that to a peculiar American "rights consciousness." However, rules create spaces for claims—that the rules were inappropriately applied or that they should be interpreted in light of some other generally agreed-upon principle—and it makes sense to expect that such spaces would be used in Britain as well. They have been. This chapter explores the way that claims can be constructed within a hostile system. I will focus on the legal system as it is traditionally defined: on how lawyers frame claims and what opportunities they see for doing so. Litigation regarding applications of immigration rules provides a good limiting case for evaluating the completeness of the control of claims by technical legal language.

Legal theory often romanticizes courts and judges as advocates for the individual over the state (e.g., Dworkin 1986). So does political discussion, sometimes. Seeing a comparative advantage in courts might sound similar to that romanticizing. It is not, which was made clear in the discussions I had with barristers and solicitors. Lawyers had a clear sense that some judges were more sympathetic than others and that it was important to get the right judge. But to illustrate what a low priority these cases had for many judges, a barrister told me of a comment a judge had made during a case she was trying. Immigration cases often take about half a day; commercial cases can often take much longer. When she was arguing a case, a judge asked her to hurry the case along because the court had an important commercial case coming up. She used that case to emphasize to me that the commercial cases are taken to be important while immigration ones are not. Critiques of particular judges and the immigration rules went alongside an insistence that there is some chance to win and that one must try to win for clients. No one argued that courts were some bulwark of antistatism.

The possible political gains of even ordinary litigation require reopening the question of whether rights are antithetical to politics. Doing that also implies loosening the tight link commonly made between courts and rights. What courts are for, it is often assumed, is the enforcement of rights. The task for studies of rights then becomes to define how they do it, whether they do it, and how it might be justifiable (Dworkin 1986). However, implicit definitions of rights as more fundamental than court declarations emerge in critiques of decisions as unfair and wrong. For an unfavorable decision from a court can be used to criticize publicly the practices of British institutions. To understand the making of immigration law in Britain, I turn to that next.

Making Immigration Law

Immigration laws became an issue in the courts in the 1970s. The 1971 Immigration Act restricted rights of access of immigrants from former colonies, particularly ones in Africa and the Indian subcontinent. The statute made a distinction between patrials and nonpatrials among Commonwealth citizens. Patrials had a right of abode and were either United Kingdom citizens or born abroad with a parent or grandparent who was a United Kingdom citizen. This distinction made it easier for those from New Zealand and Australia to immigrate to Britain than it was for those from the Indian subcontinent, the West Indies, or any part of the Middle East. Subsequent statutes and rules have elaborated standards and restrictions on entry, grounds for deportation, and the meaning of nationality. The 1981 Nationality Act made nationality explicit and brought it into line with immigration law, creating categories of citizens with different rights of settlement in Britain. With efforts to regulate (but not absolutely prohibit) entry came complaints that some people were being excluded improperly under the existing rules. Those complaints have expanded ever since; one commentator called immigration a "growth industry" in the 1970s (Blom-Cooper 1982). In the mid-1980s it comprised 30 percent of the judicial review caseload of the High Court, though it dropped to about 22 percent of applications for judicial review in 1991 (Sunkin 1987b; Sunkin, Bridges, and Meszaros 1993, 6).

Refugee cases surged through the judicial review system in 1987 and 1989. In 1987 Tamil refugees fleeing Sri Lanka provided at least 258 judicial review applications; in 1989 Kurdish refugees fleeing Iraq provided at least 55 applications (Sunkin, Bridges, and Meszaros 1993, 10). These waves of applications for refugee status only gave a hint of what in the 1990s would become an expansion in asylum-seeking that concerned states throughout Western Europe. The British state's strategy in the late 1980s of limiting asylum seekers via administrative strategies while stating a public commitment to international obligations would prove to be its approach in later years as well. Furthermore, the cases from the late 1980s provided the material to which the government would react in asylum bills in the 1990s. Therefore thc struggles over the doctrine in the 1980s is important to understand. Immigration cases in judicial review were common enough by the late 1980s that officials of the Immigration and Nationality Department saw judicial review as part of the ordinary environment within which they worked. Planning too carefully to avoid judicial review would distract the department from the work of making decisions (Sunkin and Le Sueur 1991, 175).

Practice around immigration law looks roughly as follows. People who want to visit or immigrate to Britain obtain a visa and entry clearance from street-level administrators. Once in the country, people are sometimes subject to deportation, also bringing them into contact with the law. Immigrants who have lost within the administration can be informed of the existence of the government-funded United Kingdom Immigration Advisory Service (UKIAS). Immigrants could either use it or go outside to a solicitor. UKIAS's staff included legally trained counselors; cases that did not win through representations to the Home Office were filtered through legally trained advisers who decide whether there is a good legal claim. If a counselor thought an immigrant has a point of law to make, he or she referred the case to an outside solicitor (Martin 1986). UKIAS was widely criticized as badly underfunded and under the control of the government (see, e.g., Harlow and Rawlings 1984). The government closed UKIAS, claiming that it was in such disarray that a new advisory body had to be constituted (*The Times*, 9 July 1992, 7); indeed, it was immediately reopened as the Immigration Advisory Service. The limited availability of legal aid representation before immigration appeals tribunals has been credited with the some of the difficulty immigrants have in succeeding before them (Legal Action Group 1992). The Joint Council for the Welfare of Immigrants, which is a political campaigning organization, also refers cases to solicitors. In addition, in recent years the number of organizations concerned with immigrants has grown. While one participant estimated that twenty-four lawyers in London handle immigration claims often enough to have developed some expertise, all the law centres (publicly financed law offices) can take immigration cases (Dhavan 1989). However, since 1982 the government has left most of the funding of the law centres to the financially strapped local governments (Legal Action Group 1992, 9–10). Many cases end up in the hands of a few London firms, which often must turn cases away because they have too many to handle; indeed, four firms of solicitors were responsible for 43.6 percent of the judicial review applications in immigration during 1987, a year with a substantial number of Tamil asylum seekers. By 1989 the cases had spread out; the top four firms were responsible for only 26 percent of the applications (Sunkin, Bridges, and Meszaros 1993, 35). Even so, that is highly concentrated practice. Solicitors get cases from referrals; firms that practice in immigration get reputations within the legal community or the immigrant community for their knowledge. One solicitor said the law reports are his best advertising. Lawyers work with claimants taking cases to the Immigration Appeals Tribunal, an internal administrative appeal system. Ordinary appeals go from there to the Court of Appeal. However, before 1993 the law did not provide for an in-country right of appeal. That is, people who are to be deported cannot appeal that decision from England, Wales, or Scotland but must go back to the country from which they emigrated to appeal. However, they may get decisions judicially reviewed from within the country. For that, they go to the High Court. The solicitors decide whether to refer the cases to a barrister to take to the High Court or whether to only work on representations to the Home Office or M.P.'s. Barristers make representations both before the Immigration Appeals Tribunal and the High Court.

Immigration law does not get an enormous amount of respect either from judges or from some barristers in other areas. One barrister said it had the reputation of being "bad lawyers arguing badly for dishonest clients." In 1986 the High Court in *R. v. Secretary of State for the Home Department ex p. Swati* ([1986] All E.R. 717) complained that too many immigration cases were coming before the court. Finally, a judge and some civil servants have argued that immigration cases are inappropriate for judicial review; they should be handled through better tribunal procedures. As Hazel Genn has argued in her study of tribunals, applicants do not necessarily prefer court procedure, for it is more expensive and complex. Businesses, too, have tried to move disputes out of the courts, even in Britain where court procedure is often less expensive and cumbersome than it is in the United States (1993, 396–97). Even so, arguing that immigration cases do not belong in the courts is symbolically important; it states what types of cases are worthy of high-status time and attention.[10]

Cases can be taken to the European Commission on Human Rights and after that to the European Court of Human Rights (ECHR) under a claim that the British government has violated the European Convention on Human Rights. While the ECHR can overturn domestic decisions, its influence can reach beyond that. Two immigration cases from the early 1980s stood out as noticeable even within the general field of administrative law and illustrate the possible subtle influence of the ECHR. In *Zamir* ([1979] 3 W.L.R. 89) the Divisional Court had held that a visitor had an obligation to come forward with any information relevant to their immigration status; the higher courts dismissed appeals from the decision. The case went before the European Commission on Human Rights, which held for the government on all issues except whether the government had handled the case with adequate speed (*Zamir v. the United Kingdom,* Application #9174/80, 1983). In response the government changed the practices governing the speed of granting legal aid in a habeas corpus case. In the meantime, the legal profession criticized the domestic *Zamir* decision (e.g., Blake 1980). The courts reconsidered *Zamir* in *Khawaja* ([1983] 1 All E.R. 765). The Law Lords did so against the background of a threat to go to the European Commission of Human Rights with the case if they did not overturn *Zamir* (interview, 1990). In *Khawaja* the Law Lords held that an applicant had an obligation not to deceive but that the burden was not on the applicant to come forward with all the information the immigration officials might possibly think relevant.

Relevant grounds of appeal to the ECHR include Articles 3 and 13 of the European Convention. The latter is most relevant to administrative law, for it requires that there be an adequate remedy in the country of origin. Lawyers practicing immigration law find being attuned to Europe necessary. The relationship between domestic judicial review and the European Convention can also be frustrating, at least given how the Home Office frames it. Some immigration lawyers believe that in Strasbourg judicial review is framed as a far-reaching remedy. It is easy to cite the broad principles of judicial review, articulated in *GCHQ*, to support that view. In Britain when arguing an immigration case, the Home Office finds it important to urge the limited nature of judicial review on the courts; courts are not to substitute their judgment for that of administrators but to review the decision for illegality. Finally, for nationals of European Union member states, claims can be made under European Union law.

In response to cases or in advance of them the Home Office, which is responsible for administering immigration law, can grant discretionary exceptions to the rules, change the interpretation of the rules, change the rules themselves after laying them before Parliament, or try to get the statute changed. Indeed, immigration statutes and rules have changed several times. A change in practice, rules, or statute, or a wide-ranging judicial decision, can in turn affect the cases that are worth bringing for practitioners.

However, no one relies only on the rules to tell them that cases are not worth bringing. A strict rule-of-law model, in which the courts make decisions that state the law and hold both administrators and claimants to the law, allows no room for legal interpretation or contesting interpretations. It does indeed treat law as an entirely closed system allowing no critique internally. That does not capture the efforts in immigration law to try for more favorable interpretations of rules. When the Home Office encroaches on areas in ways that practitioners feel are especially unjustifiable, they can decide to take claims because they *do* challenge practice under a conception of what rights people should have. Interpreting the rights people should have under existing rules requires careful and narrow framing of claims. But it does mean criticism of officials. For example, changes in immigration practice regarding exclusion of immigrants who entered the country to marry seemed unconscionable to many practitioners. That meant they needed to find cases they could use to persuade the courts that they *were* unconscionable; they did not decide to stop bringing cases because the rules excluded the cases. Legal officials adapt to each others' actions. But they do not necessarily adapt by accepting a decision from another participant as authoritative. Instead, they can use the resources they have to change unacceptable decisions from others to the extent possible within the accepted boundaries of legal knowledge. That can mean only pushing for a shift in the burden of proof rather than the overturning of a whole rule or principle. That is a prudent strategy rather than an acceptance of dominant ideology.

Barristers and solicitors in Britain organized the Immigration Law Practitioners Association in 1984. Leading members hoped that by controlling enough cases they could persuade the Home Office to listen to them. Caseloads could provide a negotiating tool, as they have for some public interest lawyers in the United States (Lazerson 1982). While the hope has been that one can shape case law and negotiate through control, members readily acknowledge that anyone can bring an immigration case and that not all practitioners might share a concern with ILPA members for shaping case law. In addition to trying to organize claims about immigration, ILPA offers a place to exchange knowledge about Home Office practices.

> [O]n a thing like immigration much of the secret practices of the Home Office are not published, of course they're useful to know about. Then you can know what's going to attract them and what's not. (interview, 1990)

Both immigration lawyers who take on cases under the rules that severely limit the options for those from the Indian subcontinent and other, less-favored areas and those who take cases for business executives therefore join the ILPA.

Despite the impossibility of completely controlling caseloads, the ILPA found itself able to negotiate with the Home Office on the rules regarding marriage because its members did bring cases. ILPA practitioners have seen it as important for negotiation that they begin to control more cases and practitioners than they now do—that they be a peak organization of immigration lawyers rather than just a loose federation. They have not achieved that. However, a lack of cohesiveness is not universally a disadvantage. In the United States centralization in litigation organizations did not allow for openness to reconsidering policy, nor did it allow for flexible adaptation to local circumstances, including what clients wanted.[11] On the other hand, the political and administrative environment in Britain is different from that in the United States. The court and administrative systems are unified and centralized in Britain. Organizations that are unified and centralized are therefore more likely to be created around them. Indeed, as the quotation above suggests, the very secrecy of bureaucratic practices in Britain is part of what makes the organization attractive. Powerful organizations provide reasons for others to organize similarly to respond to them; administrative unity suggests some real advantage to unity in response (DiMaggio and Powell 1983).

To the extent that Weberian legal rationality is pursued in this field—and it is not, for rules change frequently, they are put together as a response to circumstances and opportunities for closing out immigrants within the statute—it is highly dependent not on a universal articulation of abstract principle but on shared knowledge and a community of practice. Many of the cases are not reported, and the concentration of power is enough that individual discussions with members of the Home Office are important for finding out what immigration officials' priorities are. The ILPA also forms part of the network of practice and addresses this diffuseness of knowledge. It runs training sessions on very particular current issues in immigration law. It also provides a place to share information about what the Home Office might be doing based on individual practitioners' discussions with officials. It has also provided a model; the need for coordination that it represents works in even more specialized areas of law. For example, lawyers involved in Kurdish refugee claims formed an ad hoc committee to address common concerns regarding Home Office practice.

As an organization the ILPA takes stands on issues both of legal practice and the substance of immigration law. It has made representations specifically to the Home Office about how it thinks Home Office practices should change. In doing so it has confronted the issue faced by all expert organizations: what to include within its realm of expertise and what to avoid as a "purely political" (not legal) issue (Halliday 1987; Abel and Lewis 1989d). In taking on that distinction it accepts as real the distinction between law and politics raised in British courts in the early twentieth century and pervasive in the twentieth-century debates about courts.

On those grounds members of the association argued against taking a stand on the question of Hong Kong immigration raised first in 1990. The government wanted to allow it while Labour criticized the government both because that is the role of the opposition and because the government had limited other immigration. The ILPA did not think that it could offer anything as a legal advocate. A solicitor active in the organization explained that the Hong Kong exception to immigration exclusions was simply a giant discretion by legal means. It was not actually a legal issue.

Both the Joint Council for the Welfare of Immigrants (JCWI) and the Immigration Law Practitioners Association point out the problem of insisting on a distinction between political organizing and the individuation of claims through litigation. Instead, we need to recognize the blurring of such boundaries. It is not hard to do so: political activity and changes in the rules are portrayed as a collective good while litigation to stay in the country is portrayed as a private good. However, they are all part of a continuum. Some collective goods have benefits so largely concentrated on one participant that they resemble private goods in the incentives they establish (Hardin 1981). Conversely, litigation can offer selective benefits to claimants as well as having benefits for political organizing. Furthermore, case pressure itself can gain some changes in rules or practices, and it seems to have done so with regard to procedures in deportation cases.

The next section uses particular issues that have emerged in immigration law to address what practitioners within immigration law think they have been able to get out of litigating cases. Litigation has been used to win gains for clients, in the process raising political discussion of immigration rules, winning reconsiderations from the Home Office, and changing Home Office interpretations of rules.

Adaptation and Resistance: From Genuine Visitors to Refugees

Many of the early 1980s immigration cases concerned applicants who tried to enter as visitors but were turned away based on an immigration official's decision that they were using a visitor's visa with the intention to settle. In 1986 the High Court refused relief to an applicant who claimed that he had been wrongly denied entry because an immigration official had determined that he was not a genuine visitor. The court did not just hold that the person was not a visitor, but it administered a scolding to lawyers pursuing immigration cases, claiming that they were clogging the courts. Lawyers were, the judge argued, bringing cases just to gain their clients time in the country rather than because they actually had good cases (*R. v. Secretary of State for the Home Dept. ex p. Swati* [1986] All E.R. 717). The next year, the number of immigration cases dropped; so did the percentage of applications granted leave (Sunkin 1987). Solicitors and barristers said that *Swati* had knocked out the visitor cases but that the exclusion seemed to be largely limited to them. The hostility toward immigration cases expressed in the *Swati* opinion had not excluded political asylum cases, for example. But *Swati* certainly meant that most visitor cases were no longer worth taking. Lawyers reacted to other cases that limited their ability to pursue claims by carefully working to win revisions of the legal interpretations.

Practitioners fit that case into their understanding of a problem in immigration law: that people are desperate to stay, judicial review is their last hope, and it is possible to find solicitors and barristers who will take their cases, even with little point to be made in law and little chance of the client's winning. Bad cases provide an open invitation to condemn the area more broadly and therefore have effects beyond the individual cases.

Primary purpose (of marriage) cases and asylum cases were unaffected by that particular decision. Criteria for what constitutes a genuine refugee are unrelated to those that describe genuine "visitors." It would be difficult to learn anything about whether refugee cases are worth bringing from *Swati.* What it means to be a genuine refugee has been litigated substantively—for example, whether someone can claim refugee status when, as the British courts understand it, people purposely put themselves in danger. More importantly, lawyers and clients have been able to work through the courts for changes in the procedures for deciding refugee cases.[12]

Trouble in countries throughout the world has meant that there have been people looking for asylum (Zolberg, Suhrke, and Aguayo 1989). The established practice of immigration law has meant that there were people who could take on the business in Britain. According to data collected by the Home Office, the number of people applying for settlement as refugees changed between 1984 and 1990 from 2,905 to 26,205 (Home Office 1994, table 1.2). Since then, applications for refugee status have soared but the government has been less willing to grant it (The Refugee Council 1994). The rising numbers of applications for refugee status throughout Europe alongside European integration have made the problems of transnational recognition acute (Webber 1991).

In the course of deciding immigration cases, the courts have elaborated what the requirement of danger means. According to elaboration of the rules by the courts, the claimant cannot have acted so to enhance his political danger in order to gain refugee status. This issue came up regarding an Iranian who had shown up at demonstrations without wearing the mask customary at such rallies (*R. v. Immigration Appeal Tribunal ex p. "B"* [1988] CO/1852/87).

A group of Tamil cases attracted substantial public attention in 1987, focused in part on the exclusiveness of the immigration rules (Plender 1987). One can only qualify as a refugee if the country to which one would be returned poses a serious threat of persecution. One must leave one's country and then apply for refugee status. Furthermore, applying for a passport as a politically active person from the country of origin can be dangerous. Finally, destroying one's passport after leaving one's country would make it more difficult to return. Applicants for refugee status, therefore, may have no papers or may have destroyed their papers; yet from the point of view of advocates the applicants may be quite genuine. This issue came up in the Tamil cases, where fifty-three Tamils who were seeking refugee status were being returned quickly on the grounds that they were not real refugees because they had destroyed their passports. As one participant saw it:

> We applied for leave [for judicial review] on the grounds of the fact that they destroyed their passports and came without visas was not against their being refugees; it might even be a factor in establishing it. The Home Office realized the problem and so abandoned the decisions and at the same time announced they were going to penalize any aircraft that carried a refugee without a valid passport or visa.

Provoked by these cases, the government sponsored and Parliament enacted the Carriers' Liability Act in March 1987 (Boyd 1989; Cruz 1991). It imposed a fine on airlines that allowed passengers to come to Britain without valid papers. No fine would be imposed if any forgery of travel documents was not reasonably apparent. Reflecting on that, a solicitor involved in the case noted that

> there was a ferocious fight, I mean it went on for about a year and a half. And while I like to think that we've actually won that fight, I remember thinking at the end of 1987 that we had won every single legal battle but

> we definitely lost the political struggle because they had retreated far and passed legislation.[13]

Some of the cases continued after that. Six Tamil refugees were deported in February 1988 because they did not, according to the immigration tribunal, satisfy the requirements for refugee status. Several people, including David Burgess, a solicitor for the applicants, visited Sri Lanka in 1988 to document the troubles of the Tamils once they were returned. The Immigration Appeals Tribunal on a subsequent application allowed the reentry of five. In May of 1989 the Home Secretary was granted his application for judicial review (*The Guardian,* 18 May 1989, 3). In July of 1989 the High Court held against the secretary of state because he had filed the application to the Immigration Appeals Tribunal late. Burgess told the newspapers that he hoped the Home Secretary would now abide by his "moral and legal duty" to allow the five Tamil refugees to stay in the country (*The Times,* 28 July 1989, 2). In 1990 the Court of Appeal refused to hear an appeal against the High Court's decision (*R. v. Immigration Appeal Tribunal and Another, ex p. Secretary of State for the Home Department* [1990] 1 W.L.R. 1126). The case offered a moral publicity not readily available from other strategies, in addition to the substantial legal victory for the claimants. The meaning of that publicity was dependent on the meaning of legal judgments as significant and fair in the political culture. Burgess had insisted that the secretary of state had a moral duty. Yet the secretary had lost not on the grounds that the applicants were genuine refugees but because he filed late. The decision came as Parliament was recessing for the summer, and hence it was not discussed. Each stage previous in the legal process had been the subject of a written question and answer in Parliament (e.g., *Parliamentary Debates,* 6th series, Commons vol. 155, col. 194w [22 June 1989]).

These Tamil cases finally made their way into the European Court of Human Rights. The Tamils' situation was still uncertain in Britain. They had applied for asylum, and they had exceptional leave to stay in Britain until 1992. Their application to the European Commission and the court claimed that Britain did not provide an adequate legal remedy for violation of rights protected by the convention, as Article 13 requires. They also claimed that being sent back to Sri Lanka amounted to a violation of Article 3, which prohibits "torture or . . . inhuman or degrading treatment or punishment." The European Commission chose to refer the case to the court, and the court issued a judgment on 30 October 1991.

A key issue was the adequacy of judicial review as a matter of human rights: what had started in the 1960s as a technical revision of the law had become elevated as the basis of a human rights claim under the European Convention on Human Rights.

Within Britain legal textbook writers have insisted on the distinction between appeal, wherein the court can substitute its judgment for the decision maker's, and review, wherein the court is only to decide whether a decision is legal. But within the European Court of Human Rights the government had every reason to blur that distinction. Indeed, the court quoted from the expansionist decision discussed in the last chapter, *GCHQ,* in which the House of Lords held that judicial review allowed for three grounds of review: illegality, irrationality, and procedural impropriety. Those grounds sound very broad, allowing the government to say that the courts hold administrators accountable. The European Court agreed with that reading of judicial review (*Vilvarajah v. United Kingdom* [1991] 30–31). However, on most big issues the government wins, as it did in *GCHQ,* and the executive routinely insists domestically that the remedy of judicial review is narrow. An immigration barrister bitterly mentioned the different ways the executive presents judicial review, depending on whether cases are before domestic courts or the European court. Indeed, the dissent in the European court noted that "judicial review controls only the procedure and not the merits of the impugned decision" (*Vilvarajah,* 42).

The making of multiple meanings for cases is also evident in the European Court's citation of *Wednesbury,* the 1948 English case holding that courts could only overturn administrative action when it was quite unreasonable. The example used in *Wednesbury* was that of a local government firing a teacher because she had red hair. Yet in the human rights framework of the 1990s the legal profession—in this case the government lawyers arguing before the European Court—had transformed that case so that it was the basis of a claim that there is rights-based protection within a system of parliamentary supremacy (*Vilvarajah,* 30). The European Court of Human Rights can have rather subtle effects beyond its ability to overturn domestic decisions. As in this case, it can provide an environment that encourages reinterpretation of domestic law to fit current concerns.

The European Court of Human Rights, often held out as the main hope for bringing rights to British politics, played a complex role. It mattered in encouraging the government to read domestic case law in a new way, if only for strategic reasons. However, the refugees lost in the European Court. They won neither on Article 3 grounds, which protect against torture, nor on Article 13 grounds, on the adequacy of internal remedies. However, the European Court decision did help keep the issue in the news. The existence of the cases domestically, which worked against the background of the court, pressured the Home Office both to change its procedures and to propose a bill changing the law. Although the institutional bases of power are different, as in the United States the courts play a part in provoking action from other branches as well as imposing costs on them.

Procedures within the Home Office were also changed through refugee cases, though in a way that has been more favorable to those claiming refugee status. With the Tamil cases in 1987, the Home Office gave potential refugees a brief interview, then refused refugee status if that interview did not prove to its satisfaction the claimant's refugee status. What is more, the Home Office would threaten to put claimants on an airplane in twelve hours. Lawyers described getting judges up in the middle of the night or going to their homes on weekends to get signatures on applications for leave to apply for judicial review; one barrister called it a time of "hand to hand combat" with the Home Office. With those applications the lawyers could prevent the person from being deported immediately. The ILPA asked the Home Office to agree upon a timetable, one that would mean they didn't have to ask judges on croquet lawns for signatures. When they did not obtain a more favorable timetable, they pressed cases. Applications for leave were granted, and the Home Office found itself waiting for a hearing on the case; as one plaintiff's lawyer put it, "back of the queue, wait nine months for it to come up."[14] Pressing cases gave the Home Office some reason to listen to the ILPA.

Through pressing cases, the lawyers were able to obtain a second interview. If the immigrant raised a new point of law or new information relevant to the case, the immigration officer had to refer the case back. If the new information was true and could not have been found earlier, it was considered by immigration officers. Immigration officials also had to offer reasons for exclusion (*R. v. Secretary of State for the Home Dept., ex p. Thirukumar and Others* [1988] Q.B., *The Times,* 27 December, 18; [1989] C.A., *The Times,* 10 March, 36). The cases were useful in gaining a change in administrative procedures.

When Kurdish claims came up in 1989, the Tamil cases provided a background for criticism of Home Office practice. David Burgess applied for judicial review in June of 1989, claiming that Kurdish applicants were being denied the interviews to which they were entitled. Subsequent applications also insisted on the importance of information for good immigration decisions (*The Times,* 22 June 1989; 31 August 1989). With the second batch of Kurdish refugee cases, from early 1990 on, practitioners were getting more favorable decisions from the Home Office without taking the cases to court. Fewer victories for Kurds claiming refugee status would appear in the courts, but that would be because the pressure from the cases meant that they were settled favorably beforehand in the Home Office. Indeed, the outcome in cases decided by judges could actually look worse for those refugees than they had previously, as the most winnable cases were settled.[15] Once the Home Office fixed its procedures to give good reasons for decisions and offer interviews, there was nothing for the courts to review. And the Home Office was likely to concede the best cases in its preliminary review. A reinterview cured the procedural irregularity claimed in the case, making the case virtually impossible to bring. Lawyers agreed that substantive critiques of decisions cannot often be run in judicial review. Judges have seemed more reluctant to rule in a claimant's favor in substantive cases.

The change in Home Office policy, provoked by favorable court decisions and the time delay litigation afforded, rippled through the litigation system. However, the change came not from changes in judges and their attitudes, though lawyers did note that they needed judges who were concerned. Nor did changes in policy come even from very real changes in the substance of law from Parliament or the Home Office, which an interpretation emphasizing the powerlessness of courts would argue. The change in policy came in part from the most narrow use of the law: challenges in court under existing rules. The process costs imposed by the courts on the administration by way of the efforts of attorneys and claimants were enough to get practices changed. Resistance to Home Office practice, based on the claim that it was ridiculous and unfair, and the possibility of playing one institution against another provided the basis for challenge in the courts. In order to make progress on this issue no one had to believe that the courts were sympathetic to refugees. Instead, one needed only to be able to ask for further procedures.

As the numbers of applications for refugee status rose in the late 1980s, so did the percentage of cases granted full refugee status. In addition to granting full refugee status, the government could and did grant a status called exceptional leave to remain, which is discretionary permission outside the rules.[16] The percentage of applicants granted that status stayed roughly steady, again as numbers were increasing. Between 1987 and 1989 the numbers of applications went from 2,432 to 6,955. The percentage granted refugee status went from 11 percent to 32 percent in those same years. The percentage granted exceptional leave to remain moved between 63 percent and 55 percent (Home Office, 1994: Table 1.2). The increases were not because the government was eager to grant either status; in the 1990s the numbers and percentages dropped again, culminating in substantial cutbacks under the new Asylum and Immigration Appeals Act in 1993.

Decisions from the courts regarding refugees led to adaptation, which in turn would influence the caseload in the courts. That adaptation came from resistance on the part of lawyers to Home Office practice. The courts did not simply lay down the rules for everyone to obey. Lawyers could frame resistance in a limited and appealing fashion for the courts. One asked only for a reinterview to hear information relevant to the decision; one did not ask the courts to grant refugee status to a claimant. Such a shift did not come from political change outside the litigation system nor from an acceptance on all sides that the word of any one authority—the Home Office or the immigration officials—was final. Rather, an estimation of the strategic availability of principles in the courts made resistance to Home Office practice possible. That strategic estimation has meant that it works better to argue for better or more elaborate procedures than to criticize the substance of a decision in court. The hoped-for result, of course, is to change the substance of decisions. That points out the similarity of British administrative legal ideology to that of Americans. While there have been important elaborations of administrative law in the courts, ones that have made substantive differences, they have largely been made in terms of procedure (Stewart 1975; Melnick 1983, 1994).[17]

The importance of procedure is curious in the context of revived emphasis on holding administrators and states to law. That would imply that administrators can make substantively wrong decisions, ones that courts would overturn. Yet that is not considered a useful approach by immigration lawyers, at least not for judicial review as against internal administrative rights of appeal. As one interviewee noted:

> It is a legal decision, and you have got to have some sort of error of law. Either failure to take into account relevant factors, or taking into account irrelevant factors, or some sort of procedural irregularity or breach of natural justice. And, as I said, a manifestly unreasonable element is very, very, rarely successful in refugee cases.

But winning on procedures provides opportunities to win for particular clients and to try to influence the immigration debate in Britain.

The government proposed an asylum bill in 1991, cutting rights of asylum and changing appeal rights. The bill would have cut legal aid for immigrants pursuing their cases; the government backed down in response to widespread criticism both from the legal profession and refugee interest organizations (*The Times,* 7 March 1992, 7). In particular the bill also limited rights of statutory appeal. The bill was left unfinished for the coming election, then reintroduced in October 1992 (*The Observer,* 18 October 1992, 3). The government rescinded some of the provisions limiting appeal rights for those claiming asylum, but not for visitors or students, in response to the criticism (*The Times,* 12 October 1992, 10). However, the government received extensive criticism, criticism that attracted attention in the press, raising racism as a problem in practices of asylum. The Roman Catholic and Anglican churches strongly objected to the bill. Finally, the House of Lords, which had increasingly become a source of criticism of the government, had an extensive debate critical of the asylum bill. The Lord Chief Justice also criticized the bill (*The Times,* 7 February 1993, 22), highlighting the role judges can and do take in Britain in political debate in part by virtue of their having a position in the House of Lords (Stevens 1993). The Asylum and Immigration Appeals Act took effect in 1993. For the first time this act provided for in-country right of appeal to the Court of Appeal against decisions by the Immigration Appeals Tribunal. A leading judge, Lord Justice Woolf, had recommended such a right of appeal in the hope that it might relieve the judicial review caseload (Chowdhury 1994a, 1994b; Woolf 1990).

The courts provided another opportunity to criticize the government regarding its handling of refugees in 1993 when the Home Secretary was found guilty of contempt of court. In 1991 the Home Office had deported a man whose refugee case was under consideration in the courts, despite the government's lawyer agreeing that it would not deport the man. The government claimed that it was not subject to contempt of court proceedings; in this claim immigration was connected with the constitutional issues of accountability discussed in the last chapter. The Law Lords held in 1993 that the former home secretary was subject to injunctions and contempt of court (*M. v. Home Office* [1994] A.C. 377). The entire issue reinforced the discussion in the newspapers over whether the government must be held to the law (Wade 1993; *The Times,* 4 May 1993, 29; *The Times,* 28 July 1993, 1). In newspaper discussion it escaped the hostility to immigration so often expressed because it did play to the cultural issue of whether the government had to obey the law (Wade 1993). Indeed, the question had emerged in the first place in part because the courts had decided in 1990, in *Factortame Ltd. v. Secretary of State for Transport* ([1990] 2 A.C. 85), a commercial law case, that the Crown, or the central government, was not subject to interim injunctions.

The news coverage did not guarantee sympathy for refugees; in the midst of this discussion a Conservative member of Parliament spoke against what he called the "relentless flow of immigrants." However, that speech occasioned still more criticism and discussion of race, politics, and British refugee policy (*The Times,* 29 May 1993, 1). Lawyers see contributing to debate as one part of what case law can do.

This mixture of domestic law, European court decisions, Parliament, and political debate was replayed in family settlement issues, the other major source of immigration in Britain. Family settlement turns from procedures to how courts substantively interpret statutes, reading the responsibilities of the government "between the lines" (Melnick 1994).

Elaborating the Rules: Compassionate Circumstances and Primary Purpose

While lawyers tried to build favorable interpretations of the rules, at the same time they claimed that immigration is "hard law," not something that is shapeless and dependent entirely on the facts of cases. This point is illustrated in a barrister's interpretation of refugee cases.

> So however strong your case is on its facts—and I've had a Tamil woman who had lost virtually the whole of her family—on the face of it, on the facts, you have an incredibly strong claim, but we couldn't find an error of law. The [immigration officials] had come to a decision neither of the

courts was prepared to find was manifestly unreasonable. They just back away from that. You're stuck. (interview, 1990)

"Manifestly unreasonable" is an extravagant claim within British legal practice, asking judges to rule that officials got the law wrong. Yet that is exactly what legal scholars argue for in the literature when advocating an expanded judicial review (Jowell and Lester 1989).

Procedural issues are the most attractive course to take and a broad declaration of unreasonableness the most difficult ruling to get. Something in between is possible. This section turns to the question of interpreting statutory standards, addressing how lawyers and claimants make room for substantive challenge to the rules without asking the courts to hold a claim manifestly unreasonable.

As practitioners see it, it is difficult for the Home Office to change the rules all the time, especially if an interpretation from the courts looks sensible and humane. Even if the Home Office changes rules in response to a victory for claimants, the previous particular clients have won. Parliament does not change that retroactively.

Lawyers worked on rule interpretation for the dependency rules, which allowed dependents of people already settled in Britain to immigrate there. The immigration rules only allowed parents of immigrant residents to live in Britain if they were dependent on their children and if their standard of living would not go up with the move to Britain. One lawyer, citing a sympathetic decision by Justice Simon Brown, pointed out how strange that was; if the parent had been dependent on children when abroad, as required by the dependency rules, his or her standard of living had to go up with the move to Britain (*R. v. Immigration Appeal Tribunal, ex p. Begum* [1986] Imm. A.R. 385. In a case on judicial review, the court held that "emotional needs" could be considered in deciding whether a parent is dependent on a child (*The Times*, 19 April 1989). It is that kind of issue that is taken as possible to change: one does not argue that the Home Office ought to consider everything as part of dependency nor that the dependency rules are ridiculous. One argues points of law, narrowly construed in statutory or rule terms but based on principled concerns such as the importance of emotional dependence within families or communities.[18]

Similar questions of the meaning of family and community connection arose with the grounds for deportations. Under the statute before 1988, the immigration officials before deciding to deport had a duty to consider compassionate circumstances as reasons not to deport. An administrative law duty requires officials to consider all relevant circumstances. Compassionate circumstances rules were elaborated through litigation. An important decision came out of the House of Lords, holding that "compassionate circumstances" need not be personal. They could include community support (*R. v. Immigration Appeal Tribunal ex p. Bakhtaur Singh,* [1986] *The Times,* 27 June, 35).

Perhaps it is a measure of the success of litigation that the Immigration Act of 1988 limited appeals of deportation to the grounds of deportation themselves. That is, one could challenge the accuracy of the basis for the decision to deport; one could no longer raise compassionate circumstances as grounds for a favorable decision. The ILPA objected to that change, but it became part of the statutory law. It is difficult to achieve permanent change in the British legal system through litigation. Difficulty can be ascribed too readily both to the lack of a written constitution and to the ministries' control over Parliament. No written constitution would enshrine rights of settlement; interpretive questions would always arise. The organization of Parliament and the executive are important. However, even in the United States, while it is more difficult to overturn a judicial decision, legislatures do alter statutes in response to judicial interpretations (Lindgren 1983). Reflecting on the problems of rule changes, one barrister said:

> One's duty as a lawyer is to one's client, not to the mass of other potential clients. So if there's a point you can get a result for your client on you have to pursue it. You can't say I won't take this point because it might be worse for other people unless the client wants to adopt altruistic self-sacrifice as part of his or her instructions to you. So the short answer is that if it's a point you can win on, even though the Home Office might reverse it, you have to take it. Secondly, it becomes, the more things they have to reverse on the more it clogs up parliamentary time, the more difficult, and depending on what the issue is, it may provoke a parliamentary debate. . . . And it took the Home Office five years to reverse the *Bakhtaur Singh* case.

Winning for individual clients might have long-term costs. But without, for example, arguing for the importance of community support the Home Office would not have allowed anyone to stay on those grounds anyway. Without the cases, clients still would have been excluded under the rules. Furthermore, the exclusive focus on rule changes doesn't attend to a meaning of politics in Britain. Debate in Parliament is always considered either an achievement or a substantial cost to be avoided whether or not it achieves immediate public policy changes. Lawyers see cases as sometimes achieving that, and they have been right.

This mixture of achievement for clients and participation in public debate also characterized the rules regarding marriage and settlement. The 1983 immigration rules required the claimant to show that the "primary purpose" of a marriage was not settlement. This rule discriminated on the basis of sex. Women bringing in husbands had to show that the primary purpose of a marriage was not settlement; men bringing in wives did not have to show that. The rules were challenged as discriminatory to the European Court of Human Rights; in 1985 the court ruled that the rules did discriminate on the basis of sex (*Case of Abdulaziz, Cabales and Balkandali,* 28 May 1985 Series A #94). In response the government decided that men and women had to show that the primary purpose of a marriage was not settlement (WING 1985). The rules had three parts: a marriage could not have been entered into primarily to obtain admission to the United Kingdom, each of the parties had to intend to live together permanently, and the parties to the marriage had to have met. Practitioners pointed to the problem of "proving a negative." The rule was also seen as inhumane; how could the Home Office throw someone out of the country on those grounds when the person had established a family life and worked within England? Because the Home Office was sometimes trying to deport people some time after they had entered the country, they were pursuing people with established lives. The issue began to be litigated in 1984. Immigration lawyers, UKIAS, and the Joint Council for the Welfare of Immigrants were determined to challenge the rules.[19] The courts and the Immigration Appeal Tribunal saw a number of cases.

From the point of view of lawyers practicing routinely in immigration, a change in the rules depends on claiming it is just for a particular claimant. Judges' concerns about opening the floodgates to new cases require a limited form of argument. Rather than making sweeping statements of principle, it is important to make claims of simply interpreting the rules *in this case.* Then, as one lawyer said, one simply finds that there are many cases like that particular one. But it is important to never run an argument in general terms, not "at any stage" (interview, 1990). The conservative and limited sense of their power that the courts often have has not meant that it is impossible to challenge rules. Rather, it has limited the types of challenges that are possible.

> You've got to narrow it [a claim in a case] down to the facts of your case rather than make it a big general submission that in every case things have got to be looked at again. I've succeeded on applications for leave just by doing that, by narrowing it down, looking at the facts for this case, and pointing to reasons why in this particular case the secretary of state had a duty of fairness which wasn't complied with. And then by doing that you are reassuring judges, because they are always susceptible to the floodgates argument, that if we let this one in we'll have to let them all in, so you are dealing with that, you are reassuring them that it is only on these particular facts, but then of course when you find another case the facts are fairly similar, and there are quite a lot, then you can say ah, but, it was accepted in this other case. (interview, 1990)

Through those efforts, lawyers were able to pursue a change in the consideration of marriages. These changes have depended on working the rules before judges who might be willing to hear arguments framed for a particular client. They have not depended on having judges wholly sympathetic to immigrants. Setbacks and small victories illustrate that. An approach critical of litigation would ask what that could possibly mean in the long run. However, as Patricia Williams has argued (1987), it is far from a settled question that individual victories actually hinder long-term political change. Litigation is simply unlikely, in Britain or the United States, to change everything.

Practitioners who specialize in immigration law are insistent that opening big issues of principle is a losing proposition. That does not mean that such issues do not come before the courts. And lawyers use them as lessons for what not to do (*R. v. Immigration Appeal Tribunal, ex p. Bhatia* [1985] Imm. A.R. 24, 1986, 42). Immigration lawyers bitterly cited *Bhatia* as an example of a bad case to bring, one that dismantled much work that had previously been done in pushing for favorable interpretation of the primary purpose rules. The barrister in *Bhatia* argued that the burden of proof shifted to the Home Office once a genuine marriage had been proven, "which it doesn't and which you can't say, but because of that then the whole thing was set back for about a year because this case then got up to the Court of Appeal, with very bad submissions, which resulted in it being much more difficult," as a barrister critical of the decision said. Out of that case came a Court of Appeal decision reaffirming that the burden of proof was on immigrants (*The Times,* 9 August 1985).

Rather than halting the challenges to primary purpose, *Bhatia* meant that they had to start again. Barristers were certainly concerned, and the year after *Bhatia* UKIAS tried to refer even more primary purpose cases so as to challenge the interpretation of the rules. Lawyers cited *Bhatia* as a reason for concentrating practice within an organized group of lawyers and as a reason for providing educational seminars through the ILPA. *Bhatia* also highlights how very cautious claims before the courts must be. After all, no one in the case argued that the immigration rules were ultra vires or that the immigration officials had a manifestly unreasonable interpretation. They only tried to shift the burden of proof.

In July of 1986 the Court of Appeal issued an important decision revising *Bhatia* though claiming to be following it. While the court insisted that there were three separate criteria, as listed previously, it held that "evidence of intervening devotion might make it easier to satisfy the officer that the parties' purpose at the time of the marriage was not primarily to obtain entry to the UK" and that "evidence bearing on one [question] would often cast a 'flood of light' on the other" (*R. v. Immigration Appeal Tribunal, ex p. Kumar* [1986] *The Times,* 13 August, 29). The lives that people had made together would count in determining whether the marriage had been genuine. *Bhatia* and *Kumar* have continued to be cited together as touchstones for deciding primary purpose cases.[20] That has not, however, meant that the judges are always sympathetic.

They have since then even held, for example, that the Immigration Appeals Tribunal could hold that children are not enough of a sign of intervening devotion when a married couple with their children was able to live in the country of the spouse not settled in Britain (*R. v. Immigration Appeal Tribunal ex p. Hussain* [1992] CO/2027/90).

Finally this issue went before the European Court of Justice, and that court issued a decision in July of 1992 (*R. v. Immigration Appeal Tribunal and Surinder Singh ex p. Secretary of State for the Home Department* [1992] Common Market Law Reports 358; *The Times,* 8 July 1992, 2). The court held that the primary purpose rules that are applied to a British citizen who has lived in another European Community (Union) state violate the Community right to travel. That decision made the rules more unworkable and provoked further public criticism of them. Indeed, the Home Office instituted an informal policy in June of 1992 that no one who has made a family life for five years would be deported under the primary purpose rules (House of Commons, Parliamentary Debates 6th series vol. 30 June 1992 col. 714).

The cultural meanings of these cases are fraught and contested. It would be easy to think of the problems of marriages arranged between people living in Britain and those living in another country as simply a problem of cultural difference in the meaning and organization of marriage. That is, the English are simply suspicious of a practice of arranged marriage relied on by people who still maintain cultural ties with India. But feminist organizations among communities in Britain have questioned the dominance of men in defining cultural-political issues to the British state (Sahgal and Yuval-Davis 1993). Nevertheless, to say that arranged marriages may not always reflect the preferences of young women in Britain is not to concede that the British state should determine whether marriages are legitimate. Indeed, black women's organizations have maintained that the existing rules have been used to intimidate women at home (*The Observer,* 18 October 1992, 3; Southall Black Sisters 1993).

Kumar came from an effort to challenge the courts' and the government's understanding of marriage. A sense of fairness provided energy to the narrow legal claims. That sense of fairness did not depend on the legal system's definition of what was fair. It depended on concern with the "endless stream of misery" that activists saw the primary purpose rules were causing.[21] Assessing what is worth bringing requires a dense understanding of what can seem unfair within the culture and in the context of immigration rules and in turn an understanding of how to convert that into legal language.

Gaining from Cases: Public Debate

In a context in which immigration as an issue will receive no favorable attention from either party, litigation can be an important way of gaining public time.

Cases can be part of an effort to elevate an issue to the political agenda, occupying time in Parliament and the newspapers. Litigation has been useful for organizing in the United States. But that issue might be especially important in Britain. Parliament, more than the U.S. Congress, is organized around partisan debate. Judicial decisions, along with issues, provide material for that debate. The importance of the neutrality (or, in the debunked version, the "Toryness") of the law provides a framework for debate (Griffith 1991). Because of that, cases are part of a strategy of "jumping the queue" to gain debate in Parliament. Time in Parliament is valuable and a scarce resource. There is certainly competition on the government side among departments for the time needed to get bills through. Civil servants often prefer to change practices without using parliamentary time, in part because there is such competition for it. From outside government, strategies that get one into public partisan debate are useful because time *is* difficult to get and time wins media attention. Some of the important cases, for example, the Tamil suit, have gained time in Parliament. While the attention on the issue was not just about law but about the plight of refugees, the lawsuit did provide an occasion for comment. That the lawsuit was simply one part of a successful effort to gain attention for the issue and win also highlights the fact that the law is not a self-contained, authoritative, governing discourse.

One barrister put the question of the public usefulness of cases this way:

> I think if politicians intrude too grossly upon perceived due process rights—that's a nebulous conception, what it should be—I think there is the beginnings of an emerging sense of impropriety and foul play. . . . I think politicians are creating trouble for themselves. A constitution is increasingly on the agenda because of the way they respond to judicial decisions. They're perfectly entitled to reverse a judicial decision. I'm not saying they're not entitled to. But if it impinges upon what would be seen as fundamental norms of procedural propriety, and I think that taking away a deportation appeal [does,] . . . to take away their right of appeal is, I think, offensive to what a democratic and accountable government would be. It goes against a trend of devolvement of decision making where executive government ought to be prepared for their decisions to be reviewed by others.

Furthermore, the political debate has relied on different anecdotes to highlight the different stories one could tell about immigration—whether it is about persecution or about people unfairly taking advantage of the riches of Britain. Even after the five Tamil deportees were receiving sympathetic attention in the national press, the news regarding immigration was dominated in early 1989 by Viraj Mendis, who took refuge in a Manchester church to avoid deportation to

Sri Lanka. While people marched to protest his deportation, he was also criticized as manipulating the system. Yet even that case provoked commentary in the conservative *Times* on the shameful restrictiveness of British immigration rules, noting in particular their race-based restrictiveness (Pimlott 1989). The home secretary used the occasion to proclaim the limited ability of Britain to absorb refugees, that it could not provide a home for all "economic refugees" (*The Times,* 22 January 1989, 3). Breaking into official political debate in a political-administrative system known to be one of the most closed in the Western world is a real accomplishment. It is certainly not divorced from political organizing, even if it occurs in part through lawsuits.

Not only do cases gain publicity for the issue of immigration. Rather, publicity and taking cases can provide alternative or complementary strategies, depending on the strength of a case and an issue. For example, some of the lawyers who have litigated the primary purpose rules wrote the JUSTICE report criticizing those rules. Lawyers also worked for Iraqi nationals in Britain during the Gulf War in 1991. The Home Office was detaining people on the grounds that they could pose security risks. It was a blanket detention, not dependent on risks particular people posed. National security claims made cases more difficult to take to court; publicity could play on sympathy for people detained.

The gloomy conclusions from the analysis of the worth of test cases say that it is not worth bringing them because the rules can be changed so easily. While the Home Office does change practices and rules, practitioners share a sense that it is not always so easy. Clogging up parliamentary time is valuable, and it is difficult and embarrassing to revise judicial decisions too frequently (though that might be more true in areas other than immigration, and it is possible that lawyers in the field overestimate the government's embarrassment). That is in part because of the meaning the High Court (and its judges) carry in British culture: that they articulate "the law" and only Labour would engage in debunking them (Griffith 1991). Gaining public statements or debates in part through bringing cases means that participants sometimes see litigation as one more strategy within a political system that focuses on debate in Parliament. One analysis of the development of administrative law in Britain concluded that it might disrupt and refocus the continual insistence on partisan debate as the meaning of politics, bringing instead legal accountability. However, litigation fits into parliamentary practice by providing material for debate.[22] Finally, "what else can be done?" Parliament was called a "desert" on gaining relief for immigrants about to be ejected from the country, though representations to particular M.P.'s for clients are part of constituency service.[23] Believing that courts could help has involved no romanticism about the possibilities courts offered. Rather, it was a question of comparative advantage, one that needs to be considered even with its limits. The courts do not need to seem ready to rule in favor of all immigrants to offer the possibility of victory to a particular claimant who wants very badly to stay in the country. Nor do the courts have to be critical of the very basis of immigration rules to provide a way of criticizing the practices of immigration officials.

Conclusion

In understanding what litigation might have to offer it is important to attend to context-specific, interpretive issues of areas of law rather than looking to general assertions about activism in the British courts, deference to Parliament, or the conservative nature of British courts. Those assertions deflect attention from the meaning attributed to court cases. They also assume that the judges are completely in control of that meaning and that when ruling in favor of individual claimants they are doing no more than applying the law. However, lawyers who raise the questions effect change "millimeter by millimeter" (interview, 1990).

The courts cannot simply apply the law. They have choices to make. But it is not possible to raise large-scale claims of fairness in the courts either. In the choices that lawyers and judges make we can see the work of making common sense of British immigration law. As Sally Falk Moore has written of legal interpretation, ideology's "instance-by-instance use permits the kind of reinterpretation, redefinition and manipulation that is associated with processes of situational adjustment" (1978, 51). It is in those instance-by-instance uses that it becomes possible to understand commitments to what is fair as they intersect with what is possible.

Lawyers can frame winnable cases, but that incorporates an estimation of how to make claims before the courts when the claims are not in accord with what the Home Office's interpretation of its statute is. Those claims must be narrowly and cautiously stated. The Home Office and lawyers struggle for control of the procedures and the substantive standards that will make it easier or more difficult for claimants to stay. They struggle over the meaning of "compassionate circumstances" and how one shows the primary purpose of a marriage. All those issues incorporate cultural norms of what is fair, and those norms as lawyers and judges see them are not what the Home Office sees.

Looking at litigation as something for particular clients, but in addition as a form of resistance to policy, allows a better analysis of the use of litigation than does a perspective focusing on the ideologies of the judges. Britain highlights the importance of looking at the elaboration of rules: the shape of the constitutional system and the reluctance of judges to get drawn into some kinds of issues make it too easy to dismiss what the courts do as irrelevant to politics. While scholarship has revised the argument that courts are irrelevant to governing in Britain (Atkins 1990; Steamer 1987; Waltman 1984), interpreting the use and meanings of the law provides a much better way of embedding litigation in politics and governance than attending solely to judicial decisions does. That means we need to understand the usefulness of litigation to participants as well as the ideology constructed in doctrine. The blurring of publicity, political campaigning, and winning for clients also shows that the dry, technical language of the law need not dominate an issue. Even the unity of the British state and parties around the problems raised by immigration provide resources and institutions for political critique.

Conclusion

The focus in most discussions of legal accountability in Britain has been on what appellate courts have been doing. New judges with different attitudes have become "active" and have imposed the rule of law on government, as the standard story goes (Schwartz 1987). Understanding what appellate courts have been doing is clearly one part of the story of legality in the British state. But I have argued that it is more interesting to understand the place of legality in governing, for approaching that opens myriad questions. To understand the place of legality it is necessary to understand how broad, policy-level choices are made. In turn to understand that it is necessary to examine the meaning of legality in British culture. Rather than deciding whether the courts are inactive or active, understanding the place of legality requires an understanding of why that question seems so important. I have argued in this study that rather than asserting anything about the rule of law or its demise in Britain one must embed the courts in the political arguments, meanings, and context in which they work.

Explanations that address the closure of other political institutions in Britain are also necessary to address the closure and what once was the seeming irrelevance of the courts. That is, the control the ministries have over the parliamentary agenda means that it has been very difficult to gain access to policy negotiation for nonproducer groups. That control also means that it is difficult to write statutes that encourage court involvement in decision making.

A brief comparison with the United States highlights the significance of that control, for the configuration of interests is also different in the two countries. In Britain the question of legal accountability in the 1950s immediately raised the possibility of more extensively legalizing social welfare claims. The integration of the unions into the Labour party and the extensiveness of social welfare programs meant that by the 1950s raising the question of imposing court-based accountability raised the specter of the courts governing social welfare claims. In contrast, legalizing administrative procedure did not raise that specter in the United States in the 1940s, for unions were largely not part of discussions of legal accountability at that time. In Britain, unions did not support it. Groups that did, primarily traditional property holders, could not overcome the control ministries had over Parliament. Choices about the structure of legal accountability are important; explaining them requires attending to factors similar to those that matter in explaining other political choices.

At the same time, the cultural meanings of court decision making are crucial to understanding commitments to a rule of law in Britain; that too goes well beyond the attitudes of individual judges. Cultural meanings have publicized and amplified court decisions. Amplifying court decisions first establishes at least among legal elites an expectation that the government can be held to law. But the importance of that in the culture almost immediately leads to disappointment; law is but one consideration within complex organizations, and organizations are not, in any simple sense, "held to" the law (Loveland 1991). Rather than joining the debate over how active courts should be and are in Britain, I have argued that it is important to understand why their decisions are taken to be significant both among legal elites and in the elite newspapers. The cultural meanings of courts as holding lawless administrators to something static, neutral, and universally fair called "the law" is in turn a partial explanation for the continuing reemergence of legality as an issue. Without that meaning, the issue makes no sense. The limits on the effectiveness of considering changes that would expand legality, however, depend entirely on a political explanation of how British political organization shapes choices.

Administrative Procedures, Structural Choice, and Courts

Legal change works from and in its context. Meanings of reform depend on the conditions from which they emerge. Administrators in Britain shape the structuring of review; while they do not control the actual outcomes in cases, they can control enough of the procedure to ensure that the role of courts in administration will be limited. The limits in the efforts to enact the Tribunals and Inquiries Act and gain reform through the Law Commission, both elite-led efforts that need not have been seen as fundamental challenges to governing in Britain, illustrate that point. The reforms that were gained did not even begin to open the administration by requiring it to respond, inform, and justify. While the parliamentary system shaped the limits of changing administrative accountability, it has not controlled meanings of legality in Britain. To explain the institutionalization of legality requires attention to both structure and meaning.

One of the few efforts to explain choices about legal procedures in the United States quite purposely ignores the concern lawyers often state for uniform procedures and general availability of judicial review. With regard to the United States, Mathew McCubbins, Roger Noll, and Barry Weingast have argued that administrative procedures are put into place so as to control bureaucracies by building in processes that favor the constituents also favored in the substance of legislation (1989). A contradiction enters here. They assume that it is impossible to specify favored outcomes in the substance of legislation because the future is so uncertain. Yet somehow advocates can determine which procedures will favor constituents. In the United States, legislatures are able to enforce a concern to monitor bureaucracies through procedures the bureaucracies do not welcome because Congress has independent sources of power. Congress is not directly responsible for administrative programs, so members have an interest in monitoring bureaucracies. This approach suggests that Britain has less reason to enact administrative procedures. Parliament has less reason to want to control bureaucracies through legal procedures since members of Parliament head the ministries. Clearly the unity between Parliament and the administration mattered in limiting the changes of both the Tribunals and Inquiries Act and the Law Commission's efforts in administrative law. However, this explanation relying on procedures to control outcomes emphasizes strategy far too much. From this perspective it is not at all clear why there should be any group to advocate legality in administration in Britain, other than those that seemed to be permanently out of power. Groups would be certain to get their favored outcomes more directly. Furthermore, this explanation does not address why lawyers, rather than groups committed to particular policies, worked for reform. It does not attend to the significance of legal ideology. Such an explanation does not address the insistence on the importance of uniform procedures, both in the United States and Britain. Not only should procedures vary by policy area if the wholly strategic explanation is correct, so should the efforts for them. Yet the question of uniformity provided an important point of contention and uniformity of procedure is a lawyer's concern.

Substance and procedure are not completely separable, but a concern for procedure on the part of lawyers is also not merely a guise for opposition to the substance of programs. Legal concerns are somewhat independent of concerns about the substance of policy. In the United States, for example, while those who worked on the enactment of the Administrative Procedure Act tried to separate substance and procedure, many were opposed to the substance of new administrative programs. However, some also thought such opposition was illegitimate based in part on a formal legal commitment to neutrality with regard to the substance of democratic choice. Some advocates within the American Bar Association instead tried to structure programs through the availability of judicial review by courts that might be hostile to the programs (Sterett 1992b). However, legal elites in the United States and Britain are the ones who pursued administrative procedures. In the United States in particular conservative lawyers worked on uniform procedural control in the face of support for some longstanding administrative programs from the lawyers representing those who were regulated and in the face of those lawyers' opposition to further procedure. Legal ideology as a ground for policy was inextricably mixed with the political evaluation of programs.

The approach focusing on procedures only as a means to some other end cannot explain the push toward uniform procedures and standards for judicial review, emphasized in particular by conservative lawyers but pursued to a certain extent by left-leaning lawyers in Britain. Attention to legal ideology accounts for that effort. It also accounts for lawyers working on the issue without any visible or obvious push from some other, more "substantive," policy constituency. Lawyers worked on reform as conservative or socialist lawyers, with legal ideology forming a clear and constitutive part of preferences.

For the United States, McCubbins, Noll, and Weingast (1989) note the importance of the Constitution as the source of preferences for courts, though in administrative law much of what the courts do is statute-based (see Shapiro 1988). That view of the Constitution is analytically convenient because it is difficult to contend with the specificities of statutory interpretation. In trying to address the vagaries of statutory interpretation, McCubbins, Noll, and Weingast argue that either the courts are ensuring that the bureaucracies do not drift away from their legislative mandate or that the courts are imposing "random policy shocks"—virtually inexplicable decisions. McCubbins, Noll, and Weingast even suggest that legislatures impose statutory standards in part to control these impositions of judicial preferences. To argue that the courts are ensuring that bureaucracies are not drifting from the statutory mandate or that statutory standards are in turn to prevent courts from imposing their preferences is to take statutory interpretation as far more clear than it is. To argue that judicial decisions not comprehensible in these terms are simply "random policy shocks" is to treat judges' decisions as though they are not drawn from any systematic set of concerns.

In Britain judicial principles are loosely tied to constitutional presumptions. Furthermore, the courts have elaborated principles of review somewhat independently of what Parliament has done. The imposition of duties on administrators comes more from judges' rereading of statutes than it does from any ideological shift in Parliament or the administration in favor of judicial review, as McCubbins, Noll, and Weingast would argue that it should, given parliamentary and executive control over policy. Judges impose choices based not just on policy preferences in the sense of preferences about outcomes but also based on preferences favoring due process or natural justice and some circumscription of administrative authority. Such a general statement tells little about the actual choices judges make. As we have seen, the concerns and complaints regarding the British administrative system are actually quite specific to that system rather than emanating from a general commitment to what Americans call due process and the British call natural justice. For example, the U.S. system even in the most abstract theory does not enforce a duty to always keep one's mind open so as to make the best decision in changing circumstances, an approach necessary under British political justifications. To understand how courts fit into the administrative process, it is necessary to attend to the way they understand and use the deep justifications for action within the particular state while interpreting through a statutory framework. To say that courts simply apply the law does not suffice, nor does it explain anything to say they bring personal preferences to interpretation disconnected from analyses of the legal system.

The path dependency of political change shapes more than the administration-imposed limits on reform. It shapes what court decisions can mean in broader political debate. Rather than meliorate the dichotomous partisanship in British politics, which is what some have argued an expanded rule of law could do (e.g., Ashford 1981), legality participates in that partisanship. Since partisan debate is the political debate treated as most real, court decisions when they are significant for their value in debate are valuable for the partisan uses to which they can be put. Changing that depends on change that would decrease everything reinforcing partisanship in Britain, not solely on what the courts do.

As we have seen in this study, many organizations, most notably local governments, that were foreclosed from any effective political action via ordinary lobbying in the 1980s and onward, took cases to court using the remedy of judicial review. Local governments in particular lost most of the time against the central government. They often did not gain even a hollow victory of a declared win but a loss when it came to implementation, which is what critics of the use of courts argue is what happens with judicial decisions (e.g., Rosenberg 1991). When the government was so difficult to challenge in other forums, the courts could seem to provide a way of challenging central policies such as the changes in local government finance. The cases that did have more bite were the repetitive case level claims in homelessness, immigration, and education where applicants sometimes actually won. These cases provide a more serious evaluation of the claim that courts cannot offer anything useful because it is in these cases that claimants did win.

Courts, Law, and Change

Addressing the place of decisions in the culture turns us away from focusing solely on the courts' reasoning and what they think of themselves as doing. For example, in immigration decisions the courts can be very narrow and fact based even while ruling in favor of a particular claimant. The courts participate in political and social life not just by virtue of how they rule but by virtue of how rulings fit into politics more broadly. Many have argued, both in the United States and in Britain, that law is simply not useful for those who are disadvantaged through other political means. That statement works at too broad a level of generality.

The reasons offered for the limits to legal change are manifold, but three stand out for my purposes. First, the legal system requires that one ask officials to rule against other officials; they are likely to do so only in the most limited way. Second, in resisting dominant political practices through law one uses the same categories used by officials; one does not transcend or transform them. One is caught within the categories rather than abolishing them. Finally, and perhaps more pragmatically, enforcement of court decisions depends on the cooperation of other institutions (Rosenberg 1991). To take an American example, the legislature must finance court-ordered school funding equalization. That cooperation is unlikely to appear unless the legislature was already inclined to change the funding. Surely, given the centralization of control in Britain, real change is even less likely. Attending to this problem—what litigation can actually mean for change—through the lens of the problems and possibilities in political resistance could illuminate change questions for both societies.

In Britain and the United States, the limits to change are not exclusive to courts. In Britain, the strategic openings that are available, even those based sometimes on technical legal points, provide something not always available elsewhere. The limit might well be less with courts than with expecting sweeping social change through any particular institution or practice.

At the same time that we recognize that there are real limits to what courts can bring to administration in Britain—that there are real limits to what the administration will allow them to do and that there are real limits developed and encouraged through the narrowness of legal training—we need to recognize that legal officials are not able to wholly contain what court decisions mean. Cases can be put to the purpose of political argument, as the London Fare's Fair decision was. Cases can contribute to changes in central government decisions as they did in local government finance. Court decisions can be useful for victories in individual cases, as they are in immigration. They also can be useful for both, as they are in immigration.

Most substantial political change begins within the existing framework of dominant ideology, taking advantage of the spaces within it to turn it to the benefit of challengers (Scott 1990). Even such a narrow legal system as the British contains those spaces for change. In that system it would make the most sense to find and use small openings, making claims well within the technical legal language. Those are the only forms possible. Furthermore, the closed organization of the British state would also imply that one must work with institutions that offer possibilities, no matter how small those possibilities are. If we do not expect total political change from other strategies, there is no reason to expect it from legal challenges.

This question of political possibilities in law engages issues regarding the nature of law raised within critical and feminist legal theory. Scholars usually address two possibilities: first, that law's essence or nature is against the interests of those who would use it to change governing practices. Carol Smart (1989) has argued from a British point of view that law is intrinsically narrow and technical, unavailable for feminist uses and dangerous when used because it requires that political claims be framed in limited legal language. Legal language excludes all others, and it is impossible to challenge on its own terms. Certainly the British legal system and its reasoning constitute one of the more narrow systems in the Western world. Indeed, Smart's argument that law is closed and self-referential might hold best for Britain. However, Smart specifies her claim in part through reference to Carol Gilligan, who argues that law is rational and detached, emphasizing autonomy, and therefore impossible to reform from a perspective that emphasizes context and particularity (Smart 1989).

Alternatively, and raised more recently in the United States by Patricia Williams (1987), Mari Matsuda (1987), and Richard Delgado (1987), the particular victories one can gain matter and are not antithetical to the concerns of whoever might be trying to address state policies. The presumption that law is total is simply wrong from this latter perspective; nothing is so inflexible and complete as to offer no openings. These analyses of law help to specify and evaluate the question outlined above, of the possibilities of political resistance made in part through dominant cultural forms, particularly litigation.

The first perspective argues that legal frameworks emphasizing rights and rationality rather than political commitments allow little room for change. Using litigation requires acquiescing to a form that excludes an acknowledgment of connectedness and collective responsibility, for those are not law's characteristics. Yet even that perspective admits of another possibility: that claims to universality and rationality made in the name of legal principles are wrong. Such claims only provide a way of obscuring a particular vantage point.

Patricia Williams has made this critique effectively. She has argued that legal reasoning wrongly represents itself as consisting of "transcendent, acontextual, universal legal truths or pure procedures." The cost of that is that judges "disparage anything that is nontranscendent (temporal, historical), or contextual (socially constructed), or nonuniversal (specific) as 'emotional,' 'literary,' 'personal,' or just Not True." Finally, judges and others claim to have "objective, 'unmediated' voices by which those transcendent, universal truths find their expression" (1989). Through these approaches, Williams argues: "Law too often seeks to avoid this truth [that life is complicated] by making up its own breed of narrower, simpler, but hypnotically powerful rhetorical truths" (10). One point of analysis, then, is to note the particularity of perspectives that presume universality. As we have seen throughout this study, legal reasoning has been based on particular professional concerns that also shape and react to assessments of the problems in the British state. Arguments about legal accountability are not "just" partisan politics by other means, but neither are they something separate from the particularities of the British state.

A second point is to once again take seriously those claims made for legal reasoning and to see how and what they mean in a culture. For, as we have seen, in Britain those very claims to apolitical neutrality provide political grounds for a critique of the government. There is nothing especially rational or universal about administrative law. The aspirations and language are there—for example, that ministers are to use universal principles in limiting local governments' rates. Despite the three basic principles of review, there is little to make up a cohesive body of law in the statutes, administrative interpretations of them, or judicial interpretations of both. Administrative law judgments have been quite particular. Indeed, that is one part of the explicit ideology of the British legal system—that the common law system decides particular cases rather than declaring general principles. Perhaps that is all we should expect from judgments and we are wrong to think there can be general rules to decide particular cases. Martha Nussbaum has argued (1991b) that we work from quite heterogeneous values, making it certain that principles we believe will come into conflict. Particularism is a necessary part of our moral and legal judgments. It is not surprising that understanding the decisions and the reasons for them requires an understanding of the particular history from which they emerge. The problem with legal reasoning is less that it is universal and abstract and perhaps more that legal officials claim a universality for legal reasoning that on examination is difficult to find.

That law is always self-contained and self-referential misses the assumptions that are necessary to decide any particular case, even a fairly technical one under a statute. Legal officials make assumptions about personal and political responsibility. For example, judges have asserted the importance of deference to elected or administrative officials who can best judge what circumstances require. In immigration they have made assumptions about what makes for a valid marriage and why those conditions are not met in marriages between people residing in different countries. Attending to assumptions provides a more realistic understanding of what exactly the rationality is in legal reasoning. Furthermore, noting the rich political arguments embedded in these cases means that we need not believe that law is a closed structure admitting of no criticism outside itself and therefore useless in challenging dominant political meanings. Immigration law has raised questions of race in political discussion; legal decisions are one resource in political disputes. The very expectation that the law is something universal, clear, and rational makes decisions by courts more important as political criticism, no matter how much we note the particularities of reasoning. The furor in Britain over the case of *M* in 1993 illustrates that point; that the government could claim it did not have to obey the law shaped the public political argument.

Not only do the universalist aspirations of law make it available as criticism of political practices. Individual clients do sometimes win. As Richard Delgado and Patricia Williams have argued for the United States, it is far from clear that a victory for a particular person somehow delays any other substantial change. Using the existing legal framework in immigration law it is possible to ask at minimum for women's interests to be taken into account as much as men's are, and for respect to be accorded to marriage and affection in marriage as much as it is in native-born marriages (WING 1985). Such claims can be used to make room for critiques of racism within Britain.

A concern that law is by its nature closed in its reasoning, self-contained, and internally rational has allowed analysts to argue that it is somehow in the nature of law that some unfavored group will lose. But attention to the particular commitments of legal officials and embedding legal decision making in the broader political system allow a shift in focus. If statutes have dismantled local governments, administrative officials have implemented that policy, and courts have allowed them to, it is because of a closed political system that allows leadership to follow its commitments. There is nothing in the nature of law to require that to happen. Similarly in interpreting the Homeless Persons Act we can substantively point out that courts largely (not exclusively) defer to state purposes while occasionally reading statutes as binding local governments or central state officials. Legal form does not require courts to defer to government.

Even if legal reasoning were wholly closed and self-contained, legal decisions could still be important to those trying to disrupt dominant meanings of law. Paradoxically, the meaning of law as universal is important because it sometimes carries so much weight in the popular culture. Williams notes that while critiquing claims of universality made for law she does not want to abandon them as meaningless (1987, 14); the neutrality they promise has provided aspirations for some who have been disadvantaged in law, and dismissing legal categories and reasoning would dismiss the promise inherent in the rule-of-law rhetoric. As we have seen in the law concerning local government finance, the aspiration to universality actually provided some critique when the law could be shown to be partial in perspective. Court decisions that could be portrayed as generous to the central government provided the opportunity to criticize the government through one of the central state's institutions—the courts. In immigration, taking cases provides an opportunity to gain time for clients, organize politically, and sometimes gain attention in debate in Parliament. How the judges reason and what their reasoning means to them do not control these different deployments of legal decisions.

As Nancy Fraser (1987) has argued with regard to social welfare rights, whether or not rights are useful is probably not something intrinsic to right-ness but dependent on the substance of the rights and the organization of the social world supporting the claiming of rights. "Rights" is a widely contested concept. It incorporates everything from bare-bones individual assertion, which is indeed difficult to use for those without extensive social resources, to substantive claims against the state considered important enough to enjoy protection through state bureaucracies or public interest organizations. In Britain, as in the United States, individualized rights claims have been part of a strategy to claim status as a collectivity. Rights claims are not antithetical to making group claims. This has been particularly visible within immigration law where individual rights claims have been seen by lawyers as necessary to framing group claims.

Rather than attending to a perhaps nonexistent, all-encompassing rationality in law as the form that exclusion takes, we can attend to the particular strategies, often in the control of administrators, that exclude claims. In chapter 5 I argued that the procedures for taking things to court in themselves limit how much courts will participate in judging government practices; those procedures are the creation both of the government and of the judges. These points can be extended to the areas that Smart discusses as excluding women's interests. Sex and race discrimination laws have been difficult to use in England in part because so little damages were awarded that it seldom makes it worthwhile to take a case (Kenney 1992). The extent to which litigation is unsuccessful is due to the closed nature of British politics and the substantive resistance of political officials. That is, they are simply not sympathetic to those claims. In race discrimination cases, though indirect discrimination can be claimed, one cannot and does not use the statistical evidence of exclusion by group status that was once useful in the United States. Limits to legal strategies are not due to a universalizing logic that legal commentators believe exists. The point that there are multiple cultural meanings to law, and that it can be deployed in multiple ways, is a useful way to escape the aridity of claims to dry objectivity made for the legal system.

That Fraser's argument that rights have no one particular meaning has not arisen in Britain among academics could reflect the deeply closed nature of British policy making. The state has been able to close access to anyone other than significant sectoral groups or group representatives the state has selected (Vogel 1986; Schmitter 1985). The state has been able to marginalize feminism, for example—which has allowed feminism in turn to develop a more radical and anti-institutional critique than much of American feminism has. (However, in recent years feminist organizations have engaged state power more directly. See Lovenduski and Randall 1993.) Put bluntly, the depth of the radicalism in its rejection of working with state institutions is in part made possible by the lack of institutional power to which it has access (Gelb 1989). Law, whether through the courts or through lawmaking in Parliament, is one of the organizationally very closed institutions in British governance. There is no essence of law that makes it hostile to counterclaims or practices. Indeed, given the variety of legal practices and the variety of rules enforced (or not) by the state, there may be no essence to institutions. Institutional practices are bounded and not infinitely flexible. They are not, however, determined by the narrow meaning their officials give them.

At the same time, to expect dramatic change from judicial review in Britain would be to expect too much. To expect "law" to be brought to administration, and thereby hold administration accountable, is to take the normative value of law as clear and, concerning equal treatment under general rules, as true when it is not. When legal judgments are tied to facts, and when legal principles require discretion rather than rules, one ought not to expect enormous change in a discretion-based system wherein the routines of policy are insulated from a highly partisan politics.

Conclusion: Reorganization and the Rule of Law

Even in Britain, with its judiciary conventionally understood to be so conservative, it would be a mistake to take too formalist a view of law. Judges' decisions are not politically meaningless simply because there is no formal written constitution from which to build a critique of dominant practices. Nor do court decisions that lawyers and others have reason to highlight mean the submission of partisanship to rules. Instead, judicial decisions have to be understood in the context in which they are made. The attention they sometimes get in partisan debate is significant, a partisan way to criticize government that is useful precisely because it looks nonpartisan. Second, the decisions have meant a reorganization in the field of administrative law, in part because it is important to try to avoid noticeable losses regarding central policy decisions. While the reorganization implies a very human pursuit of a "rule of law," or consistency and lack of partisanship across cases, it does so in the context of rather unpredictable and changing cases under a combination of a variety of statutes and very abstract and general principles of judicial review. The human process of this making of ideology is important to remember at a time when the rule of law is being elevated as a reality of the West, one pursuable by adhering closely yet fairly to clear rules. (For discussion see Krygier 1990; Elster 1991.) For in Britain the enthusiastic reception of a revived rule of law misses the uncertainty intrinsic to the enterprise of interpreting statutes through broad principles. That uncertainty is not exclusive to Britain; the role of courts in administration in the United States is also one of sometimes substantial uncertainty (Melnick 1983).

New readings of statutes are dependent on the concern about accountability; while not wholly predictable, the new readings are not random. McCubbins, Noll, and Weingast (1989) suggest for the United States that because judges do have commitments legislatures in part write statutes so as to control the courts and keep them from drifting from legislative intent. That approach shows the importance of attending to legal interpretation and what it means for participants. For in Britain excluding judges was once generally understood to require simple statutory statements with broad grants of discretion to ministers. And, as we saw in the discussion of legal administrative reform, ministers and civil servants see little reason to write a new and more elaborate statute governing administration for fear that it would just give judges more hooks on which to hang review.

The new administrative law has increased the relevance of lawyers and legal expertise to administrative policy making in England and Wales. Related interest in a new constitution has made it more possible for legal expertise to seem relevant to governing in a way that both fits into partisanship as the relevant debate in Britain and offers something separate from partisanship, since both major parties have proven quite cautious about adopting anything like a written constitution. The interest of the Administrative Law Bar Association in legal accountability is proving to be a very statist interest, one that institutes critique of governing practices not oriented toward individual complaints about the delivery of services but toward public management issues between organizations. *GCHQ* provides an important example: the judge-stated duty of the government to consult was abrogated in that case due to national security. State priorities are treated as separable from partisan purposes. In trying to develop principles for governance, judicial review borrows implicitly from European perspectives, particularly from French administrative law, which has long been fascinating to English administrative lawyers. (Conseil d'Etat decisions are still reported in the major journal in the field, *Public Law.*) Much of the way that Europe has been integrated into judicial review is as a state management issue, outside of immigration. For example, the privatization of the water authorities in Britain has in part been challenged through Europe (Graham and Prosser 1991). Interorganizational management does not raise questions of rights in any real sense, individuals must choose to take cases for courts to decide but water privatization does not raise rights as ordinarily understood (Sen 1983). Instead, questions of state authority between organizations are crucial to new meanings yet they are far from the earlier concerns of the place of individuals in an administrative state. Constitutionalism through Europe and through the debate over the issues the courts actually decide means drawing lawyers into state management.

Immigration law does not entirely capture that statist interest; nor does homelessness litigation. Elites within the profession often treat these questions as separable, not crucial to a general administrative law. Homelessness and immigration illustrate how administrative law is relevant to people's lives. Yet at the moment of its institutionalization in Britain as a critique of governance, it has become more abstracted from people's lives. Immigration and homelessness claims are still the main component of the judicial review caseload. However, leading lawyers have urged the more extended use of tribunals and ombudsmen for the routine complaints people have about government programs, including both immigration and homelessness. The courts have also decided cases, such as *Pulhofer* and *Swati,* that have impatiently deplored the existence of so many cases. Lawyers cite these issues as a warning sign of retrenchment: too many applications are made "without a proper basis." Both immigration and homelessness cases were selected as important examples of that problem (interviews, 1990). Interorganization litigation was not, though lawyers also bring those cases as a way of bargaining in a climate of legal uncertainty. In attending to how the legal ideology of fairness and uniformity can be used in the culture, we can move beyond questions about how the courts reason and whether they are "active" or "passive." It is only in doing so that we will be able to situate law in all its manifestations as worth studying in comparative politics.

Notes

Introduction

1. Parliament debated the decision twice in December. See *Parl. Deb.,* Commons, 6th ser., 15 (1981): 532–49, 889–929.

2. However, some excellent scholarship attends to the complexity and significance of statutory interpretation. See Melnick 1983, 1994; and Shapiro 1988.

3. See, for example, Bingham 1991, 64.

4. For a discussion of the significance of this justification for rule, see Greenhouse 1989, 1631.

5. I am grateful for discussions at the Cause Lawyering Conference in Amherst, Massachusetts, in August 1994 that clarified to me the wide range of legal systems in which this is true.

6. For a suggestive discussion of the relationships between law as hegemonic and as offering space for resistance, see Lazarus-Black and Hirsch 1994, introduction. See also Sterett 1994.

7. I am grateful to Carrie Menkel-Meadow for raising this point to me. See also Handler 1992. At least some of the time participants keep an eye on links between small victories and the broad issues they engage. For a recent statement of the link in Britain between a generous refugee policy and the importance of rethinking foreign policy, see Blom-Cooper et al. 1991.

Chapter 1

1. For an analysis that reads elite cultural ideas about political structure and deference from legal texts, see Messick 1988, 637–61.

2. Mertz 1988, 661–85, 662. See also Starr 1989.

3. Ashford 1981, 35–38, 63–65; Thomas 1980. In turn, this means that a focus for much of British work on the civil service is whether or not it is partisan or how partisan it is. It draws less on theories about how organizations work. For criticism, see Heclo and Wildavsky 1981.

4. For a discussion of the creation of public law as a field in Britain, see Sugarman 1991.

5. Critiquing Dicey continues to provide a first step in reinterpreting the place of law in British politics (Arthurs 1980; Carty 1991; Craig 1990a).

6. For a discussion of this issue, see Shapiro 1981.

7. For an excellent discussion of the politics of labor law in Britain at this time, see Forbath 1991, 25–30. See also Stevens 1980, 92–98.

8. For a discussion of the way conservative legal scholars also took law as part of the natural order in the United States, see Tushnet 1991.

9. The concern that courts in the nature of being courts must oppose collective solutions to problems has continued to shape both conservative and socialist discussions of law and courts. For critiques of the courts from this perspective, see McAuslan 1983; and Hutchinson 1985.

10. See, for example, Stevens 1980. However, David Sugarman (1991) has noted that there was a realist movement that paralleled the one in the United States.

11. In fact, between 1900 and 1930 American and British lawyers shared concerns about administrative power. See Keller 1980.

12. Harold Laski knew Americans who were concerned with the courts and social legislation, including Oliver Wendell Holmes, Felix Frankfurter, and Roscoe Pound. Laski had also spent some time teaching at Harvard before 1920. See Ekirch 1983.

13. Hollis 1987, esp. 461–85. See also Anderson and Zinsser 1988, 371–406.

14. For a recent discussion of the significance of Poplarism in British politics, see Loveland 1991.

15. For a discussion of feminist lawyering in the United States and the way it has shaped feminist political activity, see Zimmerman 1991.

16. See chapter 3 for a discussion of the strategies used to bring legal form to administration.

Chapter 2

1. See, for example, Diplock 1961.

2. For an examination of how some tribunals worked in the 1940s, see Pollard 1950.

3. There are, of course, other problems with official statistics. Sometimes they are produced for reasons other than stating what they claim to state. The police manufacture arrest rates and clearance rates. For a few years the Lord Chancellor's Office published the amount of time it took to get a case heard in court. When cases began to be heard more quickly and the backlog was cleared up, the office stopped publishing those numbers. There is no reason to think the numbers of cases are reported for any particular reason in this instance.

4. See, for example, Blom-Cooper and Drewry 1976.

5. See Council on Tribunals 1959.

6. See, for example, Stevens 1980; Paterson 1982; and H. Wade 1961.

7. See, for example, *Miller v. Minister of Health* (1946) 1 K.B. 626; *Johnson and Co. (Builders) Ltd. v. Minister of Health* (1947) 2 All E.R. 395; and *R. v. Industrial Injuries Commissioner ex p. Amalgamated Engineering Union* (1966) 2 Q.B. 31.

8. See, for example, *R. v. Medical Appeal Tribunal ex p. Gilmore* (1957) 1 Q.B. 574; and *R. v. Greater Birmingham Appeal Tribunal ex p. Simper* (1974) 1 Q.B. 543.

9. For example, in *Baldwin and Francis Ltd. v. Patents Appeal Tribunal* ([1959] A.C. 663) the House of Lords (affirming the Court of Appeal) held that the tribunal had not erred in law. See also *Judd v. Minister of Pensions and National Insurance* [1966] 2 Q.B. 580.

10. *Brain v. Minister of Pensions* (1947) K.B. 625.

11. *Minister of Pensions v. Horsey* (1949) 2 K.B. 526.

12. Both *Brain* and *Gilmore* were decisions by Lord Denning, well known for his hostility to administration. However, it would be a mistake to ascribe these trends in the law to the idiosyncrasies of one judge. Other judges used similar approaches, and Denning's decisions were noted by other judges as well. *Horsey* relied on *Brain*, and Denning was not a judge in that case.

13. See, for example, *Colleen Ltd. v. Minister of Housing* (1971) 1 W.L.R. 433, in which the statutory standard was that a minister could order the purchase of land "reasonably necessary" for redevelopment.

14. See, for example, Stevens 1980, 343–45.

15. These cases are *Franklin v. Minister of Town and Country Planning* ([1948] A.C. 87); and *Robinson v. Minister of Town and Country Planning* ([1947] K.B. 702).

16. Public inquiries are hearings the government holds to solicit public opinion and expert evidence when it is deciding where to put nuclear power plants, schools, and highways, and when there is an objection to some kinds of land use planning decisions. The government also presents its case at these hearings. See Vogel 1986, chap. 3.

17. Only one law journal, however, noted it when it was decided (*Solicitor's Journal* 14:133.

18. Following British practice, I will use the term *local authority* to describe any local elected government. Britain has many different forms of local authority: rural district councils, urban district councils, metropolitan borough councils, and London borough councils, to name just a few. The differences are not important for the purposes of this volume. When a case involves more than one local authority, I will explain their relationship and distinguish between the two.

19. The two justices—Reid and Somervell—believed precedent established that actions in bad faith simply fell outside statutory powers. They cited Lord Greene's dicta in *Wednesbury* as providing some support for the position.

20. See, for example, *Law Quarterly Review* 72:460; and *Cambrian Law Journal* (1956): 143.

21. For an interesting discussion of tribunals and courts, see Arthurs 1983, 188–214.

22. The case in question is *R. v. St. Marylebone and Paddington Rent Tribunals ex p. Bell London and Provincial Properties Ltd.* ([1949] 1 K.B. 666).

23. *R. v. Northumberland Compensation Appeal Tribunal ex p. Shaw* (1952) 1 K.B. 338.

24. *Racecourse Betting Control Board v. Secretary of State for Air* (1944) Ch. 114.

25. See, for example, *R. v. Birmingham Compensation Appeal Tribunal of the Minister of Labour and National Service ex p. Road Hauling Executive* (1952) 2 All E.R. 100; *Baldwin and Francis Ltd. v. Patents Appeal Tribunal* (1959) A.C. 663; and *R. v. Patents Appeal Tribunal ex p. Swift and Co.* (1962) 2 Q.B. 647.

26. *Nakkuda Ali v. Jarayatne* (1951) A.C. 66.

27. For the concept of strong discretion, see Dworkin 1977, 32.

28. Similarly, Marc Galanter (1983) has argued that the perceptions of those decrying a litigation explosion need explaining as much as anything else: what do they see, what do they ignore, and why?

29. See, for example, *R. v. Deputy Industrial Injuries Commissioner ex p. Jones* (1962) 2 Q.B. 677.

30. Other than unions, interest groups organized around land use planning are some of the best established in British politics (Vogel 1986). For an outline of the procedures regarding compulsory purchase orders in the 1940s, see deSmith 1950.

Chapter 3

1. The case is still discussed as an example of ministerial responsibility (Marshall 1989).

2. For a discussion of administrative reform as a symbolic struggle over the meaning of the state, see March and Olsen 1989.

3. For recent efforts to explain the institutionalization of procedure rather than just what courts do about it, see McCubbins, Noll, and Weingast 1989.

4. Carol Harlow and Richard Rawlings (1984: chap. 3) use "red light" and "green light" to designate lawyers who wanted to stop state programs and those who wanted to facilitate them. But that perspective ignores that red light lawyers wanted to facilitate state protection of private property rights via judicial governance. It also ignores the substantial shared ground that professional ideology allowed, for the green light lawyers were also in favor of imposing legal accountability.

5. For an alternative argument, that Labour lawyers were in favor of enabling administration and Conservative lawyers favored hindering it, see Harlow and Rawlings, 1984, chaps. 1–2.

6. This framework takes very seriously the Marxist understanding of what law is. See Beirne and Quinney eds. 1982.

7. The Conservative party did change the law to give former owners first option to purchase land the government was releasing (*The New Statesman,* 24 July 1954).

8. Committee on Tribunals 1957, *Minutes of Evidence,* 486.

9. For this approach to the choice of administrative procedure, see McCubbins, Noll, and Weingast 1989.

Chapter 4

1. This perspective recurred in participants' discussions of the Law Commission. See Scarman 1971, 867–70.

2. See Law Commission, 1966a.

3. For these criteria, see Schmitter 1985.

4. See par. 5 of the note prefacing the *First Programme* (Law Commission 1967c).

5. For a good summary of ideas about reform in the 1950s, see Cmnd. 218, 1957.

6. For ambiguities in Weber's concepts of rationality, see Levine 1985, chap. 7.

7. A market control model takes such reform efforts as attempts by the profession to expand markets. The most recent exponent of this perspective is Richard L. Abel. For a synthesis, see his "A Comparative Sociology of Legal Professions," in Abel and Lewis 1989c. For my purposes it is enough to say that even finding such motives by the profession is not the end of the story about what changes mean for public policy or how the particular choices about change are made. For a discussion of the market control perspective on reform, see Halliday 1987, 347–51.

8. See the essays in Meyer and Scott 1983.

9. Law Commission 1967a, 4–5. Politicians hardly cared, however. Richard Crossman, then a leading Labour minister, said of the seminar (which he missed): "Fortunately, everyone said it was nonsense" (Crossman 1976, 2:46).

10. See, for example, Griffith and Street 1951; H. Wade 1961; and Davis 1961.

11. Halliday 1987, 37. For a critique, see Abel and Lewis 1989d, 502–4.

12. On the importance of agenda setting and power, see DiMaggio and Powell 1983, 157.

13. On the importance of attending to divisions within the central state, see Suleiman 1987.

14. This discussion is adopted from Law Commission 1976, 5–16.

15. Law Commission 1971, 54–55. Much of the following account is also based on interviews I conducted in 1984, 1985, and 1990 with solicitors in the central administration and other lawyers (barristers and solicitors) involved with the Law Commission, practicing in administrative law, or in academia. The interviews were granted on the basis of confidentiality.

16. Law Commission 1971, 57. In its final report (Law Commission 1976) the commission also drew on a statute in Ontario (20).

17. Terence Halliday in a suggestive essay on Australia (1989) argues for the importance of these divisions for the ability of the profession to advise states.

18. Law Commission 1971, 103. Though the commission favored an administrative court, it did not have the authority to recommend establishing one. Its second-best solution was to have the Queen's Bench hear all administrative appeals. See also Wade 1968, 90.

19. See, in particular, testimony before the Committee of Inquiry on Tribunals and Inquiries, in *Minutes of Evidence* 1957.

20. *R. v. Secretary of State, ex p. Butt and Swati* (1986) 1 All E.R. 717; *Puhlhofer v. London Borough of Hillingdon* (1986) 1 All E.R. 467. See also Sunkin 1987b.

21. JUSTICE/All Souls Group 1988. For a discussion of the role of academics in a professional division of labor, see Freidson 1986, chap. 10.

22. On professions as setting the terms of debate, see Larson 1984.

23. For the concept of public jurisdiction, see Abbott 1988, 68, 163–65.

24. See Note 1969; and "The Law Commission: Reform of Grounds of Divorce," *The Solicitors' Journal* 111 (1967): 614–15.

25. Cohen, March, and Olsen 1972, 1–25. Similarly, lawyers noticed the divorce law problem in the United States and worked to put it on the legislatures' agendas (Jacob 1987).

Chapter 5

1. An American example, in which the Supreme Court held that the administration could not justify abandoning a regulatory effort simply by saying a new president had been elected, is *State Farm Insurance* (see Sunstein 1983). For a discussion and critique from a legal perspective of the concept of public duty in Britain, see Harding 1989.

2. For a discussion of whether the courts were illegitimately involved in politics in *Tameside,* see Lord Devlin in *The Times,* 27 October 1976, 12.

3. However, since then the courts have used the language in that case to allow standing for the Child Poverty Action Group in challenging a new form of distributing social security benefits (*R. v. Secretary of State for Social Services ex p. Stitt,* [1990] CO/1026/89).

4. For a discussion of law and order as a liability for the Conservative government since crime rates have increased, see Loveday 1992.

5. Morris 1984; Young 1984; Pannick 1984; Griffith 1991. *The Times* in an editorial chose to emphasize the courts' discovery of a legitimate expectation of consultation and therefore called the decision part of the "postwar invigoration of judicial review" ("The GCHQ Case for Judicial Review," *The Times,* 23 November 1984, 13.

6. For the discussion in Parliament, see *Parl. Deb.,* Commons, 5th ser., 15 (1981): 532–49, 889–929. For the newspaper discussion, see "Thatcher Welcomes Fares Judgment," *The Guardian,* 18 December 1981, 19; Stephenson 1981, 15; Hebert 1981, 13; "London Transport and the Law," *The Times,* 18 December 1981, 13; and *The Times,* 20 December 1981, 12.

7. See *R. v. Secretary of State for the Environment ex p. Hackney L.B.C.* (1983) 1 W.L.R. 524; *R. v. London Bourough of Hackney ex p. Fleming* (1985) CO/339/85; *R. v. Secretary of State for the Environment ex p. Sheffield City Council* (1985) CO/472/85; *R. v. Secretary of State for the Environment ex p. Borough of Greenwich* (1985) Q.B. (Crown Office List). The local governments did win in *R. v. Secretary of State for the Environment ex p. Nottinghamshire City Council* (1985) *The Times,* 19 July.

8. Since *O'Reilly* and *Cocks,* lawyers have struggled over which of their quasi-governmental bodies, such as the Tourist Board and the Jockey Club, are subject to judicial review. See *R. v. Jockey Club ex p. RAM Racecourses Ltd* (1991) 5 Admin L.R. 265. See also *R. v. Panel on Takeovers and Mergers, ex p Datafin* [1987] 1 Q.B. 815. For discussion, see Parpworth 1993.

9. See Woolf 1986b, 1990; Laws, 1989. For a discussion of the continuous nature of public goods, in which the excludability of benefits is a matter of less or more, see Hardin 1981.

10. For a discussion of this debate, see Harlow and Rawlings 1984, chap. 3.

11. See, for example, Beatson 1987, 34–65.

12. See, for example, Sedley 1986.

13. McCubbins, Noll, and Weingast 1987. The unity of the executive and legislature would suggest indeed that there would be less administrative procedure structuring administration and less opportunity for judicial review in the first place. That seems to be a good explanation for the limits on judicial review in Britain today (Sterett 1992b).

14. See, for example, Sunstein 1986. For a skeptical discussion of this as simply elevating lawyers above everyone else, see Shapiro 1988, esp. chap. 5.

15. For the American case, see Sunstein 1990b.

16. In 1992, Mr. Sedley became a High Court judge.

17. See Woolf 1992, 226–27, for that argument for homelessness claims.

18. For an illustration, see Woolf 1990, 111–12.

19. One former Treasury solicitor believed this was generally a problem with judicial review (Kerry 1986).

20. Interview, 1990. Bridges et al. (1987) point out the myriad ways lawyers were brought into consultation with local governments after the Fare's Fair case. For publicity concerning this and discussion of it as illegitimate, see Lomas 1985.

21. Interviews, 1990. See also Sunkin and LeSueur 1991.

22. For an example of how broad a category "constitutional" has become, see Graham and Prosser 1990.

23. Hitchens 1990, 757. See also Siedentop 1990.

24. For the Social Fund case, see *R. v. Secretary of State for Social Services ex p. Stitt*. For a discussion of the design of discretion into the plan, see Drabble and Lynes 1989.

25. Courts in the United States as well have generally been more willing to elaborate procedures than require particular decisions in administrative law. That seems to have been changing since the 1980s, when courts seemed to be more interested in insisting on the one technically best policy. They insisted on that when at times there was not, nor could there be, any such thing (see Shapiro 1988). However, for the argument that courts in the United States are willing to address substantive standards while in Britain they address procedures, see Atiyah and Summers 1987.

26. The central government responded to the *Tameside* decision by strengthening the powers of the minister to order local governments to follow central education policy (Bull 1986). The British government has been widely critiqued as profoundly undemocratic. Voting reform to bring the system closer to proportional representation has long been advocated.

27. See Woolf 1992, 223.

Chapter 6

1. See also Kureishi 1989, 270–89.

2. For an extended discussion of the handling of citizenship in Britain, see Rose 1968.

3. For a discussion of the cultural politics of race in Britain, see Gilroy 1987.

4. See the discussion in Kramer 1993.

5. See Salyer 1995.

6. On "activism" in the British courts, particularly in administrative law, see Stevens 1980; and Paterson 1982.

7. A good synthetic discussion of this issue is in Sunstein 1990a, 111–57.

8. Hazel Genn and Yvette Genn completed an excellent study of client satisfaction and tribunals; part of it addressed immigration tribunals (Genn and Genn 1989).

9. Martha Minow provides a good summary of critical legal studies approaches to rights (1990, 167–78).

10. Stephen Sedley, a barrister and now a judge, has argued (1990) that court reorganization has been about freeing the courts for international business disputes.

11. Bell 1976. For the contrasting advantages of a more decentralized litigation strategy in the United States, see Olson 1984.

12. For the argument that procedure is an important part of British law, see Atiyah and Summers 1987.

13. For a discussion of carriers' liability in the European Community, see Cruz 1991.

14. In 1987, when the Tamil refugee cases first came through the system, 33.7 percent of all judicial review cases took between six months and one year from the time of application to the time of decision. I do not know what proportion of those cases involved immigration. Forty-two percent of all judicial review cases took less than six months. In 1988 the percentage of cases that took between six months and a year went

up to 49.6 percent (Sunkin, Bridges, and Meszaros 1993, 58). Lord Justice Woolf expressed concern about the amount of time these cases were taking (1992, 221–22). In 1993 judges also complained about the amount of time cases were taking and urged the government to appoint more judges (*The Times,* 7 February 1993, sec. 1, 22).

15. In 1987 there were 348 withdrawals of applications for leave to apply for judicial review. The number dropped to 98 in 1988 when there were many fewer applications. The reasons why applicants withdrew their applications are not publicized (Sunkin, Bridges, and Meszaros 1993, 20).

16. Whether the government has the legal authority to do that has been questioned (Vincenzi 1992).

17. However, Patrick Atiyah and Robert Summers argue that American law focuses more on substance (Atiyah and Summers 1987).

18. For an argument about the importance of recognizing emotion in law, see Nussbaum 1991b.

19. UKIAS has long argued that the Home Office does the same thing, choosing cases to bring on the basis of how it would like to shape the rules (UKIAS 1978). Immigrant advocacy groups have also made such choices (Joint Council for the Welfare of Immigrants 1979).

20. In December of 1987 the Court of Appeal restated and affirmed *Bhatia* and *Kumar* in a case on appeal. The Court of Appeal pointed out that the burden of proof does not shift once there is evidence of a genuine marriage and that the evidence of intervening devotion should help entry clearance officers to determine the genuineness of a marriage (*Immigration Appeal Tribunal v. Hoque and Singh* [1988] Imm. A.R. 216).

21. That phrase appears frequently in criticisms of the primary purpose rules (Pannick 1993).

22. For the argument that administrative law would make for a breakthrough in the insistent focus on partisan debate in British politics, see Ashford 1981, 18.

23. At other times representations to individual members of Parliament have seemed more favorable at least than internal administrative appeals (Joint Council for the Welfare of Immigrants 1979; United Kingdom Immigrant Advisory Service 1982).

References

Abbott, Andrew. 1988. *The System of Professions.* Chicago: University of Chicago Press.

Abel, Richard L. 1988a. Lawyers in the United States. In *Lawyers in Society.* Vol. 1, *The Common Law World,* edited by Richard L. Abel and Philip S. C. Lewis. Berkeley: University of California Press.

Abel, Richard L. 1988b. *Lawyers in England and Wales.* London: Basil Blackwell.

Abel, Richard L. 1988c. *The Legal Profession in England and Wales.* Oxford: Basil Blackwell.

Abel, Richard L., and Philip S. C. Lewis. 1988a. *Lawyers in Society.* Vol. 1, *The Common Law World.* Berkeley: University of California Press.

Abel, Richard L., and Philip S. C. Lewis. 1988b. *Lawyers in Society.* Vol. 2, *The Civil Law World.* Berkeley: University of California Press.

Abel, Richard L., and Philip S. C. Lewis. 1989c. *Lawyers in Society.* Vol. 3, *Comparative Theories.* Berkeley: University of California Press.

Abel, Richard L, and Philip S. C. Lewis. 1989d. Bringing Law Back into the Sociology of Lawyers. In *Lawyers in Society.* Vol. 3, *Comparative Theories,* edited by Richard L. Abel and Philip S. C. Lewis. Berkeley: University of California Press.

Adams, Tenley. 1991. Charter 77 and the Workers' Defense Committee (KOR): The Struggle for Human Rights in Czechoslovakia and Poland. *East European Quarterly* 26:219–38.

Adams, Tenley. 1992. Charter 77 and the Workers' Defense Committee. *East European Quarterly* 26:219–38.

Allen, Sir Carleton Kemp. 1931. *Bureaucracy Triumphant.* London: Oxford University Press.

Allen, Sir Carleton Kemp. 1945. *Law and Orders.* Oxford: Oxford University Press.

Ames, Jonathan. 1993. Dearth of Expertise on Judicial Review. *Law Society's Gazette* 90:5.

Anderson, Bonnie S., and Judith P. Zinsser. 1988. *A History of Their Own: Women in Europe from Prehistory to the Present.* Vol. 2. New York: Harper and Row.

Anwar, Muhammad. 1991. The Context of Leadership: Migration, Settlement and Racial Discrimination. In *Black and Ethnic Leadership in Britain: The Cultural Dimensions of Political Action,* edited by Pnina Werbner and Muhammad Anwar. New York: Routledge and Chapman Hall.

Arthurs, Harry. 1980. Rethinking Administrative Law: A Slightly Dicey Business. *Osgoode Hall Law Journal* 17:1–45.

Arthurs, Harry. 1985. *Without the Law.* Toronto: University of Toronto Press.

Ashford, Douglas. 1981. *Policy and Politics in Britain.* Philadelphia: Temple University Press.

Ashford, Douglas. 1983. *British Dogmatism and French Pragmatism.* London: Allen and Unwin.

Atiyah, P. S. 1979. *The Rise and Fall of Freedom of Contract.* New York: Oxford University Press.

Atiyah, P. S., and Robert S. Summers. 1987. *Form and Substance in Anglo-American Law.* Oxford: Oxford University Press.

Atkins, Burton. 1990. Interventions and Power in Judicial Hierarchies: Appellate Courts in England and the United States. *Law and Society Review* 24:71–92.

Atkins, Burton. 1991. Communication of Appellate Decisions: A Multivariate Model for Understanding the Selection of Cases for Publication. *Law and Society Review* 24:1171–96.

Atkinson, Michael M., and William D. Coleman. 1989. Strong States and Weak States: Sectoral Policy Networks in Advanced Capitalist Economies. *British Journal of Political Science* 19:47–67.

Baker, J. H. 1979. *An Introduction to English Legal History.* London: Butterworths.

Baldwin, John, Nicholas Wikeley, and Richard Young. 1992. *Judging Social Security: The Adjudication of Claims for Benefit in Britain.* New York: Oxford University Press.

Baldwin, R., and D. Horne. 1986. Expectations in a Joyless Landscape. *Modern Law Review* 49:685–711.

Baldwin, R., and John Houghton. 1986. Circular Arguments. *Public Law* 1986:239.

Bardach, Eugene, and Robert Kagan. 1980. *Going by the Book.* Philadelphia: Temple University Press.

Barnett, Anthony. 1990. Rule from Below. *New Statesman and Society.* 27 April, 16–17.

Barron, Anne, and Colin Scott. 1992. The Citizen's Charter Programme. *Modern Law Review* 55(4): 526–46.

B.B.C. 1990. Analysis: Q.C. vs. M.P. 6 April. Radio broadcast.

Beatson, Jack. 1987. "Public" and "Private" in English Administrative Law. *Law Quarterly Review* 103:34–65.

Beer, Samuel. 1969. *British Politics in the Collectivist Age.* New York: Vintage.

Beer, Samuel. 1983. *Britain against Itself.* London: Faber and Faber.

Beirne, Piers, and Richard Quinney, editors. 1982. *Marxism and Law.* New York: John Wiley and Sons.

Bell, Derrick. 1976. Serving Two Masters. *Yale Law Journal.*

Bell, John. 1984. *Policy Arguments in Judicial Decisions.* Oxford: Clarendon.

Beloff, Michael J. 1995. Judicial Review—2001: A Prophetic Odyssey. *Modern Law Review* 58(2):143–59.

Bingham, Sir Thomas. 1991. Should Public Law Remedies Be Discretionary? *Public Law* (spring): 64–75.

Blake, C. G. 1980. Death of Habeas Corpus. *New Law Journal* 130: 772.

Block, Fred. 1987. *Revising State Theory.* Philadelphia: Temple University Press.

Blom-Cooper, Louis. 1982. The New Face of Judicial Review: Administrative Changes in Order 53. *Public Law* 1982: 250–55.

Blom-Cooper, Louis, and Gavin Drewry. 1976. *Final Appeal.* Oxford: Oxford University Press.

Blom-Cooper, Louis, David L. Astor, M. Campbell-Johnston, Jane Ewart-Biggs, Victor Guazzelli, Ronald Hoar, Robert MacLennan (for In Defence of Asylum). 1991. Letter. *The Times,* 6 December, 19.

Bourdieu, Pierre. 1987. The Force of Law: Toward a Sociology of the Juridical Field. *Hastings Law Journal* 38:805–53.

Boyd, Fiona. 1989. The Carriers' Liability Act, 1987. *Public Law* 1989:23–27.

Boyron, Sophie. 1992. Proportionality in English Administrative Law: A Faulty Translation? *Oxford Journal of Legal Studies* 12(2): 237–64.

Bradley, A. W. 1987. The Judge Over Your Shoulder. *Public Law* 1987:485–88.

Bradley, A. W. 1988. Protecting Government Decisions from Legal Challenge. *Public Law* 1988:2.

Bradley, A. W. B. 1989. The Treasury Solicitor and the Separation of Powers. *Public Law* 1989:374–78.

Bradley, Anthony. 1989. The Crown Office Digest. *Public Law* 1989:11–13.

Bridge, Lord. 1988. An English Judge's View of the Conseil d'Etat. Paper presented to the Administrative Law Bar Association.

Bridges, Lee, Chris Game, Owen Lomas, Jeremy McBride, and Stewart Ranson. 1987. *Legality and Local Politics.* Aldershot: Avebury.

Brint, Steven. 1990. Rethinking the Policy Influence of Experts: From General Characterizations to Analysis of Variation. *Sociological Forum* 5(3): 361–80.

Britain's Constitution: The Case for Reform. 1995. *The Economist* 337 (14 October): 25–26.

Brodkin, Evelyn Z. 1986. *The False Promise of Administrative Reform.* Philadelphia: Temple University Press.

Brown, R. Dugdale. 1955. *The Battle of Crichel Down.* London: Bodley Head.

Bull, David. 1987. *Tameside* Revisited: Prospectively "Reasonable"; Retrospective "Maladministration." *Modern Law Review* 50:307–44.

Bulmer, Martin. 1982. *The Uses of Social Research.* London: Allen and Unwin.

Bulpitt, Jim. 1986. Continuity, Autonomy and Peripheralization: The Anatomy of the Centre's Race Statecraft in England. In *Race, Government and Politics in Britain,* edited by Zig Layton-Henry and P. B. Rich. London: Macmillan.

Burger, Warren E. 1983. Today's Challenges: Improving the Administration of Justice. *Judicature* 66:394–407.

Burrage, Michael. 1989. Revolution as a Starting Point for Comparative Analysis of French, American, and English Legal Professions. In *Lawyers in Society,* vol. 3, Comparative Theories, edited by Richard L. Abel and Philip S. C. Lewis. Berkeley: University of California Press.

Cain, Bruce, John Ferejohn, and Morris Fiorina. 1987. *The Personal Vote.* Cambridge: Cambridge University Press.

Cain, Maureen. 1983. The General Practice Lawyer and the Client: Toward a Radical View. In *The Sociology of the Professions,* edited by Robert Dingwall and Philip Lewis. New York: St. Martin's Press.

Cain, Maureen, and Christine Harrington. 1994. *Lawyers in a Postmodern World: Translation and Transgression.* New York: New York University Press.

Campbell, Colin, ed. 1980. *Do We Need a Bill of Rights?* London: Temple Smith.

Cane, Peter. 1992. Private Rights and Public Procedure. *Public Law* 1992: 193–200.

Cane, Peter. 1993. The Law Commission on Judicial Review. *Modern Law Review* 56(6): 887–96.

Cannell, Fenella. 1990. Concepts of Parenthood: The Warnock Report, the Gillick Debate, and Modern Myths. *American Ethnologist* 17(4): 667–86.

Caporaso, James A., ed. 1989a. *The Elusive State.* Newbury Park, Calif.: Sage.

Caporaso, James A. 1989b. Introduction. In *The Elusive State,* edited by James A. Caporaso. Newbury Park, Calif.: Sage.

Carty, Anthony. 1991. English Constitutional Law from a Postmodernist Perspective. In *Dangerous Supplements: Resistance and Renewal in Jurisprudence,* edited by Peter Fitzpatrick. Durham, N.C.: Duke University Press.

Carvel, John. 1984. *Citizen Ken.* London: Chatto and Windus.

Cawson, Alan. 1986. *Corporatism and Political Theory.* London: Basil Blackwell.

Charter 88. 1990. Redress for All State Abuse. London: Charter 88.

Charter 88. N.d. Statement of Purpose. London: Charter 88.

Chester, Sir Norman. 1954. Crichel Down. *Public Administration* 32:389.

Chorley, Lord. 1946. Law-Making in Whitehall. *Modern Law Review* 9:26.

Chowdhury, Zahir. 1994a. From the Tribunal to the Court. *New Law Journal* 144(6635): 240–41.

Chowdhury, Zahir. 1994b. From Tribunal to the Court, Part 2. *New Law Journal* 144(6636): 207–8.

Cmd. 4060. 1936. United Kingdom. Parliament. *Report of the Lord Chancellor's Committee on Minister's Powers.* London: HMSO.

Cmnd. 218. 1957. United Kingdom. Parliament. *Report of the Committee on Tribunals and Enquiries.* London: HMSO.

Cohen, M. D., James March, and Johan Olsen. 1972. A Garbage Can Model of Organizational Choice. *Administrative Science Quarterly* 17:1–25.

Cohen, Nick. 1990. Capped Councils Win a Judicial Review. *The Independent,* 25 April, 4.

Cohen, Nick. 1995. The Long Arm of the Law. *The Independent on Sunday,* 5 November, 18.

Comment. 1954a. *British Journal of Administrative Law* 1:1–2.

Comment. 1954b. *British Journal of Administrative Law* 1:34.

Comment. 1956. *Public Law* 1956:1.

Commission for Racial Equality. 1988. *Annual Report.* London: HMSO.

Commission for Racial Equality. 1989. *Annual Report 1988.* London: Commission for Racial Equality.

Committee on Tribunals and Enquiries. 1957. *Minutes of Evidence.* London: HMSO.

Constable, Marianne. 1993. Sovereignty and Governmentality in Modern American Immigration Law. *Studies in Law, Politics, and Society* 13:249–71.

Cooper, Jeremy, and Rajeev Dhavan, eds. 1986. *Public Interest Law.* New York: Basil Blackwell.

Cooper, Philip. 1986. *Hard Judicial Choices.* New York: Oxford University Press.

Cornell, Drucilla. 1991. *Beyond Accommodation: Ethical Feminism, Deconstruction, and the Law.* New York: Routledge.

Craig, Paul P. 1989. Bentham, Public Law and Democracy. *Public Law* (August): 407–27.

Craig, Paul P. 1990a. Dicey: Unitary, Self-Correcting Democracy and Public Law. *Law Quarterly Review* 106 (January): 105–43.

Craig, Paul. 1990b. *Public Law and Democracy in the United Kingdom and the United States of America.* New York: Oxford University Press.

Craig, Paul. 1994. *Administrative Law.* 3rd ed. New York: Oxford University Press.

Crick, Bernard. 1990. How Scotland Can Set the Example. *The Guardian,* 3 May, 19.

Cross, Rupert. 1961. *Precedent in English Law.* Oxford: Clarendon.

Cross, Rupert. 1977. *Statutory Interpretation.* Oxford: Clarendon.

Crossman, Richard. 1976. *The Diaries of a Cabinet Minister,* vol. 2. London: Hamish Hamilton and Jonathan Cape.

Crouch, Colin, and Ronald Dore. 1990. Whatever Happened to Corporatism? In *Corporatism and Accountability,* edited by Colin Crouch and Ronald Dore. Oxford: Clarendon.

Cruz, Antonio. 1991. Carrier Sanctions in Four European Community States: Incompatibilities Between International Civil Aviation and Human Rights Obligations. *Journal of Refugee Studies* 4:63–81.

Davis, K. C. 1961. The Future of Judge-Made Public Law in England: A Problem of Practical Jurisprudence. *Columbia Law Review* 61:201–20.

Davis, K. C. 1962. English Administrative Law—An American View. *Public Law* 1962:139–50.

Delgado, Richard. 1987. The Ethereal Scholar: Does Critical Legal Studies have What Minorities Want? *Harvard Civil Rights-Civil Liberties Law Review* 22: 301–23.

Denning, Alfred. 1949. *Freedom under the Law.* London: Hamlyn Lectures.

deSmith, S. A. 1946. Abuse of Statutory Powers. *Law Quarterly Review* 63:237.

deSmith, S. A. 1950. Appeals in Town and Country Planning Law. In *Administrative Tribunals at Work: A Symposium,* edited by Robert S. W. Pollard. London: Stevens and Sons.

deSmith, S. A. 1955. A Conservative Approach to Administrative Law. *British Journal of Administrative Law* 2:3.

deSmith, S. A. 1959. *Judicial Review of Administrative Action.* London: Stevens and Sons.

Devlin, Patrick. 1956. The Common Law, Public Policy and the Executive. *Current Legal Problems* 9:1.

Dhavan, Rajeev. 1989. So Why Are There So Few Cases? Anti-discrimination and Race Relations Law and Policy in the United Kingdom. Paper presented at the annual meeting of the Law and Society Association.

Diamond, Aubrey. 1977. Law Reform and the Legal Profession. *Australian Law Journal* 51:397.

Dicey, A. V. 1920. *Introduction to the Law of the Constitution.* 4th ed. London: Oxford University Press.

Dicey, A. V. 1926. *Lectures on the Relation Between Law and Public Opinion in England during the Nineteenth Century.* 2d ed. London: Macmillan.

DiMaggio, Paul, and Walter Powell. 1983. The Iron Cage Revisited: Institutional Isomorphism and Collective Rationality in Organizational Fields. *American Sociological Review* 48:147–60.

Diplock, Lord. 1961. The Courts as Legislators. *Current Legal Problems* 14:1.

Douglas, Mary. 1986. *How Institutions Think.* Syracuse: Syracuse University Press.

Drabble, Richard, and Tony Lynes. 1989. The Social Fund: Discretion or Control? *Public Law* 1989:297–322.

Drewry, G. 1992. Judicial Politics in Britain: Patrolling the Boundaries. *West European Politics* 15:9–29.

Drewry, Gavin. 1993. Mr. Major's Charter: Empowering the Consumer. *Public Law* 1993:248–56.

Dummett, Ann. 1994. Immigration and Nationality. In *Individual Rights and the Law in Britain,* edited by Christopher McCrudden and Gerald Chambers. New York: Clarendon.

Dworkin, Ronald. 1977. *Taking Rights Seriously.* Cambridge: Harvard University Press.

Dworkin, Ronald. 1986. *Law's Empire.* Cambridge: Harvard University Press.

Dworkin, Ronald. 1990. *A Bill of Rights for Britain.* London: Chatto and Windus.

Eastwood, David. 1994. *Governing Rural England: Tradition and Transformation in Local Government, 1780–1840.* New York: Oxford University Press.

Ekirch, A. A. 1983. Harold J. Laski: The American Experience. *American Studies* 24:53.

Ellis, Caroline. 1990. Talking about Degeneration. *The Guardian,* 1 May, 23.

Elster, Jon. 1991. Constitutionalism in Eastern Europe: An Introduction. *University of Chicago Law Review* 58:447–82.

Elster, Jon, and Rune Slagstad. 1988. *Constitutionalism and Democracy.* New York: Cambridge University Press.

Evans, Peter, Dietrich Rueschemeyer, and Theda Skocpol, eds. 1985. *Bringing the State Back In.* New York: Cambridge University Press.

Evershed, Raymond. 1956. Government under Law in Postwar England. *Law Quarterly Review* 72:460.

Evershed, Raymond. 1961. The Judicial Process in Twentieth Century England. *Columbia Law Review* 61:761.

Farmer, J. A. 1974. *Tribunals and Government.* London: Weidenfeld and Nicolson.

Farmer, James. 1982. *Administrative Tribunals.* London: Weidenfeld and Nicolson.

Feldman, David, and Mark Gould. 1992. Legalism and English Administrative Law. *Law and Social Inquiry* 17:89–100.

Fineman, Martha L. 1989. Neither Silent nor Revolutionary. *Law and Society Review* 23:945–49.

Fitzpatrick, Peter, ed. 1991. *Dangerous Supplements: Resistance and Renewal in Jurisprudence.* Durham, N.C.: Duke University Press.

Forbath, William. 1991. Courts, Constitutions and Labor Politics in England and America: A Study of the Constitutive Power of Law. *Law and Social Inquiry* 17:1–34.

Fraser, Nancy. 1987. *Unruly Practices.* Minneapolis: University of Minnesota Press.

Freidson, Eliot. 1986. *Professional Powers.* Chicago: University of Chicago Press.

Friedmann, W. 1946. The New Public Corporations and the Law, Part 2. *Modern Law Review* 10:377.

Fuller, Lon. 1969. *The Morality of Law.* New Haven: Yale University Press.

Galanter, Marc. 1983. Reading the Landscape of Disputes: What We Know and Don't Know (and Think We Know) about Our Allegedly Contentious and Litigious Society. *UCLA Law Review* 31:4.

Gamble, Andrew. 1988. *The Free Economy and the Strong State.* Durham, N.C.: Duke University Press.

Gardiner, Gerald, and Andrew Martin. 1963. *Law Reform NOW.* London: Victor Gollancz.

Geertz, Clifford. 1983. *Local Knowledge.* New York: Basic Books.

Gelb, Joyce. 1989. *Feminism and Politics: A Comparative Perspective.* Berkeley: University of California Press.

Genn, Hazel. 1993. Tribunals and Informal Justice. *Modern Law Review* 56:393–411.

Genn, Hazel, and Yvette Genn. 1989. The Effectiveness of Representation at Tribunals. London: Lord Chancellor's Department.

Gibbon, Peter, and David Steyne, eds. 1986. *Thurcroft: A Village and the Miners' Strike.* Nottingham, England, and Atlantic Highlands, N.J.: Spokesman.

Giddens, Anthony. 1979. *Central Problems in Social Theory.* Berkeley: University of California Press.

Gilroy, Paul. 1987. *There Ain't No Black in the Union Jack.* Chicago: University of Chicago Press.

Gilroy, Paul. 1994. *Small Acts.* London: Verso.

Gordon, Richard, and Helen Rogers. 1990. 1989: A Year in the Life of Administrative Law. *New Law Journal* (16 February): 220–21.

Gordon, Robert. 1984. Legal Thought and Legal Practice in the Age of American Enterprise, 1870–1920. In *Professions and Professional Ideologies in America,* edited by Gerald L. Geison, 70–110. Chapel Hill: University of North Carolina Press.

Gower, L. C. B. 1946. The Future of the Legal Profession. *Modern Law Review* 9:211.

Gower, L. C. B. 1973. Reflections on Law Reform. *University of Toronto Law Journal* 23:257–69.

Graham, Cosmo, and Tony Prosser. 1990. *Waiving the Rules: The Constitution under Thatcherism.* London: Open University Press.

Graham, Cosmo, and Tony Prosser. 1991. *Privatizing Public Enterprises: Constitutions, the State, and Regulation in Comparative Perspective.* New York: Oxford University Press.

Grant, Wyn. 1985. Private Organizations as Agents of Public Policy: The Case of Milk Marketing in Britain. In *Private Interest Government: Beyond Market and State,* edited by Wolfgang Streeck and Philippe C. Schmitter. Beverly Hills: Sage.

Green Legal Challenge to Patten. 1990. *Time Out.* 18–25 April, 9.

Greenhouse, Carol. 1986. *Praying for Justice.* Ithaca: Cornell University Press.

Greenhouse, Carol J. 1989. Just in Time: Temporality and the Cultural Legitimation of Law. *Yale Law Journal* 98:1631–51.

Griffith, J. A. G. 1954. Judicial Attitudes toward Administrative Power. *British Journal of Administrative Law* 1:41.

Griffith, John A. G. 1988. Principles and Politics and Public Law. *Osgoode Hall Law Journal* 26:834–65.

Griffith, J. A. G. 1991. *The Politics of the Judiciary.* 4th ed. London: Fontana.

Griffith, J. A. G., and Harry Street. 1951. *Principles of Administrative Law.* London: Allen and Unwin.

Hailsham, Lord [Quentin McGarel Hogg]. 1976. *Elective Dictatorship.* London: Macmillan.

Haines, C. G. 1932. Effects of the Growth of Administrative Law upon Traditional Anglo-American Legal Theories and Practices. *American Political Science Review* 26:875–94.

Haines, C. G. 1940. Constitutional Law, Administrative Law. *American Political Science Review* 34:1–30.

Hall, Stuart, and David Held. 1990. Citizens and Citizenship. In *New Times: The Chang-*

ing Face of Politics in the 1990s, edited by Stuart Hall and Martin Jacques. London: Verso.

Hall, Stuart, and Martin Jacques, eds. 1983. *The Politics of Thatcherism.* London: Macmillan.

Halliday, Terence. 1987. *Beyond Monopoly.* Chicago: University of Chicago Press.

Halliday, Terence. 1989. The Fractured Profession: Structural Impediments to Collective Action by the Australian Legal Profession. ABF Working Paper, no. 8712. Manuscript.

Hamson, C. J. 1954a. The Real Lesson of Crichel Down. *Public Administration* 32:201–2.

Hamson, C. J. 1954b. *Executive Discretion and Judicial Control.* London: Stevens.

Handler, Joel. 1992. Postmodernism, Protest and the New Social Movements. *Law and Society Review* 26(4): 697–732.

Haraway, Donna. 1991. *Simians, Cyborgs, and Women.* New York: Routledge, Chapman, Hall.

Harden, Ian, and Norman Lewis. 1986. *The Noble Lie.* London: Hutchinson.

Hardin, Russell. 1981. *Collective Action.* Baltimore: Johns Hopkins University Press.

Harding, A. J. 1989. *Public Duties and Public Law.* Oxford: Clarendon.

Harlow, Carol. 1986. Public Interest Litigation in England: The State of the Art. In *Public Interest Law,* edited by Jeremy Cooper and Rajeev Dhavan. New York: Basil Blackwell.

Harlow, Carol. 1987. *Public Law and Public Interest.* London: Butterworths.

Harlow, Carol, and Richard Rawlings. 1984. *Law and Administration.* London: Weidenfeld and Nicolson.

Harrington, Christine, and Sally Engle Merry. 1988. Ideological Production: The Making of Community Mediation. *Law and Society Review* 22:708–35.

Harris, B. V. 1992. The "Third Source" of Authority for Government Action. *The Law Quarterly Review* 108:626–51.

Harris, William F. II. 1982. Bonding Word and Polity: The Logic of American Constitutionalism. *American Political Science Review* 76:34–45.

Hartog, Hendrik. 1987. The Constitution of Aspiration and the Rights that belong to Us All. *Journal of American History* 74:1013–34.

Hartsock, Nancy. 1990. Foucault on Power: A Theory for Women? In *Feminism/Postmodernism,* edited by Linda J. Nicholson. New York: Routledge.

Harvey, David. 1989. *The Condition of Postmodernity.* Cambridge, Mass.: Basil Blackwell.

Hawkins, Keith. 1984. *Environment and Enforcement.* New York: Oxford University Press.

Hebert, Hugh. 1981. Ruling Class. *The Times,* 18 December, 13.

Heclo, Hugh. 1974. *Modern Social Politics in Britain and Sweden.* New Haven: Yale University Press.

Heclo, Hugh, and Aaron Wildavsky. 1981. *The Private Government of Public Money.* London: Macmillan.

Heuston, R. F. V. 1952. Book Review of Bernard Schwartz, *American Administrative Law. Law Quarterly Review* 68:250.

Hewart, Gordon B. 1929. *The New Despotism.* New York: J. J. Little and Ives.

Hitchens, Christopher. 1990 Lessons Maggie Taught Me. *The Nation,* 17 December, 757.

Hollis, Patricia. 1987. *Ladies Elect: Women in English Local Government, 1865–1914.* Oxford: Clarendon.

Home Office. 1994. *Statistical Bulletin.* Issue 17/94 (14 July).

Hutchinson, Alan. 1985. The Rise and Ruse of Administrative Law and Scholarship. *Modern Law Review* 48:293.

Inns of Court Conservative and Unionist Society. 1953. *The Rule of Law.* London: Conservative Political Centre.

Irons, Peter. 1982. *The New Deal Lawyers.* Princeton: Princeton University Press.

Irvine, Alexander [Lord Irvine of Lairg]. 1995. Judges and Decision Makers: The Theory and Practice of *Wednesbury* Review. Paper presented to a meeting of the Administrative Law Bar Association.

Jacob, Herbert. 1987. *The Silent Revolution.* Chicago: University of Chicago Press.

Jaffe, Louis L. 1956. The American Administrative Procedure Act. *Public Law* 1956: 218–21.

Jennings, W. Ivor. 1933. *Law and the Constitution.* London: University of London Press.

Jennings, W. Ivor. 1936. Courts and Administrative Law: The Experience of English Housing Legislation. *Harvard Law Review* 49:426–56.

Jessop, Bob, Kevin Bonnett, Simon Bromley, and Tom Ling. 1984. Authoritarian Populism, Two Nations and Thatcherism. *New Left Review* 147:32–60.

Johnson, Nevil. 1982. Select Committees and Administration. In *The House of Commons in the Twentieth Century,* edited by S. A. Walkland. Oxford: Clarendon.

Joint Council for the Welfare of Immigrants. 1978–1995. *Annual Report.* London: JCWI.

Jones, Nicholas. 1986. *Strikes and the Media: Communication and Conflict.* New York: Basil Blackwell.

Jowell, Jeffrey, and Anthony Lester. 1989. Beyond *Wednesbury:* Substantive Principles of Administrative Law. *Public Law* 1989:368–82.

Jowell, Jeffrey, and Dawn Oliver. 1985. *The Changing Constitution.* Oxford: Clarendon.

Jowell, Jeffrey, and Dawn Oliver. 1990. *The Changing Constitution.* 2nd ed. Oxford: Oxford University Press.

JUSTICE/All Souls Committee for the Review of Administrative Law in the United Kingdom. 1988. *Administrative Justice: Some Necessary Reforms.* Oxford: Oxford University Press.

Katznelson, Ira. 1973. *Black Men, White Cities: Race, Politics and Migration in the United States, 1900–1930 and Britain, 1948–1968.* New York: Oxford University Press.

Katznelson, Ira. 1986. Rethinking the Silences of Social and Economic Policy. *Political Science Quarterly* 101:307.

Kean, Hilda. 1990. *Challenging the State? The Socialist and Feminist Educational Experience 1900–1930.* New York: Falmer.

Keller, Morton. 1980. Anglo-American Politics, 1900–1930, in Anglo-American Perspective: A Case Study in Comparative History. *Comparative Studies in Society and History* 22:458.

Kelley, Robin D. G. 1990. *Hammer and Hoe: Alabama Communists During the Great Depression.* Chapel Hill: University of North Carolina Press.

Kelman, Steven. 1981. *Regulating America, Regulating Sweden.* Cambridge: MIT Press.

Kenney, Sally J. 1992. *For Whose Protection? Reproductive Hazards and Exclusionary Policies in the United States and Britain.* Ann Arbor: University of Michigan Press.

Kent, Susan Kingsley. 1993. *Making Peace: The Reconstruction of Gender in Interwar Britain.* Princeton: Princeton University Press.

Kerry, Sir Michael. 1986. Administrative Law and Judicial Review—The Practical Effects and Developments Over the Law 25 Years on Administration in Central Government. *Public Administration Review* 64:163–70.

Kilmuir, Lord [David Maxwell-Fyfe]. 1959. Individual Freedom under an Unwritten Constitution. *Virginia Law Review* 45:629.

Koven, Seth. 1993. Borderlands: Women, Voluntary Action, and Child Welfare in Britain, 1840–1914. In *Mothers of a New World: Maternalist Politics and the Origins of Welfare States,* edited by Seth Koven and Sonya Michel. New York: Routledge.

Koven, Seth. 1994. Remembering and Dismemberment: Crippled Children, Wounded Soldiers and the Great War in Great Britain. *American Historical Review* 99(4): 1167–1202.

Kramer, Jane. 1993. Letter from Europe. In *The Graywolf Annual 10: Changing Community,* edited by Scott Walker. Saint Paul, Minn.: Graywolf.

Krasner, Stephen D. 1989. Sovereignty: An Institutional Perspective. In *The Elusive State,* edited by James A. Caporaso. Newbury Park, Calif.: Sage.

Krieger, Joel. 1986. *Reagan, Thatcher, and the Politics of Decline.* New York: Oxford University Press.

Krygier, Martin. 1990. Marxism and the Rule of Law. *Law and Social Inquiry* 15:633–65.

Kureishi, Hanif. 1989. London and Karachi. In *Patriotism: The Making of British Identity,* vol. 2, *Minorities,* edited by Raphael Samuel. New York: Routledge.

Kureishi, Hanif. 1990. *The Buddha of Suburbia.* New York: Macmillan.

Labour Party. 1953. *Personal Freedom.* London: Labour Party.

Laitin, David. 1986. *Hegemony and Culture.* Chicago: University of Chicago Press.

Lakin, Alan, and John Whitmore. 1989. The Future of Discrimination Law. Paper presented at a meeting of the Administrative Law Bar Association.

Larson, Magali Sarfatti. 1977. *The Rise of Professionalism: A Sociological Analysis.* Berkeley: University of California Press.

Larson, Magali Sarfatti. 1984. The Production of Expertise and the Constitution of Expert Power. In *The Authority of Experts,* edited by Thomas L. Haskell. Bloomington: Indiana University Press.

Laski, Harold. 1938. *Parliamentary Government in England.* New York: Viking.

Laumann, Edward, and Knoke. 1990. *The Organizational State.* Madison: University of Wisconsin Press.

Law Commission. 1967a. Exploratory Working Paper on Administrative Law. Published working paper #13. London: Law Commission.

Law Commission. 1967b. *First Annual Report.* Law Commission #4. London: HMSO.

Law Commission. 1967c. *First Programme.* Law Commission #14. London: HMSO.

Law Commission. 1969. *Administrative Law.* Law Commission #20. Cmnd. 4059. London: HMSO.

Law Commission. 1971. Remedies in Administrative Law. Law Commission working Paper #40. London: Law Commission.

Law Commission. 1976. *Remedies in Administrative Law.* Law Commission #73. London: HMSO.

Law Commission. 1994. *Administrative Law: Judicial Review and Statutory Appeal.* Law Commission #226. HC 669. London: HMSO.

Laws, John G. McK. 1989. Judicial Review I: The Ghost in the Machine: Principle in Public Law. *Public Law* 1989:27–31.

Laws, Hon. Sir John. 1995. Law and Democracy. *Public Law* 1995:72–93.

Layton-Henry, Zig. 1992. *The Politics of Immigration: Immigration, "Race" and "Race" Relations in Post-war Britain.* Cambridge, Mass.: Blackwell.

Lazarus-Black, Mindie, and Susan F. Hirsch. 1994. *Contested States: Law, Hegemony and Resistance.* New York: Routledge.

Lazerson, Mark. 1982. In the Halls of Justice, the Only Justice is in the Halls. In *The Politics of Informal Justice,* vol. 1, *The American Experience,* edited by Richard Abel. New York: Academic.

Lee, Simon. 1988. *Judging Judges.* London: Faber.

Lee, Simon. 1990. Moral High Ground of Poll-Tax Refuseniks. *The Independent,* 27 April, 17.

Legal Action Group. 1992. *A Strategy for Justice.* London: Legal Action Group.

Legomsky, Stephen H. 1987. *Immigration and the Judiciary: Law and Politics in Britain and America.* New York: Oxford University Press.

Lehmbruch, Gerard, and P. C. Schmitter. 1982. *Patterns of Corporatist Policymaking.* Beverly Hills: Sage.

Lester, Anthony. 1987. Not on Her Majesty's Service. *Public Policy and Administration* 2(3): 1–10.

Lester, Anthony. 1988. The Overseas Trade in the American Bill of Rights. *Columbia Law Review* 88:537–61.

Lester, Anthony. 1990a. Bringing State Power to Heel. *The Guardian,* 2 May, 19.

Lester, Anthony. 1990b. Charter 88. *The Times,* 25 October, 15.

Levine, Donald. 1985. *The Flight from Ambiguity.* Chicago: University of Chicago Press.

Lewis, Jane. 1983a. Dealing With Dependency: State Practices and Social Realities, 1870–1945. In *Women's Welfare Women's Rights,* edited by Jane Lewis. London: Croom Helm.

Lewis, Jane, ed. 1983b. *Women's Welfare Women's Rights.* London: Croom Helm.

Lindgren, Janet S. 1983. Beyond Cases: Reconsidering Judicial Review. *Wisconsin Law Review* 1983(3): 583–638.

Lloyd, Trevor O. 1979. *From Empire to Welfare State: English History, 1900–1976.* London: Oxford University Press.

Lomas, Owen. 1985. Law as a Resource. In *Between Centre and Locality: The Politics of Public Policy,* edited by S. Ranson, G. W. Jones, and K. Walsh. London: Allen and Unwin.

Loughlin, Martin. 1992. *Public Law and Political Theory.* New York: Oxford University Press.

Loughlin, Martin, and Peter M. Quinn. 1993. Prisons, Rules and Courts: A Study in Administrative Law. *Modern Law Review* 56(4): 497–527.

Loveday, Barry. 1992. Right Agendas: Law and Order in England and Wales. *International Journal of the Sociology of Law* 20:297–319.

Loveland, Ian. 1991. Legal Rights and Political Realities: Governmental Responses to Homelessness in Britain. *Law and Social Inquiry* 16:249–319.

Loveland, Ian. 1995. *Housing Homeless Persons*. Oxford: Oxford University Press.

Lovenduski, Joni, and Vicky Randall. 1993. *Contemporary Feminism: Women and Power in Britain*. Oxford: Oxford University Press.

Luker, Kristin. 1984. *Abortion and the Politics of Motherhood.* Berkeley: University of California Press.

MacDonald, Ian, and Nicholas Blake. 1991. *Immigration Law in the United Kingdom.* London: Butterworths.

MacKinnon, Catherine. 1988. *Toward a Feminist Theory of the State.* Cambridge: Harvard University Press.

Mansbridge, Jane J., ed. 1990a. *Beyond Self-Interest.* Chicago: University of Chicago Press.

Mansbridge, Jane J. 1990b. The Rise and Fall of Self-Interest in the Explanation of Political Life. In *Beyond Self-Interest,* edited by Jane J. Mansbridge. Chicago: University of Chicago Press.

March, James G., and Johan Olsen. 1989. *Rediscovering Institutions.* New York: Basic Books.

Marshall, Geoffrey, ed. 1989. *Ministerial Responsibility*. Oxford: Oxford University Press.

Martin, Ian. 1986. Combining Casework and Strategy: The Joint Council for the Welfare of Immigrants. In *Public Interest Law,* edited by Jeremy Cooper and Rajeev Dhavan. New York: Basil Blackwell.

Mashaw, Jerry. 1983. *Bureaucratic Justice.* New Haven: Yale University Press.

Matsuda, Mari J. 1987. Looking to the Bottom: Critical Legal Studies and Reparations. *Harvard Civil Rights–Civil Liberties Law Review* 22:323–99.

McAuslan, Patrick. 1980. *The Ideologies of Planning Law.* London: Pergamon.

McAuslan, Patrick. 1983. Administrative Law, Collective Consumption, and Judicial Policy. *Modern Law Review* 46:1.

McAuslan, Patrick. 1989. Administrative Justice: A Necessary Report? *Public Law* 1989:402–12.

McCann, Michael. 1991. Legal Mobilization and Social Reform Movements: Notes on Theory and Its Application. *Studies in Law, Politics, and Society* 11:225–54.

McCubbins, Mathew D., Roger G. Noll, and Barry R. Weingast. 1987. Administrative Procedures as Instruments of Political Control. *Journal of Law, Economics, and Organization* 3:243–77.

McCubbins, Mathew D., Roger G. Noll, and Barry R. Weingast. 1989. Administrative Procedures as Political Control. *Virginia Law Review* 75:423–81.

McGuire, O. R. 1939. The American Bar Association's Administrative Law Bill. *Louisiana Law Review* 1:550–54.

Meidinger, Errol E. 1987. Regulatory Culture: A Theoretical Outline. *Law and Policy* 9:355–86.

Melnick, R. Shep. 1983. *Regulation and the Courts.* Washington, D.C.: Brookings Institution.

Melnick, R. Shep. 1994. *Between the Lines.* Washington, D.C.: Brookings Institution.

Meredith, Paul. 1988. Legitimate Expectations and School Closures. *Public Law* 1988: 4–13.

Merry, Sally Engle. 1985. Concepts of Law and Justice Among Working Class Americans: Ideology as Culture. *Legal Studies Forum* 9:59.

Merry, Sally Engle. 1990. *Getting Justice and Getting Even.* Chicago: University of Chicago Press.

Mertz, Elizabeth. 1988. The Uses of History: Language, Ideology, and Law in the United States and South Africa. *Law and Society Review* 22:661–85.

Messick, Brinkley. 1988. Kissing Hands and Knees: Hegemony and Hierarchy in Shari`a Discourse. *Law and Society Review* 22:637–59.

Messina, Anthony. 1989. *Race and Party Competition in Britain.* Oxford: Oxford University Press.

Meyer, John W., John Boli, and George M. Thomas. 1987. Ontology and Rationalization in the Western Cultural Account. In *Institutional Structure: Constituting Race, Society, and the Individual,* edited by George M. Thomas, John W. Meyer, Francisco O. Ramirez, and John Boli. Beverly Hills: Sage.

Meyer, John W., and Brian Rowan. 1983. Institutionalized Organizations: Formal Structure as Myth and Ceremony. In *Organizational Environments,* edited by John W. Meyer and W. Richard Scott. Beverly Hills: Sage.

Meyer, John W., and W. Richard Scott, eds. 1983. *Organizational Environments.* Beverly Hills: Sage.

Minow, Martha. 1990. *Making All the Difference.* Ithaca: Cornell University Press.

Mitchell, J. D. B. 1967. The Anatomy and Pathology of the Constitution. In *Crisis in British Government,* edited by W. Stankiewicz. London: Macmillan.

Moe, Terry. 1985. Control and Feedback in Economic Regulation: The Case of the NLRB. *American Political Science Review* 79:1094–1116.

Moe, Terry. 1987. Interests, Institutions, and Positive Theory: The Case of the NLRB. *Studies in American Political Development* 2:236–302.

Mohanty, Chandra Talpade. 1991. Introduction. In *Third World Women and the Politics of Feminism,* edited by Chandra Talpade Mohanty, Ann Russo, and Lourdes Torres. Bloomington: Indiana University Press.

Moore, Sally Falk. 1978. *Law as Process: An Anthropological Approach.* New York: Routledge and Kegan Paul.

Morgan, Kenneth. 1985. *Labour in Power, 1945–1951.* New York: Oxford University Press.

Morris, John. 1984. There to Rule on the Law—Not to Make It. *The Times,* 23 November, 13.

Morrison, Fred. 1973. *Courts and the Political Process in England.* Beverly Hills: Sage.

Munir, Edward. 1993. One Step Forward and Two Steps Back. *New Law Journal* 143:1149–50.

Murie, Alan, Pat Niner, and Christopher Watson. 1976. *Housing Policy and the Housing System.* London: Allen and Unwin.

Murphy, Paul L. 1979. *World War I and the Origin of Civil Liberties in the United States.* New York: W.W. Norton.

Navasky, Victor. 1980. *Naming Names.* New York: Penguin.

Nelken, David. 1982. *The Limits of the Legal Process.* London: Academic.

Nelson, Robert L. 1988. *Partners with Power.* Berkeley: University of California Press.

Nicolson, I. F. 1986. *The Mystery of Crichel Down.* Oxford: Oxford University Press.

Noble, Dennis. 1990. In Search of a Launching Pad for Science. *The Guardian,* 2 May, 19.

Nonet, Philippe. 1969. *Administrative Justice.* New York: Russell Sage Foundation.

Note. 1969. A Comparative Approach: The Divergent Paths of English and American Divorce Reform—to Take the Step from Fault to Breakdown? *University of Florida Law Review* 22:101–28.

Novak, William. 1994. Common Regulation: Legal Origins of State Power in America. *Hastings Law Journal* 45:1061–97.

Nussbaum, Martha. 1991a. The Discernment of Perception: An Aristotelian Conception of Private and Public Rationality. In *Love's Knowledge,* edited by Martha Nussbaum. Oxford: Oxford University Press.

Nussbaum, Martha. 1991b. Distinction and Perception. In *Love's Knowledge,* edited by Martha Nussbaum. Oxford: Oxford University Press.

Offe, Claus. 1985. *Disorganized Capitalism.* Cambridge: MIT Press.

Olson, Susan. 1984. *Clients and Lawyers: Securing the Rights of Disabled Persons.* Westport, Conn.: Greenwood.

Orloff, Ann Shola, and Theda Skocpol. 1984. Why Not Equal Protection? Explaining the Politics of Public Social Spending in Britain, 1900–1911 and the United States, 1880s–1920. *American Sociological Review* 49 (December): 726–50.

Pannick, David. 1984. Why Criticism Should not Make M'lud Flip His Wig. *The Guardian,* 6 August, 16.

Pannick, David. 1987. *Judges.* New York: Oxford University Press.

Pannick, David. 1993. End this Purposeless Immigration Rule. *The Times,* 2 March, 31.

Parpworth, Neil. 1993. The Jockey Club and Judicial Review. *The Solicitor's Journal* (19 March): 252–53.

Paterson, Alan. 1982. *The Law Lords.* London: Macmillan.

Pederson, Susan. 1994. *Family, Dependence, and the Origins of the Welfare State: Britain and France, 1914–1945.* Cambridge: Harvard University Press.

Pimlott, Ben. 1989. Britain Leads in Politics of Closed Door. *The Sunday Times,* 22 January, sec. B, 3.

Pitkin, Hanna. 1967. *The Concept of Representation.* Berkeley: University of California Press.

Plender, Richard. 1987. Tamil Immigration. *The Times,* 4 March, 14.

Pollard, Robert S. W., ed. 1950. *Administrative Tribunals at Work: A Symposium.* London: Stevens and Sons.

Ponting, Clive. 1985. *The Right to Know.* London: Sphere.

Pound, Roscoe. 1933. A Comparison of Ideals of Law. *Harvard Law Review* 47:1–17.

Powell, Michael. 1985. Developments in the Regulation of Lawyers: Competing Segments and Market, Client, and Government Controls. *Social Forces* 64:281–305.

Powell, Michael. 1988. *From Patrician to Professional Elite.* New York: Russell Sage Foundation.

Priest, G. L. 1980. Selective Characteristics of Litigation. *Journal of Legal Studies* 9:399–427.

Prosser, Tony. 1982. *Test Cases for the Poor.* London: Child Poverty Action Group.

Public Law Project. 1990. *Prospectus.* London: Public Law Project.

Rawlings, Richard. 1994. Legal Politics: The United Kingdom and Ratification of the Treaty on European Union (Part One). *Public Law* 1994:254–391.

Reclaiming Britain's Constitution. 1995. *The Economist* 337 (14 October): 18.

Refugee Council. 1994. Increase in Refusals since the Asylum Act. 22 November.

Reich, Charles. 1964. The New Property. *Yale Law Journal* 73:733–87.

Rifkin, Janet. 1984. Mediation from a Feminist Perspective: Promise and Problems. *Law and Inequality: A Journal of Theory and Practice* 2:1–13.

Robson, Peter, and Paul Watchman. 1981. *Justice, Lord Denning and the Constitution*. Farnborough, England: Gower.

Robson, W. A. 1932. The Report of the Committee on Ministers' Powers. *Political Quarterly* 3:346.

Robson, W. A. 1970. *Justice and Administrative Law*. 3d ed. Westport, Conn.: Greenwood.

Robson, W. A. 1975. The Study of Public Administration Then and Now. *Political Studies* 23:193.

Rockman, Bert A. 1989. Minding the State—Or A State of Mind? Issues in the Comparative Conceptualization of the State. In *The Elusive State*, edited by James A. Caporaso. Newbury Park, Calif.: Sage.

Rose, E. J. B. 1968. *Colour and Citizenship*. London: Institute for Race Relations.

Rosenberg, Gerald. 1991. *The Hollow Hope*. Chicago: University of Chicago Press.

Rowbotham, Sheila. 1973. *Hidden from History*. London: Pluto.

Rueschemeyer, Dietrich. 1986. *Power and the Division of Labor in Society*. Stanford: Stanford University Press.

Ruff, Anne. 1989. The Immigration (Carriers' Liability) Act 1987. *Public Law* 1989: 222–32.

Ruggie, Mary. 1983. *The State and Working Women in Britain and Sweden*. Princeton: Princeton University Press.

Sahgal, Gita, and Nira Yuval-Davis. 1993. *Refusing Holy Orders: Women and Fundamentalism in Britain*. London: Virago.

Salyer, Lucy. 1995. *Laws Harsh as Tigers: Chinese Immigrants and the Shaping of Modern Immigration Law*. Chapel Hill: University of North Carolina Press.

Samal, Mary Hrabik. 1988. Dissent's Challenge to the East European Political System: The Case of Charter 77 in Czechoslovakia. *East European Quarterly* 21:469–90.

Samuel, Raphael, Barbara Bloomfield, and Guy Boanas, eds. 1986. *The Enemy Within: Pit Villages and the Miners' Strike of 1984–1985*. New York: Routledge and Kegan Paul.

Save Our Railways Win Right to Challenge Privatization Plans in Court. 1995. *The Times*. 25 November, 2.

Scarman, Sir Leslie. 1971. Inside the English Law Commission. *American Bar Association Journal* 57:867–70.

Scarman, Sir Leslie. 1974. *English Law—The New Dimension*. London: Hamlyn Lectures.

Scheingold, Stuart. 1994. The Contradictions of Radical Law Practice. In *Lawyers' Work: Translation and Transgression*, edited by Maureen Cain and Christine Harrington. Buckingham: Open University Press.

Scheingold, Stuart, and Stephen Sugarman. 1991. Comparing Left Lawyering in Britain and the United States. Paper presented at the annual meeting of the Law and Society Association, Amsterdam, the Netherlands.

Schmitter, Philippe C. 1985. Reflections on Where the Theory of Neo-Corporatism Has Gone and Where the Praxis of Neo-Corporatism May be Going. In *Patterns of Corporatist Policy-Making*, edited by Gerhard Lehmbruch and Philippe C. Schmitter. Beverly Hills: Sage.

Schuck, Peter. 1986. *Agent Orange On Trial.* Cambridge: Harvard University Press.

Schwartz, Bernard. 1947. The American Administrative Procedures Act, 1946. *Law Quarterly Review* 63:43.

Schwartz, Bernard. 1948. American Administrative Justice. *Law Quarterly Review* 64:519.

Schwartz, Bernard. 1950. *American Administrative Law.* Oxford: Oxford University Press.

Schwartz, Bernard. 1954. *French Administrative Law and the Common Law World.* New York: New York University Press.

Schwartz, Bernard. 1987. *Lions Over the Throne.* New York: New York University Press.

Schwehr, Belinda, and Paul Brown. 1991. Legitimate Expectations—Snuffed Out? *Public Law* 1991:163–70.

Scott, James C. 1990. *Domination and the Arts of Resistance.* New Haven: Yale University Press.

Scrivens, William, and K. F. Goodfellow. 1955. The Law of Rating. *The Conveyancer* 18:48.

Searing, Donald. 1987. New Roles for Postwar British Politics: Ideologues, Generalists, Specialists and the Progress of Professionalization in Parliament. *Comparative Politics* 19:431–52.

Sedley, Stephen. 1986. What's Next? In *Public Interest Law,* edited by Jeremy Cooper and Rajeev Dhavan. New York: Basil Blackwell.

Sedley, Stephen. 1987. Now You See It, Now You Don't: Judicial Discretion and Judicial Review. *Warwick Law Working Papers* 8(4).

Sedley, Stephen. 1989. Rule of Law. *The Times.* 20 May, 11.

Sedley, Stephen. 1990. Improving Civil Justice. *Civil Justice Quarterly* 9:348–52.

Selznick, Philip. 1969. *Law, Society, and Industrial Justice.* New York: Russell Sage Foundation.

Sen, Amartya. 1983. Rights and Agency. *Philosophy and Public Affairs* 11:3–39.

Shapiro, Martin. 1981. *Courts: A Comparative Perspective.* Chicago: University of Chicago Press.

Shapiro, Martin. 1988. *Who Guards the Guardians?* Athens: University of Georgia Press.

Shapiro, Martin. 1990. Judicial Review in France. *Law and Politics* 6:531–48.

Shepsle, Kenneth, and Barry R. Weingast. 1987. The Institutional Foundations of Committee Power. *American Political Science Review* 81:85–105.

Siedentop, Larry. 1990. Thatcherism and the Constitution. *Times Literary Supplement,* no. 4530, 88–89.

Simon, J. E. S. 1954. Administrative Procedure and the Rule of Law. *British Journal of Administrative Law* 1:12.

Simon, W. H. 1985. The Invention and Reinvention of Welfare Rights. *Maryland Law Review* 44:1–44.

Sinfield, Alan. 1989. *Literature, Politics, and Culture in Postwar Britain.* Berkeley: University of California Press.

Sivanandan, A. 1990. All that Melts into Air Is Solid: The Hokum of New Times. *Race and Class* 31(3): 1–30.

Skocpol, Theda. 1985. Bringing the State Back In. In *Bringing the State Back In,* edited by Peter Evans, Dietrich Rueschemeyer, and Theda Skocpol. New York: Cambridge University Press.

Skocpol, Theda, and Gretchen Ritter. 1991. Gender and the Origins of Modern Social Policies in Britain and the United States. *Studies in American Political Development* 5(1): 36–93.

Smart, Carol. 1989. *Feminism and the Power of Law.* New York: Routledge, Chapman, and Hall.

Smith, David G. 1986. British Civil Liberties and the Law. *Political Science Quarterly* 101:637.

Smith, Roger. 1986. How Good Are Test Cases? In *Public Interest Law,* edited by Jeremy Cooper and Rajeev Dhavan. New York: Basil Blackwell.

Smith, Rogers M. 1988. Political Jurisprudence, the "New Institutionalism," and the Future of Public Law. *American Political Science Review* 82:89–108.

Southall Black Sisters. 1993. *Against the Grain.* London: Southall Black Sisters.

Stacey, Frank. 1975. *British Government 1966–1975: Years of Reform.* Oxford: Oxford University Press.

Stacey, Frank. 1976. *The British Ombudsman.* Oxford: Oxford University Press.

Stankiewicz, W., ed. 1967. *Crisis in British Government.* London: Macmillan.

Starr, June. 1989. The "Invention" of Early Legal Ideas: Sir Henry Maine and the Perpetual Tutelage of Women. In *History and Power in the Study of Law,* edited by June Starr and Jane L. Collier. Ithaca: Cornell University Press.

Steamer, Robert J. 1987. Judicial Leadership: English and American Experience. In *Comparative Judicial Systems,* edited by John R. Schmidhauser. London: Butterworths.

Steinmo, Sven. 1989. Political Institutions and Tax Policy in the United States, Sweden and Britain. *World Politics* 41:500–35.

Stephenson, Hugh. 1981. Lords' Logic. *The Guardian,* 19 December, 19.

Sterett, Susan. 1990. Keeping the Law Up to Date: The Idiom of Legalism and the Reform of Administrative Law in England and Wales. *Law and Social Inquiry* 15: 731–66.

Sterett, Susan. 1992a. Expertise and Comparative Politics. *Law and Social Inquiry* 17:101–7.

Sterett, Susan. 1992b. Legality in Administration in Britain and the United States: Toward an Institutional Explanation. *Comparative Political Studies* 25(2): 195–228.

Sterett, Susan. 1994. "Entitled to Have a Hearing": Due Process in the 1890s. *Social and Legal Studies* 3:47–70.

Stevens, Robert. 1980. *Law and Politics: The House of Lords as a Judicial Body, 1800–1976.* Chapel Hill: University of North Carolina Press.

Stevens, Robert. 1993. *The Independence of the Judiciary.* New York: Oxford University Press.

Stewart, Richard. 1975. The Reformation of American Administrative Law. *Harvard Law Review* 88:1667–1813.

Stone, Alec. 1992. *The Birth of Judicial Politics in France: The Constitutional Council in Comparative Perspective.* New York: Oxford University Press.

Streeck, Wolfgang, and Philippe C. Schmitter. 1985. *Private Interest Government: Beyond Market and State.* Beverly Hills: Sage.

Street, Harry. 1950. Book Review of Bernard Schwartz, *American Administrative Law*. *Yale Law Journal* 59:590.

Stryker, Robin. 1989. Limits on the Technocratization of the Law: The Elimination of the National Labor Relations Board's Division of Economic Research. *American Sociological Review* 54:341–58.

Sugarman, David. 1983. Law, Economy and the State in England, 1750–1814: Some Major Issues. In *Legality, Ideology and the State,* edited by David Sugarman. New York: Academic Press.

Sugarman, David. 1986. Legal Theory, the Common Law Mind, and the Making of the Textbook Tradition. In *Legal Theory and Common Law,* edited by W. Twining. Oxford: Basil Blackwell.

Sugarman, David. 1991. "A Hatred of Disorder": Legal Science, Liberalism and Imperialism. In *Dangerous Supplements: Resistance and Renewal in Jurisprudence,* edited by P. Fitzpatrick. London: Pluto.

Sugarman, David. 1994. Blurred Boundaries: The Overlapping Worlds of Law, Business, and Politics. In *Lawyers in a Postmodern World: Translation and Transgression,* edited by Maureen Cain and Christine Harrington. New York: New York University Press.

Suleiman, Ezra N. 1987. *Private Power and Centralization in France.* Princeton: Princeton University Press.

Sunkin, Maurice. 1986. Judicial Review after *Puhlhofer* and *Swati:* Is the Administration Still Challengeable? *New Law Journal* 136:304–6.

Sunkin, Maurice. 1987a. What is Happening to Applications for Judicial Review? *Modern Law Review* 50:432–67.

Sunkin, Maurice. 1987b. Trends in the Use of Judicial Review Before and After *Swati* and *Puhlhofer. New Law Journal* 137:731–32.

Sunkin, Maurice. 1988. Judicial Review: How Is the Leave Filter Working? *New Law Journal* 138:257–59.

Sunkin, Maurice, Lee Bridges, and George Meszaros. 1993. *Judicial Review in Perspective: An Investigation of Trends in the Use and Operation of the Judicial Review Procedure in England and Wales.* London: Public Law Project.

Sunkin, Maurice, and A. P. Le Sueur. 1991. Can Government Control Judicial Review? *Current Legal Problems* 1991:161–83.

Sunstein, Cass. 1983. Deregulation and the Hard Look Doctrine. *Supreme Court Review* 1983:177–212.

Sunstein, Cass. 1986. Factions, Self-interest and the APA: Four Lessons Since 1946. *Virginia Law Review* 72:271–96.

Sunstein, Cass. 1990a. *After the Rights Revolution.* Cambridge: Harvard University Press.

Sunstein, Cass. 1990b. Political Self-interest in Constitutional Law. In *Beyond Self Interest,* edited by Jane J. Mansbridge. Chicago: University of Chicago Press.

Swann, Dennis. 1990. *The Retreat of the State: Deregulation and Privatization in the United Kingdom and the United States.* Ann Arbor: University of Michigan Press.

Swidler, Ann. 1986. Culture in Action. *American Sociological Review* 48:273–86.

A Symposium on Administrative Law Based upon Legal Writings 1931–1933. 1933. *Iowa Law Review* 18:129–248.

Tanney, Anthony. 1994. Procedural Exclusivity in Administrative Law. *Public Law* 1994:51–68.

Tate, C. Neal. 1975. Paths to the Bench in Britain. *Western Political Quarterly* 28: 108–29.

Taylor, Michael. 1989. Culture, Structure, Action. *Politics and Society* 17:115–62.

Thane, Pat. 1993. Women in the British Labour Party and the Construction of State Welfare, 1906–1939. In *Mothers of a New World: Maternalist Politics and the Origins of Welfare States,* edited by Seth Koven and Sonya Michel. New York: Routledge.

The Times. 1989. Deported Tamils Win Right to Return to UK. *The Times,* 28 July, 2.

Thomas, George M., John W. Meyer, Francisco O. Ramirez, and John Boli. 1987. *Institutional Structure: Constituting State, Society, and the Individual.* Beverly Hills: Sage.

Thomas, Philip A. 1992. From McKenzie Friend to Leicester Assistant: The Impact of the Poll Tax. *Public Law* 1992:208–20.

Thomas, Rosamund. 1980. *The British Philosophy of Administration.* Chapel Hill: University of North Carolina Press.

Thompson, E. P. 1976. *Whigs and Hunters: The Origin of the Black Act.* New York: Pantheon.

Thompson, E. P. 1991. Custom, Law, and Common Right. In *Customs in Common.* New York: New Press.

Titmuss, Richard. 1971. Welfare Rights, Law, and Discretion. *Political Quarterly* 42:113.

Travers, Tony. 1986. *The Politics of Local Government Finance.* London: Allen and Unwin.

Treves, G. E. 1946. Administrative Discretion and Judicial Control. *Modern Law Review* 10:276.

Tushnet, Mark. 1986. *The NAACP's Litigation Strategy for Desegregated Education, 1925–1950.* Chapel Hill: University of North Carolina Press.

Tushnet, Mark. 1991. The Legitimation of the Administrative State: Some Aspects of the Work of Thurgood Marshall. *Studies in American Political Development* 5(1): 94–118.

Tweedie, Jack. 1989. The Dilemma of Clients' Rights in Social Programs. *Law and Society Review* 23:175–208.

Verkuil, Paul. 1978. The Emerging Concept of Administrative Procedure. *Columbia Law Review* 78:258–77.

Vincenzi, Christopher. 1992. Extra-statutory Ministerial Discretion in Immigration Law. *Public Law* 1992:300–321.

Vogel, David. 1986. *National Styles of Regulation.* Ithaca: Cornell University Press.

Wade, E. C. S. 1947. The Courts and the Administrative Process. *Law Quarterly Review* 63:164.

Wade, E. C. S. 1950. Introduction. In Bernard Schwartz, *American Administrative Law.* Oxford: Oxford University Press.

Wade, E. C. S. 1961. The Machinery of Law Reform. *Modern Law Review,* 24.

Wade, H. W. R. 1961. *Administrative Law.* Oxford: Oxford University Press.

Wade, H. W. R. 1968. Crossroads in Administrative Law. *Current Legal Problems* 21:75.

Wade, H. W. R. 1989. The Rule of Law. *The Times,* 18 and 20 May.

Wade, H. W. R. 1994. *Administrative Law.* 7th ed. Oxford: Oxford University Press.

Wade, Sir William. 1993. Lords Put Rule of Law Back on Rails. *The Times,* 17 August, 28.

Waltman, Jerold L. 1984. Change and Rumours of Change: Courts and the Rule of Law. In *Dilemmas of Change in British Politics,* edited by Donley T. Studlar and Jerold L. Waltman. London: Macmillan.

Ward, Ian. 1994. The Anomalous, the Wrong and the Unhappy: UK Administrative Law in a European Perspective. *Northern Ireland Legal Quarterly* 45(1): 46–52.

Ward, Stephen. 1995. Judges vs. the Government. *The Independent,* 3 November, 19.

Webber, Frances. 1991. From Ethnocentrism to Euro-racism. *Race and Class* 32(3): 11–17.

Weber, Max. 1978. *Economy and Society,* edited by Guenther Roth and Claus Wittich. Berkeley: University of California Press.

Weir, Margaret. 1992. Localism, Poverty, and Citizenship: Comparing Europe and the United States. Paper presented at the annual meeting of the American Political Science Association.

Weir, Margaret, and Theda Skocpol. 1985. State Structures and the Possibilities for "Keynesian" Responses to the Great Depression in Sweden, Britain, and the United States. In *Bringing the State Back In,* edited by Peter Evans, Dietrich Rueschemeyer, and Theda Skocpol. New York: Cambridge University Press.

Weitzman, Lenore. 1985. *The Divorce Revolution.* New York: Free Press.

Williams, Bernard. 1985. *Ethics and the Limits of Philosophy.* Cambridge: Harvard University Press.

Williams, Patricia. 1987. Alchemical Notes: Reconstructing Ideals from Deconstructed Rights. *Harvard Civil Rights–Civil Liberties Law Review* 22:401–33.

Williams, Patricia. 1989. *The Alchemy of Race and Rights.* Cambridge: Harvard University Press.

Wilson, Elizabeth. 1977. *Women and the Welfare State.* London: Tavistock.

WING [Women, Immigration and Nationality Group]. 1985. *Worlds Apart.* London: Pluto.

Woolf, Harry L. J. 1986a. Public Law—Private Law: Why the Divide? *Public Law* 1986:220–38.

Woolf, Harry L. J. 1986b. BLA's Autumn Conference: A Director of Civil Proceedings? *Solicitors' Journal* 130:762–64.

Woolf, Rt. Hon. Sir Harry. 1990. *Protection of the Public: A New Challenge.* London: Stevens and Sons.

Woolf, Rt. Hon. Sir Harry. 1992. Judicial Review: A Possible Programme for Reform. *Public Law* 1992:221–37.

Worcester, Robert M. 1995. State of the Nation Survey Update. *British Politics Group Newsletter* 81:16–17.

Yngvesson, Barbara. 1985. Legal Ideology and Community Justice in the Clerk's Office. *Legal Studies Forum* 9:71.

Young, Hugo. 1984. Lords of Magic Who Want to Keep the Ju-ju in Judiciary. *The Guardian,* 17 September, 12.

Young, Hugo. 1989. *The Iron Lady.* New York: Farrar Straus Giroux.

Zander, Michael. 1975. *A Bill of Rights?* Chichester: Rose.

Zimmerman, Joan. 1991. The Jurisprudence of Equality: The Women's Minimum Wage, the First Equal Rights Amendment, and Adkins v. Children's Hospital, 1905–1923. *Journal of American History* 78:188–225.

Zolberg, Aristide R., Astri Suhrke, and Sergio Aguayo. 1989. *Escape From Violence*. New York: Oxford University Press.

Cases

Anisminic Ltd. v. Foreign Compensation Commission [1969] 2 A.C. 147.
Aristides v. Minister of Housing and Local Government [1970] 1 All E.R. 195.
Associated Provincial Picture Houses Ltd. v. Wednesbury Corporation [1948] 1 K.B. 223.
Baldwin and Francis Ltd. v. Patents Appeal Tribunal [1959] A.C. 663.
Bell Property Trust Ltd. v. Hampstead Borough Assessment Committee [1940] 2 K.B. 543.
Berry v. St. Marylebone Corporation [1957] 3 All E.R. 677.
Blackburn v. A-G [1971] 1 W.L.R. 1037.
Brain v. Minister of Pensions [1947] K.B. 625.
British Oxygen Co. Ltd. v. Board of Trade [1971] A.C. 610.
Bromley London Borough Council v. Greater London Council [1982] 2 W.L.R. 62.
Bushell v. Secretary of State for the Environment [1981] A.C. 75.
Case of Abdulaziz, Cabales, Balkandali European Court of Human Rights. (1985) 7 E.H.R.R. 471.
Charter v. Race Relations Board [1973] A.C. 868.
Colleen Ltd. v. Minister of Housing [1971] 1 W.L.R. 433.
Commission for Racial Equality v. Amari Plastics [1982] 1 Q.B. 1194.
Congreve v. Home Office [1976] Q.B. 629.
Constantine v. Imperial Hotels [1944] K.B. 693.
Council of Civil Service Unions v. Minister for the Civil Service (*GCHQ*) [1984] 3 All E.R. 935.
Cocks v. Thanet District Council [1983] A.C. 286.
Crofton Investment Trust Ltd. v. Greater London Rent Assessment Committee [1967] 2 Q.B. 955.
Cumings v. Birkenhead Corporation [1972] Ch. 12.
DeFalco v. Crawley B.C. [1980] 1 All E.R. 913.
Din v. Wandsworth L.B.C. [1981] 3 All E.R. 881.
Dockers' Labour Club and Institute Ltd. v. Race Relations Board [1976] A.C. 285.
Ealing London Borough Council v. Race Relations Board [1972] 1 All E.R. 105.

Evans v. Collins [1964] 1 All. E.R. 808.
Factortame Ltd. v. Secretary of State for Transport [1990] 2 A.C. 85.
Franklin v. Minister of Town and Country Planning [1948] A.C. 87.
Gillick v. West Norfolk and Wisbech Area Health Authority [1986] 1 A.C. 112.
Greenwich v. Secretary of State for the Environment *The Times* (19 December 1985).
Hoffman-La Roche and Co. v. Secretary of State for Trade and Industry [1975] A.C. 295.
Home Office v. Commission for Racial Equality [1981] 2 W.L.R. 703.
Hornsey School of Art v. Edmonton Union 70 J.P. 121.
Immigration Appeal Tribunal v. Hoque and Singh [1988] Imm. A.R. 216.
In re Beck and Pollitzer's Application [1948] 2 K.B. 339.
JLG Investments Ltd. v. Sandwell District Council (1977) 75 L.G.R. 643.
Johnson and Co. (Builders) Ltd. v. Minister of Health [1947] 2 All E.R. 395.
Judd v. Minister of Pensions and National Insurance [1966] 2 Q.B. 580.
Khawaja v. Secretary of State for the Home Department [1983] 1 All E.R. 765.
Laker Airways v. Board of Trade [1977] Q.B. 643.
Lambert v. Ealing London Borough Council [1982] 2 All E.R. 394.
Liverpool Corporation v. Chorley Union [1913] A.C. 197.
Local Government Board v. Arlidge [1915] A.C. 120.
London and Provincial Properties Ltd. [1949] 1 K.B. 666.
Lord Luke of Pavenham v. Minister of Housing and Local Government [1968] 1 Q.B. 172.
Lovelock v. Minister of Transport 40 P. and C.R. 336 (1980).
Luby v. Newcastle-under-Lyme Corporation [1964] 1 All E.R. 84.
"M" v. Home Office [1994] A.C. 377.
Mandla v. Lee [1982] 3 W.L.R. 932.
Miller v. Minister of Health [1946] 1 K.B. 626.
Minister of Pensions v. Horsey [1949] 2 K.B. 526.
Mixnam's Properties Ltd. v. Chertsey Urban District Council [1965] A.C. 735.
Nakkuda Ali v. Jarayatne [1951] A.C. 66.
National Depositry Friendly Society v. Skegness U.D.C. [1958] 2 All E.R. 601.
Norwich County Council v. Secretary of State for Environment [1982] 1 All E.R. 737.
Ojutiku v. Manpower Services Commission [1982] I.R.L.R. 418.
O'Reilly v. Mackman [1983] 2 A.C. 237.
Padfield v. Minister of Agriculture [1968] 2 W.L.R. 924.
Pickwell v. Camden London Borough Council [1983] 1 All E.R. 602.
Post Office v. Nottingham City Council [1976] 1 W.L.R. 624.

Prescott v. Birmingham [1955] Ch. 210.
Puhlhofer v. London Borough of Hillingdon [1986] 1 All E.R. 467.
R. v. Birmingham Compensation Appeal Tribunal of the Minister of Labour and National Service ex p. Road Hauling Executive [1952] 2 All E.R. 100.
R. v. Brent London Borough Council ex p. Gunning 84 L.G.R. 168 (1986).
R. v. Chief Immigration Officer Heathrow Airport ex p. Bibi [1976] 1 W.L.R. 979.
R. v. Council of Legal Education ex p. Eddis. Queen's Bench Division. CO/1223/94.
R. v. Criminal Injuries Compensation Board ex p. Lain [1967] 2 Q.B. 864.
R. v. Criminal Injuries Compensation Board ex p. Schofield [1971] 1 W.L.R. 926.
R. v. Criminal Injuries Compensation Board ex p. Thompstone [1983] 1 W.L.R. 422.
R. v. Commission for Racial Equality ex p. Hillingdon L.B.C. [1982] 3 W.L.R. 159.
R. v. Commission for Racial Equality ex p. Prestige [1984] 1.
R. v. Deputy Industrial Injuries Commissioner ex p. Jones [1962] 2 Q.B. 677.
R. v. Governor of Brixton Prison ex p. Armah [1968] A.C. 192.
R. v. Greater Birmingham Appeal Tribunal ex p. Simper [1974] 1 Q.B. 543.
R. v. The Greater London Council and Another ex p. Westminster City Council (1984) *The Times,* 31 December.
R. v. Hull Prison Visitors ex p. St. Germain [1979] Q.B. 425.
R. v. Immigration Appeal Tribunal ex p. "B" (1988) CO/1852/87, 28 October.
R. v. Immigration Appeal Tribunal, ex p. Bakhtaur Singh (1986) *The Times,* 27 June.
R. v. Immigration Appeal Tribunal ex p. Bastiampillai [1983] 2 All E.R. 844.
R. v. Immigration Appeal Tribunal, ex p. Begum [1986] Imm. A.R. 385.
R. v. Immigration Appeal Tribunal, ex p. Bhatia [1985] Imm. A.R. 39.
R. v. Immigration Appeal Tribunal ex p. Enwia [1983] 2 All E.R. 1045.
R. v. Immigration Appeal Tribunal ex p. Khan (Mahmud) [1983] 2 All E.R. 420.
R. v. Immigration Appeal Tribunal ex p. Kotecha [1983] 2 All E.R. 289.
R. v. Immigration Appeal Tribunal, ex p. Kumar [1986] *The Times,* August 13.
R. v. Immigration Appeal Tribunal ex p. Weerasurya [1983] 1 All E.R. 195.
R. v. Industrial Injuries Commissioner ex p. Amalgamated Engineering Union [1966] 2 Q.B. 31.
R. v. Inland Revenue Commissioners ex p. National Federation of Self-Employed and Small Businesses Ltd. [1982] A.C. 617.
R. v. Inner London Education Authority ex p. Westminster City Council [1984] CO/1236/84, 19 December.
R. v. Jockey Club ex p. RAM Racecourses Ltd. (1991) 5 Admin. L. R. 265.

R. v. Liverpool Corporation ex p. Taxi Fleet [1972] 2 Q.B. 299.
R. v. London Borough of Hackney ex p. Fleming [1985] CO/339/85, 16 April.
R. v. London Borough of Sutton ex p. Hamlet [1986] CO/1657/85, 26 March.
R. v. L.T.E. ex p. G.L.C. [1983] 2 W.L.R. 702.
R. v. Medical Appeal Tribunal ex p. Gilmore [1957] 1 Q.B. 574.
R. v. Northumberland Compensation Appeal Tribunal ex p. Shaw [1952] 1 K.B. 338.
R. v. Panel on Takeovers and Mergers, ex p. Datafin [1987] 1 Q.B. 815.
R. v. Patents Appeal Tribunal ex p. Swift and Co. [1962] 2 Q.B. 647.
R. v. Race Relations Board ex p. Selvarajan [1975] 1 W.L.R. 1686.
R. v. St. Marylebone and Paddington Rent Tribunals ex p. Bell.
R. v. Secretary of State for Education and Science ex p. Collins [1983] CO/242/83, 20 June.
R. v. Secretary of State for the Environment ex p. Borough of Greenwich [1985] Queen's Bench Division (Crown Office List), 18 July.
R. v. Secretary of State for the Environment ex p. Brent London Borough Council [1982] 1 Q.B. 593.
R. v. Secretary of State for the Environment ex p. Brent London Borough Council [1985] *The Times,* 30 April.
R. v. Secretary of State for the Environment ex p. Hackney London Borough Council [1983] 1 W.L.R. 524.
R. v. Secretary of State for the Environment ex p. Nottinghamshire County Council [1985] *The Times,* 4 October.
R. v. Secretary of State for the Environment ex p. Sheffield City Council [1985] CO/472/85, 2 April.
R. v. Secretary of State for the Home Department ex p. Awa [1983] *The Times,* 19 July.
R. v. Secretary of State for the Home Department ex p. Brind [1989] *The Times,* 30 May.
R. v. Secretary of State for the Home Department ex p. Choudhary [1978] 1 W.L.R. 1177.
R. v. Secretary of State for the Home Department ex p. Hosenball [1977] 1 W.L.R. 766.
R. v. Secretary of State for the Home Department ex p. Hussain [1978] 1 W.L.R. 700.
R. v. Secretary of State for the Home Department ex p. Mughal [1974] Q.B. 313.
R. v. Secretary of State for the Home Department ex p. Ram [1979] 1 W.L.R. 148.
R. v. Secretary of State for the Home Department, ex p. Swati [1986] All E. R. 717.
R. v. Secretary of State for the Home Department., ex p. Thirukumar and Others [1988] Queen's Bench Division, *The Times,* 27 December.

R. v. Secretary of State for the Home Department, ex p. Thirukumar and Others [1989] Court of Appeal, *The Times,* 10 March.

R. v. Secretary of State for the Home Department ex p. Zamir [1979] 3 W.L.R. 89.

R. v. Secretary of State for Social Services ex p. Stitt Queen's Bench Division [1990] CO/1026/89, 21 February.

R. v. Social Fund Inspector and Secretary of State for Social Services ex p. Healey and others [1990] Court of Appeal. *The Times,* 5 July.

Racecourse Betting Control Board v. Secretary of State for Air [1944] Ch. 114.

Ravenseft Properties Ltd. v. Newham London Borough Council [1976] 2 W.L.R. 131.

Ridge v. Baldwin [1964] A.C. 40.

Robinson v. Minister of Town and Country Planning [1947] K.B. 702.

Royal College of Music v. Westminster Vestry [1898] 1 Q.B. 304.

Schmidt v. Home Secretary [1969] 2 Ch. 149.

Secretary of State for Education and Science v. Tameside Metropolitan Borough Council [1977] A.C. 1014.

Secretary of State for Employment v. A.S.L.E.F. (No.2) [1972] 2 Q.B. 455.

Selvarajan v. Race Relations Board [1976] 1 All E.R. 12.

Smith v. East Elloe Rural District Council [1956] A.C. 736.

Smith v. Inner London Education Authority [1978] 1 All E.R. 411.

Stafford v. Minister of Health [1946] 1 K.B. 621.

Summers v. Minister of Health [1947] 1 All E.R. 184.

Taylor v. Brighton Borough Council [1947] 1 K.B. 736.

Taylor v. Munrow [1960] 1 W.L.R. 151.

Vilvarajah and others v. the United Kingdom [1990] European Court of Human Rights 45/1990/236/302–6. Judgment of 30 October 1991.

Wandsworth London Borough Council. v. Winder [1984] 3 W.L.R. 1254.

Wednesbury Corporation v. Minister of Housing and Local Government [1966] 2 Q.B. 275.

Westminster Bank v. Beverley Borough Council [1971] A.C. 508.

Westminster Bank v. Beverley Borough Council [1968] 2 All E.R. 1199.

Westminster City Council v. Royal United Service Institution [1938] 2 All E.R. 545.

Westminster Corporation v. Southern Railway Company [1936] 2 All E.R. 326.

Index